The Female Factor

Shari Steiner

The Female Factor

Women in Western Europe

Intercultural Press Inc.   Chicago

Published by
Intercultural Press, Inc.
70 West Hubbard Street
Chicago, Illinois 60610
312-321-0075

Printed in the United States of America

Contents

Acknowledgments

Acknowledgments of special assistance received on this project goes first and foremost to the many who took time out to answer my numerous questions, often spending hours to go through the lengthy questionnaire that formed the backbone of my inquiries. In all the countries where I worked, people have been most helpful and open, and they have my deepest respect and gratitude.

My heartfelt appreciation is also extended to the many professional people, too numerous to name here, who contributed interviews and their own written reports, both published and unpublished, to this compilation.

For help with the manuscript, I would like to thank several writers who have read and commented on various sections, including Hans Jansen, Alan Levy, Robert Abel, Carole Abel and Cima Star. Two friends who have been an enormous assistance with the nitty-gritty are Susan Fisher and Linda Dicks. I would like to offer a special thanks to

7

Dr. Constance Sutton for making a particularly important point on the direction of the work. My long-suffering and careful editor, Anne Martindale, has been an invaluable aid, and I would also like to express my gratitude for the support and encouragement given the project since its inception by my publisher, Walter Minton.

Finally, I must say thanks to my husband and two children—all of whom had to live with the project daily for the past five years, doing so not only with patience but also with contributions of their own experiences and ideas. My husband, in addition, also read and reread the manuscript, offering constructive criticism and support. He deserves the biggest thank offering of all.

For Clyde,
who believes

Introduction

It's been five years since the first edition of this work was published—hardly enough time to give many points for forecasting such events as England having the first woman political leader and the U.S. having lost momentum on ERA. In fact, the major commendable point is that the work is based on what has become the mainstream of the dialogue between the sexes—the need and ability of both sides to work together to find solutions.

Because women are on the cutting edge of social change, however, this book is presented from a woman's point of view. Its aim is to explore the contour map of what life is like in five European societies. Unlike *The Second Sex, Sexual Politics, The Second Wave* and many of the other works discussing women in today's world, this report is not concerned primarily with the universal features of the feminine condition. Instead, it deals with why and how women's lives in various societies differ profoundly.

All of us feel a turmoil in today's female condition. We take our metamorphosis with us into our boardrooms and our beds. Despite a spurt of "late life" mothers, overall birthrates are plunging, until much of Europe has reached zero population growth. Women's suicide and homicide rates are on the increase everywhere. Rates of venereal disease, abortion and illegitimacy are also climbing. A smaller percentage of the population is getting married, and a larger percentage is getting divorced—to the point that in pacesetting Sweden, nearly half the population will spend the major portion of their lives single.

This, after all, is the first era where women have been able to state—and know that it is the physical truth—that biology is not destiny. First and most importantly, this is true because of the advent of successful means of birth control, but other factors also contribute to our newly constructed freedom. Twentieth century diet, hygiene and miracle drugs have given us reasonable expectations of long life and good health. Universal schooling means motherhood is not a full time, lifelong occupation. Household work is no longer a twelve hour a day, back-breaking feat. Today's labor force is valued more for intellectual ability than for muscle.

Our escape from biological destiny is as vastly central to the coming century as the advent of the industrial revolution was to the last. Shaking off the rigid concepts of who a woman is and how she must act is our exhilarating task. But our understanding of what is happening is so inadequate, we hardly know what barometers to watch or which part of our lives to adjust first.

This book grew from a desire to evaluate the directions open to women by taking stock of the various solutions already in operation. My hope was not only to record *how* people achieve their solutions, but—even more important—to analyze *what the motivating factors are* behind their achievements.

I wanted to see, from the vantage points of Europe's multifaceted cultures, how mothers react to the demands of the doom watchers of the population explosion. I wanted to record how large numbers of women behave when their futures are no longer printed in their chromosomes. Finally, I wanted to highlight the influence and importance of women in a variety of societies.

I have concentrated on five cultures—those of England, Italy, France, Germany and Scandinavia—first because these are the European cultures most conscious of change, and second because they are predominant in influencing the United States. As an American who has experienced the peculiar strains and pleasures of being an American woman,

I wanted to examine my closest cousins to compare our strengths and weaknesses.

I wanted to look at history and archetypes and statistics and expert opinions, but most of all I wanted to know how women felt and behaved in their offices, supermarkets and homes. I wanted to see and talk with them about how they interact with their children and their mothers, how they behave with other women and with men, how they deliver government reports and close business deals.

I found that daily life and work routines, as well as the modern archetypes of these societies, are very tightly woven with those of the United States. We all "do it with Dash." We all watch the same British television productions of Shakespeare and the same Italian spectaculars starring Sophia Loren. We all read Agatha Christie and Simone de Beauvoir and *Vogue*.

But conspicuous fundamental differences persist. We don't organize our lives with the same goals in mind. We don't enjoy the same legal rights and social freedoms. We don't have the same status or responsibilities in our societies. We don't give birth the same way; we don't flirt the same way; we don't even cry the same way—or if we cry, we can expect the responses of those around us to vary from bewilderment to laughter to contempt.

These deviations are important because they indicate how societies starting with similar physical surroundings and cultural heritages can develop and sustain entirely different patterns of behavior. Their existence demonstrates that new patterns can be adopted, but an examination of the dynamics of these shifts reveals that any change in the behavior of women affects all of society.

Several factors have emerged in this study as crucial forces in a woman's formulation of her self-image. Historically, Western women arise out of two fundamental traditions—that of the Lady and that of the Warrior Woman. Their basic difference was and is quite simple. The Lady carves out her own physical and emotional world separate from that of the man, and there she exercises her talents. The Warrior Woman, on the other hand, bases her values on intersexual camaraderie, taking up arms alongside her partner. Men in both these cultures, of course, are just as profoundly shaped by these philosophies of human motivation as women.

The Lady has been predominant in the South, where the development of the archetype was largely interwoven with the heritage of the Latins. The Warrior Woman has held sway in the North with the Teutons. Both have had their strengths and weaknesses, and both have certain advantages to offer today's rapidly evolving woman.

In modern times the most important factors affecting a woman's self-image involve attitudes toward the individual, toward work and toward verbal ability.

The individual-oriented society insists that everyone must achieve personal status first, with the result that the importance of the family, especially the mother, is downgraded. Women in groupist societies, however, can find themselves in an even worse position if it is not the family but the nation, the company or the male peer group that receives primary allegiance.

The work-oriented society has always granted women access to power behind the throne, where they enjoy the victory of mind over muscle. In an epoch when muscle is not so important as knowing how to control a machine, women are stepping into the foreground of power with relative ease.

Social cartography is always deeply influenced by the observer's point of view, and this attempt to cover such a vast area makes my position particularly relevant to the reader. I have approached this work as a journalist who has lived and worked in Europe for thirteen years after having spent a sheltered average childhood in a middle-class home in Colorado. Much of the research rests on interviews with authorities and ordinary individuals, but the major portion is drawn from the mountain of notes and clips I have collected in the process of analyzing life around me, at parent-teacher meetings and business conferences, in homes and doctors' offices and traffic jams.

I've used generalizations to draw national outlines. Obviously, not all Italians have pasta as the first course at midday, and not all Norwegian fathers teach their children to ski. The broad strokes have been necessary in order to begin sorting out what makes us what we are and determining what our strengths may be. In this way, each pattern can be highlighted in contrast to another. To further dramatize these contrasts, I've made references from time to time to the American experience as well.

This study is not presented as any kind of final analysis. It is only a beginning in many areas. Its purpose is certainly not to hold up any one society as the most successful. It is a glimpse of what we as women have to offer ourselves and each other through a comparison of our differing experiences, failures and victories. Ultimately, I believe, by knowing and understanding each other, we shall be able to experiment with roles and lifestyles as eagerly and as guiltlessly as today we try on dresses.

Shari Steiner

Part One

The Englishwoman—

The Eternal Teammate

1

International Admiration

The Anglophile is an international phenomenon. Americans are not the only ones impressed by BBC series on their television sets. They aren't alone in their feeling that England is the most civilized country in the world. As soon as England joined the Common Market, a poll of the other member countries established that England was the preferred place to live.[1] The Germans speak appreciatively of English diplomacy, and the French, who are particularly parsimonious with praise, admit admiration for *le confort anglais*—a phrase that includes a style of living as well as a style of furniture.

The Englishwoman comes in for her share of international regard. Films and television specials on Queens Elizabeth, Victoria and Mary of Scotland are worldwide favorites. Agatha Christie and Daphne du Maurier are best sellers in French, German and Italian, as well as in Swedish, Danish and Dutch. European plastic surgeons report that their international clients prefer the Princess Anne nose: large, but "it has character."[2] In America, the Transatlantic Woman has always enjoyed an enormous following. The same people who were incensed because Martha Mitchell curtsied to Queen Elizabeth are avid readers of biographies of Mary Queen of Scots and Jennie Churchill.

In fact, when you ask the question, "Who do you think is the most modern woman?" the answer is often, "The Englishwoman." Not only because of Mary Quant, Germaine Greer and Diana Rigg, but because there is a general impression that the Englishwoman is coping best with transition. She has a zest for adventure, a nonneurotic acceptance of the conflicts of change, a *sensible* approach to her emerging image. She isn't distant and difficult to understand like the Swede; she isn't locked into the mannerisms of the coquette like the French; she isn't nervous and overextended like the American.

Quant, Greer and Rigg have done an enormous amount to help create this image. They have a businesslike approach to their work, and in addition, are able to laugh at themselves. In fact, Greer is the only major feminist who has ever been able to laugh at herself, to the point of self-mockery for falling in love.[3] Even Julie Andrews insists on letting interviewers know she swears, and that, when she's working and her husband isn't, she expects him to have the children under control and supper on the table when she arrives home. "It's quite dicy at times," she says. Cheerful and matter-of-fact. Despite her sugar-coated image, the Nice Mystique doesn't stand in Andrews' way.

The concept of cheeky is what most people find so admirable. Despite the Pippi Longstocking irreverence taught in Scandinavia, the Englishwoman seems to have the international patent on downright, across-the-board, earthshaking iconoclasm. The strength of the woman who's not afraid to laugh at herself is that she's not afraid to keep struggling when others are laughing. Just as she's not afraid to tease and criticize others, she's not afraid to make a mistake and be teased and criticized in turn. And when she's incensed, she's not afraid to have an all-out row and put the confrontation out in the open. Crusty fearlessness is an invaluable trait that all too few women possess.

Englishwomen have occupied positions of power for a long time. England was the first European nation to have a woman as official head of state, and it has consistently had the most powerful female monarchs in history. Englishwomen were the first to organize and argue for women's voting rights and equality in the eyes of the law, and today England has not only some of the world's best-known female firebrands, but also some of the most powerful female government ministers in the West.

In other areas, the English were already employing Nannies as professional mothers over a hundred years ago, and even today they ship their children out of the family at an earlier age than in any Western society. Finally, the Englishwoman has the distinction of being the only contemporary female who wears clothes designed predominantly by women.

Oddly enough, with all these credits stacked up on her side, the Englishwoman is rarely thought to be more liberated or to have fewer problems than women of other countries. Virginia Woolf, Germaine Greer, Juliette Mitchell, Eva Figes and others have been so articulate that we are fully aware of the barriers against the Englishwoman. We know that practically speaking she is not receiving equal pay for equal work, nor does she have sufficient day nurseries. She has also failed to introduce the Scandinavian concept of housekeeping by husbands to the common Englishman.

No, the reason for the feeling that the Englishwoman is so well equipped for the future lies in the admiration for the way she is operating, despite deeply entrenched male pride and prejudice.

Switzerland, two years ago, held a conference on "Tomorrow: Woman and Man in Business and Society," which was attended by business and professional women from all over Europe and the United States. When it was over, and women had discussed ways to explore female energy and intelligence, one of them—Dilys Powell, columnist for *The Sunday Times*—commented, "In private, to tell the truth, I actually like being a woman."

One could imagine the majority of her countrywomen responding, "Hear, hear!"

2

Queens and Ladies

Female archetypes in England started out strong. In A.D. 62, Boadicea, Queen of the Iceni (a powerful Celtic tribe in East Anglia), led her army in a revolt against the governing Romans. A master of the surprise attach, she sacked Colchester, St. Albans and London, to become known in history as one of the earliest warrior women of Northern Europe.

The first woman characterized in English literature is the terrible mother of Grendel in *Beowulf*. Half monster, half human—a creature who attacks in the night and eats human flesh—she is Beowulf's most awesome enemy, the ultimate foe who must be slain before the kingdom of Hrothgar can be safe.

Guinevere, the prototype of the English Lady, comes next. Beautiful, sweet-tempered and possessing a musical voice, she destroys the harmony of the Round Table through her ignorance and selfishness. Her role in the downfall of King Arthur has none of the malicious calculation of Medea.

In the original tenth-century work, she is portrayed as a simple creature, easily swayed by the treacherous knight, Mordred. In Malory's *Le Morte d'Arthur,* written three hundred years later, she is depicted as simply succumbing to the charms of the dashing Lancelot—and then hastening to a convent to atone for her weakness.

Chaucer created the bold and jovial Wife of Bath, with her five husbands and her knowledge of "what every woman wants" ("to have her own sweet way"). *The Canterbury Tales* are full of strong, interesting female archetypes from the patient Griselda, to the unfaithful Dorigen, to the much-tried Constance, to the simple, intelligent Prioress. Some of these characters are embroidered versions of Boccaccio's creations, but Chaucer's strength lies in drawing women who are far more complicated and subtle than the virgin/whore stereotypes found throughout most of Continental literature.

What was happening to real flesh and blood women during the Middle Ages? Eleanor of Aquitaine was pulling strings behind the thrones of both France and England, particularly the latter, where she was instrumental in the crowning of three kings: her husband, Henry II, and her sons, Richard, Cœur de Lion, and John Lackland. She warded off the claims of her grandson, Arthur of Brittany, published a compilation of the maritime Laws of Oléron, and at the age of seventy-eight crossed the Pyrenees on horseback to arrange the marriage of her granddaughter, Blanche of Castile, to Louis VIII of France.

Eleanor's powerful presence was not to be duplicated until the turbulent sixteenth century when Henry VIII, for the love of several women and the need of a male heir, broke with the Pope to establish his own church in England, thereby legalizing his marriages and progeny. The resulting bloody conflicts between the Catholic and Protestant claimants to the throne cast first the ill-fated Lady Jane Grey into nomination as monarch for nine days and then Mary I into ascendancy. Mary was to be one of the most controversial monarchs of English history.

Five years later, in 1558, Elizabeth I became queen, reigning for forty-five years. At home, she quelled religious conflicts, bested her strong-willed cousin, Mary, Queen of Scots, in her counterclaims to the throne, dominated Parliament and created an atmosphere where architecture, music, literature and the theater thrived. Abroad, Elizabeth I established England as a world power. She set Francis Drake to conquer the Spanish Armada with a smaller but more maneuverable fleet. She encouraged industry and invested her coffers and the queen's ships in the fledgling charter trade companies that were to be the foundation for modern financing and capitalism. She sent Sir Walter Raleigh to colonize Virginia, launching England's empire.

The idea of women in power thus became recognized in England at a very early date. Only Margrethe I of Denmark, Catherine the Great of Russia and Maria Theresa of Austria were to wield power comparable to that of the British queens. They were largely anomalies in their countries, however, whereas in England, women repeatedly influenced commerce, culture and politics.

Elizabeth's awesome reign was followed by the Stuart dynasty which lasted for over a century, except for the Interregnum of the Puritan Commonwealth. The Stuart monarchs were male, except for Mary II—who ruled jointly with her husband, William of Orange—and Queen Anne, during whose reign the English subdued France and united with Scotland.

In 1837, Queen Victoria was crowned. Although only eighteen, she soon asserted her independence from her domineering mother and uncle, and succeeded in establishing her personal power by working with Parliament rather than against it. Her reign of sixty-four years was to be the longest in Western history, and was to see England through the Industrial Revolution and into the most opulent period of the British Empire. At the close of her life, England not only dominated the seven seas, but also considered Australia, most of Africa and a good part of Asia to be her property.

This tradition of women in power contributes to our concept of the resourceful and sturdy Englishwoman, but what was happening to the majority of women during the reigns of these indomitable queens? Unfortunately, very little. Eleanor, Elizabeth and Victoria were not interested in the problems of others of their sex. Women could be whipped for bearing illegitimate children and imprisoned for vagrancy if they did not have a man pledged to look after them.

Those who fought to be different faced formidable odds. Take Margery Kemp, an ordinary housewife of the late twelfth century: driven to madness with her first pregnancy, she regained equilibrium after a vision of Christ. She resisted her husband's "desire to commune fleshly," but was constrained to bear thirteen more children. She traveled across England and the Continent to the Holy Land on pilgrimages, was ridiculed and imprisoned for her visions and fits of weeping, attended to as many of the ill—particularly the insane—as she was allowed to, and finally set about hiring reticent scribes to write her autobiography. According to Joan Goulianos, who concluded an extensive study of women's literature in 1973, the resultant work "is the first known extant autobiography in English."[4]

Throughout Elizabeth's reign, women were taking part in the budding industry of cloth and clothing manufacture. In addition to contributing to family finances, they were articulate about their values and status. In 1589, Jane Anger (probably a pseudonym) published her *Protection for Women,* a vitriolic attack on "The Reports of a Late Surfeiting Lover, and All Other Like Venerians that Complain to be Overcloyed with Women's Kindness."

"Their [men's] unreasonable minds, which know not what reason is, makes them nothing better than brute beasts," she snapped, explaining that, "We are contrary to men because they are contrary to what is good. Because they are purblind, they cannot see into our natures, and we too well (though we had but half an eye) are into their conditions, because they are so bad. Our behaviors alter daily because men's virtues decay hourly."

Feminine archetypes found in literature of the period are equally indignant, determined and self-propelling. Portia is literature's best-known woman lawyer, Lady Macbeth is probably one of the world's most articulate villains, and the shrewish Kate is sister to the self-assured Warrior Women, Brunhild and Diana.

The 1600s found another strong female voice in Aphra Behn, an actress and at one time a spy for Charles II in Antwerp. She traveled to the West Indies, where she met the African prince, Oroonoko, and later wrote a play about him decrying slavery. She was hailed as England's Sappho for her plays, poetry, novels and translations, and is considered the first Englishwoman to have supported herself as a writer.

The times were marked by Cromwell's struggles to establish a democratic government based on the middle class. Women in that class were also stating their rights to govern their own destiny. It was another hundred and fifty years, however, before women's suffrage became a widespread issue in England.

Women's participation in the democratic governing of a country is an English tradition. Mary Wollstonecraft and her *Vindication of the Rights of Women* in 1792, the Seneca Falls Convention in 1848, England's Sheffield Female Political Association resolution presented to Parliament in 1851, Wyoming's women's enfranchisement in 1869, New Zealand's in 1893— all were firsts for feminists and all were accomplished within the English-speaking world.

Behind the fermentation of the early 1800s stand two important and pervasive attitudes. First is the English tradition of the strong and sensible woman—an archetype that was not obliterated by the popular image of the helpless and dependent Lady. Second is the egalitarian idealism of democracy itself, which had its head start in England and her colonies.

The self-sufficient woman's image survives today, whether her name is Diana Rigg, Vanessa Redgrave, Bridget Rose Dugdale or Bernadette Devlin. And yet, side by side with these outspoken women is the "typical British housewife," who insists, "I'm very well off in my little home," and disdains the feminist movement altogether. This is the country where teenagers submit to being called "birds," and the place where women gladly wore the miniskirt before central heating became a widespread phenomenon. How extensive are these surface inconsistencies?

3

The Eccentric as a Career Woman

"I hired Pamela as editor because I liked her intelligence and the cheeky way she talked and the fact that she wasn't afraid to send up somebody, even if she *should* have been nice to them. We thought that if she could find writers who wrote like that, and if she tackled a wide variety of subjects, we'd have a good magazine."[5]

This story was told to me in a cluttered office on the top floor of Chestergate House, the home of National Magazines, a publishing group that includes women's magazines for all pocketbooks and all ages. Pamela Carmichael's is called *She*. It's at the "popular" end of the scale, counterbalancing *Harper's* and *Good Housekeeping* and a few other "up market" monthlies down the hall. Like the others, *She* is backed by the American Hearst Publications, but it has absolutely no counterpart in any other country and epitomizes what makes the Englishwoman unique.

Take a look at an ordinary cover: a smiling blonde in blue print bikini with matching skies, the lead article devoted to prize cruises to Yugoslavia, followed by: "Peter Fonda—a State of Freedom," "Women Need It as Much as Men, but Mustn't Ask for It—Guess What?," "What Witches Do—the Naked Truth Will Amaze You!" and "On the Job Hunt."

The contents are as diversified as the cover. Female sexuality is the most popular theme, and it is generally treated in a humorous fashion. The major pieces are often run in pairs—one serious and one light. The first is full of facts, the second is full of puns. The rest of the magazine is balanced between the usual "women's magazine" material—i.e., sewing and cooking and gardening—and straight information on everything from dentistry and group therapy and how to do your tax forms to an in-depth report on the Japanese riot police force. Pamela Carmichael is probably the only magazine editor in the world who would assign one writer to do both an interview with a film personality and a "thought piece" on Dr. Thomas Szasz's belief that psychology is the modern form of the Inquisition. She makes such assignments based on her firm belief that, since she herself is interested in both people and new ideas, her writer will share her interests and her readers will too. The *She* reader is not limited to "women's subjects" any more than Pamela Carmichael is.

These cheeky and inquisitive qualities make *She* emphatically different from *Cosmopolitan.* The magazine is closer to *Playgirl* in its appreciation of female sexuality, but is aimed at the general audience, both married and unmarried. It reminds one of Scandinavia's *Femina* and France's *Elle* in its coverage of a wide variety of subjects, but even *Elle* and *Femina* would be reluctant to run a piece on Japanese riot police.

There is another similarity between *She* and *Femina*—the models wear little makeup and their hair is nearly always windblown and/or totally collapsed. This may be due to the fact that neither Anglo nor Nordic hair has ever yielded to the regimen of the Latin hairdresser. Since elaborate hairdos don't work, nobody in the North even tries anymore, and good cutting has taken over.

There is something else about *She* that is typically English—the attitude toward the professional woman. The "On the Job Hunt" cover-feature article, for example, lists forty-nine areas of jobs on a cross-reference tabulation of talent, temperament and skill. The emphasis is on the variety and originality of the jobs. The reader is supposedly already employed but looking for something more exciting or for a change of pace. Convenience of location and flexible hours tend to be considered job advantages. The selection runs the gamut from entering public relations to working as a farmer's secretary. Addresses of employment agencies are given; salaries and advancement prospects are not. The list does not include any position requiring long-term training, such as engineering, university teaching or medicine.

No matter what the position or how long a highly trained individual has been working at a job demanding her full-time concentration, the English professional woman is generally thought of as a "Temp." Often she is, if only because, in England, work itself does not have any particular status or mystique. Instead it is viewed as a sort of endurance test—The Daily Slog. There are little victories, but, having found a niche, one doesn't bother about "getting ahead"; one simply puts one foot in front of the other on the eternal treadmill. It's not surprising that women choose to take part only temporarily. No wonder they dream of marriage and family as an escape or value their freedom to choose to "do nothing" in the house.

To a great extent this antithesis of the work ethic predominates only in the upper and lower classes, and not in the well-entrenched middle class, which is moving upward these days. If Margaret Thatcher, a grocer's daughter, can become the Conservative Party leader, then obviously one can't say that in England hard work is futile. However, the upper class doesn't want to go anywhere, and so far the lower class hasn't seen much evidence of any real possibilities. Meritocracy is not exactly taking the country by storm.

For middle-class professional women, the equivocal attitude toward work can sometimes be an advantage. Female editors may quit and freelance for several years, then return to mastheads because publishers feel that "having had a chance to get the nesting urge out of their systems," they're "more reliable than someone who's been beavering away all the while." Female politicians may find themselves at the top of health, education or consumer affairs ministries, partially because prime ministers believe that women who are wives and mothers know more about such affairs than the experts.

On the whole, however, the professional woman suffers from her dilettante status. A female suffers as a child because neither her parents nor her teachers expect high standards of work from her. She suffers as a teen-ager because she is more likely than her brother to be forced out of school for financial reasons. She qualifies equally with men for state-subsidized higher education during her university years, but students are emphatic that the student grants (maximum $1500 per annum) cannot possibly meet the expense of living in a university area, and that parents are less likely to assist their daughters with extra living money than they are to aid their sons. In addition, if a woman marries a nonstudent while she is studying, her student grant can be cut almost in half.[6]

Aside from practical considerations, a girl wishing to continue her education runs into enormous psychological barriers as well as explicit "Sorry, No Women Allowed" rules. In 1972, five of the men's colleges that make up Oxford University decided to admit their first women undergraduates on an experimental basis, beginning in 1974. Three others agreed to open their faculties to women teaching fellows.

At the time, none of Oxford's twenty-three men's colleges had any women fellows, and of the nearly eight thousand undergraduates in the Oxford University complex, only about fifteen hundred were women. All of them belonged to one of the five colleges founded especially for them toward the end of the last century, fifty years after Mount Holyoke was founded for women in the United States.

In 1973, Rosemary Murray, fifty-nine, was appointed deputy vice-chancellor at Cambridge University. She had been president of New Hall, one of the three exclusively women's colleges at Cambridge. She is only the second woman to become a university "head" anywhere in the country. The first was Dame Lillian Lenson, who held such a post at the more sexually integrated London University from 1948 to 1951.

Theoretically, the sparseness of facilities for women students and women teachers should make no difference to the female student. Technically she is simply a social member of her college (where she is usually housed during the first two years), and should be free to utilize any of the other Oxford or Cambridge university facilities. In reality, however, each college tends to specialize. The men's colleges are better endowed, have better libraries and more extensive seminar programs. A woman from New Hall would have no access to a popular Cambridge seminar in political science given by a leading professor. The biggest drawback, of course, is that she is unlikely to get into Cambridge at all because, with fewer facilities, there are fewer places for women.

The emotional resistance to coeducation is formidable—so much so that when the Wilson government finally agreed to propose a women's equality bill at the end of 1974, it specifically avoided the issue, fearing, I was told by a student feminist, that this one clause would probably sink the whole proposal in Parliament. In Cambridge, the 1974 decision to integrate the colleges was accompanied by a report suggesting that only "two average-sized or one large college" should begin admitting women in any one year . . . and optimistically planning for communities of "not less than 25 to 30 percent women" by the end of the decade.[7]

At Oxford, Mr. R. F. S. Hamer, junior censor of Christ Church College, elaborated a remarkable thesis in his attack on the decision to integrate: "There is no proof that it is the right thing to do. This is a major decision, and it is our duty to debate the justification of such a move. . . . Most people accept that they [women] are human—except advertisers—but my position is simply that since the exclusion of women from these colleges is presumed to be an injustice, this proposition must be debated. There is a duty to explain what good this move will do. Show me the tremendous proof that there is an injustice! . . . No doubt these women liberationists will not bother to find out what the real issues are—these woolly-minded, vaguely progressive women who go prancing about making a song and dance about something they have not bothered to understand properly.[8]

England is a groupist society; i.e., the highest status and greatest satisfaction for most people come within the team, the school, the club, the social class. Even the prime minister functions only as group leader within the Cabinet. Thus, antagonism toward allowing women into the exclusively male schools is a part of the overall picture of discrimination practiced against all outsiders.

The "proper" place for women wanting more education is thought to be in the secretarial schools and the hairdressing colleges. When a woman graduates from these institutions, her biggest club is the Temp circuit, dominated by the vast Alfred Marks and Brook Street employment bureaus that place thousands of secretaries a year. Their specialty is supposed to be the well-dressed Girl Who Knows What She Wants, and demands it. But what does she want? In the end, it is likely to be a job with no future, no guarantees and pay that rarely amounts to more than $5000 a year before taxes.

Women making the Temp rounds must be flexible and able to enjoy new jobs, new people and new routines, but all they get for their imagination and adaptability is the freedom to find a new job the following week. And when business hits a slump, the woman is the first to be in trouble and the one most likely to have the lowest dole from the government. Her employment stamps (Social Security payments) are inferior to those of a steady worker, and she may not have kept them paid up anyway.

The workingwoman's image of herself is so low in England that comments such as "Oh, I could never learn to drive a car" are still not uncommon. Employment bureaus for career women have found that, when they advertise a job with a salary of $8,400, no one responds. When the job is readvertised at $3360, applications pour in.[9] Despite the impressive accomplishments of the million-plus Englishwomen since 1969 who have "decabbaged" themselves by going to work, one invariably finds that the real gains are low.

The rest of the world has the idea that the Englishwoman, like the En-

glish economy, is muddling along all right. In actuality, the country is slipping behind the rest of Europe in important areas such as GNP growth rates
and executive pay scales, and the Englishwoman isn't doing much better.
Her wages are still only a little better than half those of a man.[10]

On a comparative scale with her European sisters, the Englishwoman is
least likely to pursue a profession, except in the area of medicine. Unfortunately, medicine has less status in the United Kingdom than elsewhere and
it does not pay very well either.

In fact the long-suffering nurse has maintained England's National
Health System with her ceaseless work in near-slavery conditions. Until
the sixties, she was often confined to a woman's dormitory and paid as little as 50 cents an hour—earning in some cases less than she would receive
on welfare.

Despite having been among the first in Europe to have the vote and the
right to hold office, the Englishwoman only recently won legal guarantee of
her equality. Occasionally efforts to that end had been made in Parliament,
but, until the beginning of the seventies, such ideas were rejected out of
hand. As late as 1973, feminists protesting in the galleries were expected to
be happy that their bill wasn't rejected outright. It was instead simply
strangled by a genteel English trick known as "talking out"; namely, the
bill was not voted on by the time business was finished at 4:00 P.M. one
Friday and therefore automatically died.

By the end of 1974, the Labour Government was backing a Woman's
Rights Law. Prime Minister Harold Wilson heralded the move as progressive, although his government was still issuing lower pensions for women
as well as offering five times as much job training to male employees. Un-
derstandably, there are some reservations among feminists about the effica-
cy of the law.

Somehow, in 1970, Parliament did pass a simple law requiring equal
pay for equal work, effective in December 1975. It stipulated the five-year
delay to enable industry to prepare for the enormous change. Industry has
cheerfully done so by sending out memos to personnel directors explaining
that they should organize their staffs so that women are confined to certain
areas such as clerking and cleaning. With no men being hired for these positions, no one can complain that the men are better paid. Since the law
does not provide for equality of opportunity, this manipulation of the law
cannot be challenged.[11] Presumably, however, Wilson's Equality Bill will
end this gerrymandering.

For a society that supposedly provides for the welfare of its workers,
England offers few protections for women. A law that guarantees a woman

the right to hold her job if she becomes pregnant is only at the drafting stage. Not only can her employer fire her, but the buildings-fund manager can create trouble for her and her husband over their mortgage, since newlyweds can be required to sign forms agreeing not to have children while paying off their debt.[12]

Once a woman has her baby, she has no right to delay returning to work. If her employer has been generous enough to keep her job open for her, he usually requires that she return within three weeks, docking her pay in the meantime. The state does not give a child allowance for the first child, and weekly allocations for subsequent children—less than $3 each—are hardly adequate. The notorious Supplementary Benefits due to mothers "in unusual circumstances" are coated with forms and restrictions and served up with generous doses of pious charity. Except for the women's unions that have been forming in the seventies in the wake of the feminist movement, there is no pressure from any quarter to change these laws which place the burden of child raising so firmly and heavily on women. Society apparently assumes that motherhood is such a pleasurable and frivolous pastime that women will pay practically anything for the privilege.

By the early 1970s, women constituted more than one-third of the work force in England.[13] The greatest leap forward came in 1969, a year that saw seventy thousand more women working than the year before. Since then women have continued to maintain their importance in the work force, although both sexes have suffered layoffs in the current economic crisis.

As noted before, not everyone drifts from one job to the next in butterfly bliss until some fine morning when the wedding bells ring. If that were the case, Britain would hardly be the home of Margaret Thatcher, who successfully challenged Edward Heath for the leadership of the Conservative Party; or of Barbara Castle, Labour Minister of State for Social Services; businesswoman Mary Quant; social columnist Jilly Cooper; terrorist Bridget Rose Dugdale; theoretician Eva Figes; or playwright/director Joan Littlewood. How did such women achieve their success? There are far too many of them and they exist in too many fields to be anomalies. Where does such a strong strain fit into the picture?

The answer in England, as in France and Italy, lies in the social structure. Despite the roots of democracy, the Magna Carta, John Stuart Mill and modern welfarism, England is as class conscious as any European country. The Old Boys networks of the exclusive private schools still control the country. As Disraeli said, England is "two nations—the People and the Privileged."

The middle class is also there, of course; as noted before, it is the middle class that keeps England afloat. But somehow, when it comes to things like sending one's child to the "right" secondary school, or casting one's vote, or relying on the National Health for tonsillectomies, people revert to the traditional two-class system of values. As Nancy Mitford so accurately pointed out, in England even speaking patterns break down into U (upper) versus non-U.

The result of this U versus non-U system has been a neat division of the country into teams—Tory versus Labour, Union versus Management and Stockholders. Occasionally these forces join in monumental struggles that result in widespread and endless strikes.

How does English "bloody-mindedness" work in practice? Like this: a coal miner barely makes a living wage, has no security for either himself or his family if his mine closes down and very little if he happens to be involved in an accident or is a victim of black lung disease. But the members of the upper class will refuse to concede one jot to his demands. In fact, when Mich McGahey's Scottish miners produced their New Charter in mid-1974, asking for a £5000 ($12,500) guaranteed wage plus sickness benefits, Peter Wilsher, business columnist of the relatively liberal *Sunday Times*, promptly trotted out his own charter demanding $50,000 and an industrial health program to compensate for falling hair, overdeveloped paunch, ulcers, correspondent's alcoholism, cynicism and other related industrial diseases.[14] Naturally enough, when Peter Wilsher and the Establishment ask the workers to observe the Social Contract by politely refraining from striking, the miners refuse.

The English class system is so tightly controlled that two out of every ten people own a grand total of 84 percent of the country's wealth. A woman who is not born with the silver spoon will not be handling a six-digit bankbook in England simply because she invents the executive jet or the Barbie doll. The only outside possibilities lie in the world of pop music and fashion where Melanie and Mary Quant and Twiggy have made their marks. Even there, people are often incensed that someone from the lower classes is not only making money but being awarded with the rank of OBE (Order of the British Empire) by the queen. "I mean," carped one supposedly liberal journalist, "how could one possibly address Lord Ringo?"

In the past the Old Boys regime left women out in the cold. But an interesting trend has developed. Women are so obviously outside the system that they are not expected to participate in the regime, and thus at the top levels are accepted more on their own merits than men are. This is how Pamela Carmichael can be hired to run a magazine, not because of her connections or her experience, but because of the impression she makes in a conversation, her practicality and vivaciousness. This is how a Barbara Castle can win elections and be appointed to important ministries, how Mary Manley took over the Tory *Examiner* from Jonathan Swift in the 1700s and Nancy Astor became the first woman to be seated in English Parliament in 1919.

It is significant that feminine firsts often take place inside the Tory government. The Tories are traditionally the most class conscious and therefore the most likely to elevate a woman of class and position over a workingman. It is also important that an unusual number of women who come to prominence—from Nancy Astor through to Germaine Greer—are foreigners. As such, they are more easily accepted in the class structure where their accents cause amusement not humiliation, and where they can thus compete more freely in the work market.

Looking at the successful Englishwoman again, one notes that Pamela Carmichael—despite her cheekiness—is not one to drop her h's. Neither are any of the other women who stand out as successes in England. The "working girls" who make it may have come up through the ranks, but they all turn out to have proper backgrounds with the exception of Twiggy, whose manner of speaking is emphasized in every feature written about her.

There was a period in the mid-sixties when both sexes with Cockney accents were as popular as Eliza Doolittle was with Professor Higgins, but that fad has passed. Fortunately, the slow emergence of women in positions of power has not proved equally transient.

For the rest of the successful few, there are three common denominators. One is the class factor already analyzed. The next is eccentricity. England is such a strongly groupist country, with such an emphasis on "pulling with the team" and "holding up your part of the deal," that certain formal concessions have had to be made to the eccentric. The eccentric woman differs from the individualist because she is a unique phenomenon—that is, she's not trailblazing a new way of life, but simply giving vent to the impractical oddities in her nature. She's the Victorian explorer Daisy Bates marching through the jungle in her hat and crinoline. Admired by a few during her lifetime, and by many after death, Daisy Bates still was never permitted to join the Royal Geographical Society and assert her individualism inside the group.

Acceptance of eccentricity is what keeps *She* a thriving publication straddling both intellectual and "women's items" worlds. It is the protective coloring worn by many successful English business or professional women, as well as by English women politicians. As long as women are eccentric, they don't threaten female stereotypes and don't arouse the full ire of the tightly bonded men's groups. Conservatism only starts roaring from the rafters when women act as the shock troops for a large group to follow.

The third characteristic that is valuable for the English career woman is the license to be cheeky. Cheeky is an odd word—rarely used in the United States, and practically untranslatable in languages of other countries. For the English, it means the peculiar right to be bad accorded to someone of a lower status. It translates into the American "uppity" better than anything else. It is used to describe the actions of children, fluffy dogs and workers. It can be a fond adjective—in fact, it generally is, when giving implicit parental approval for mischievous or antiauthoritarian acts. "My, you are a cheeky one, aren't you?" is a common approbation, although, "Don't you get cheeky with me," is a warning that parental fun and games have come to an end. It always carries an undertone of condescension, implying higher status on the part of the speaker.

Because of her weaker physical strength and the assumption that she is innately more civilized, a girl is encouraged to be more cheeky than her brother. The tiny two-year-old, bedecked in curls and bows, can be seen talking back to her father and biting, kicking or slapping her mother. Parents won't accept this kind of rebellion from a son, but they'll laugh and tease an infuriated daughter.

In the same way, the feisty female adult is encouraged by society. "Only a woman could have smacked Maudling like that," people will say approvingly of Bernadette Devlin's attack on a fellow Parliamentarian. Modesty Blaise and Mrs. Peel are modern equivalents of the original Mary Poppins—eccentric, self-centered, strong and *willing to be bad.*

On the plus side of the ledger, the Englishwoman's dauntless pluck makes it possible for her to endure many situations that other women are afraid to face. It has led to England's having the only female muscle act in the West.[15] It means that newspapers regularly carry stories like the one about the woman army parachutist who fell 2400 feet on her first jump attempt when her parachute failed to open. She immediately went back for her second try with the remark, "I'll just have to forget that nasty jump." It translates into Englishwomen naturally accepting the idea of making a round-the-world voyage in a rubber raft without even knowing how to swim, or setting up home in the Arctic or the equator with only a box of tea to remind them of the comforts of home.

Not surprisingly, this phenomenon has produced a high rate of female violence. The widely praised Judith Todd, sentenced to a Rhodesian jail for her reformist views, is close kin to the Price sisters and Judith Ward and all the other Irish revolutionary women who have filled the British terrorist wards in recent years.

Bernadette Devlin simply used the House of Commons as a more acceptable way of expressing the same cheekiness as Bridget Rose Dugdale, who stole more than $20 million worth of paintings for the Irish cause. These women hark back to the firebrand, Emmeline Pankhurst, and her daughters of the suffragette days. All of them are passionate Lady Godivas, willing to do anything for their cause.

It could be argued that their acts are not antisocial, since Judith Ward and the Price sisters are heroines within their own societies. But the picture of an unusual degree of female violence does not stop with the Irish Republican Army (IRA). In 1973, the Home Office released statistics on violent crimes for the first years of the decade, and found that in one year, between 1970 and 1971, female violence had risen 16.6 percent, while male violence had risen only 11.8 percent. The biggest jump was in the fourteen- to seventeen-year-old female group, where there was an increase of 60 percent. Girls in that category were burglarizing homes and attacking old ladies with hammers while snatching their purses. Older women were found to be the brains behind frauds and husband poisoning.[16]

The pattern of violence starts young. An eleven-year-old girl, Mary Bell, was the topic of headlines for weeks in 1968 during the trial where she and a girlfriend were accused of murdering two little boys. Her friend was acquitted, but Bell was charged with manslaughter in both cases and sent to an institution for the criminally insane. Since then, according to Gitta Sereny, a journalist who is campaigning for proper treatment of these violent children, preadolescent girls have continued to murder or attempt to murder, although authorities try to keep such cases secret. This is the cheeky child carrying her rebellion to total confrontation. How does society react? With the same indulgence as before.

When Bridget Rose Dugdale was in the dock for her first burglary charge—that of taking over $300,000 worth of paintings and silver from her father's country house—the judge gave her a two-year suspended sentence and told her, "I think the risk that you will ever again commit burglary or dishonesty is extremely remote." That was in 1973. A year later she pulled off a heist nearly ten times as big, was captured and sentenced to nine years in Limerick Prison, where she is the only woman in the political ward. The authorities had finally taken her seriously. The newspapers, however, not only still referred to her as a "girl" at age thirty-three, but implied that her crimes were due to the bad influence of her boyfriend.

Society was not much more jolted by Judith Ward, who was convicted of helping to plant a bomb on a bus carrying English servicemen and their families. Twelve of the passengers were killed, a numerical high-water mark in the "Irish Problem." During Judith Ward's trial, the court was heavily guarded, and the judge termed her action heinous. But the newspapers still referred to her as a "girl" (after all, she was only twenty-five), and set out to prove that she was not to blame for her actions. They attributed her behavior to her overwrought reaction to the shooting death of her husband a few months earlier or to the malicious goading of other male members of the IRA.

For the women and girls who commit frankly antisocial crimes, the picture is much the same. Although the 1973 Home Office report noted that women accounted for only one in seven indictable offenses, there was a hidden factor indicating that the figures revealed only a small part of the overall female pattern; a senior officer can decide not to prosecute a case if he feels that "more purpose can be served by not bringing charges." In that case, an official caution is issued to the woman. The act is recorded and can be taken into account for sentencing if she is up before the court later, but it does not go on the public record. The Home Office found that approximately three times as many women are cautioned for an offense of violence as are actually convicted. In comparison, fewer men are cautioned for such offenses than are convicted. There is a greater tendency to caution female offenders involved in cases of violence than in any other type of major crime. Again the tendency is to write off the woman as cheeky but harmless.

With all this political militancy and anti-Establishment behavior, what about the Women's Movement in England? Unfortunately, despite competence, determination and a history of demanding equal rights, English Women's Liberation groups today are splintered, ineffective and laboring under widespread ridicule and misinformation. For example, Arianna Stassinopoulis, the popular essayist, will staunchly defend equal pay and opportunities in one breath, and in the next launch into a vitriolic attack on legislation and organized feminism with comments like: "In the United States, the Equal Rights Amendment [means that] . . . GENTLEMEN and LADIES signs will have to disappear from public lavatories. There will be unisex loos." And, "Because Women's Libbers disapprove of different sex roles, [American] teachers are telling their pupils that lesbianism or homosexuality are sex experiences as valid as any other."[17]

Stassinopoulis is an intelligent and well-informed woman. Why she uses such statements is a mystery, but her words are part of the general chorus of derision and deception directed toward "The Libbers." Meanwhile, the Englishwoman is not sure she wants fundamental changes. She is not sure of her ability to change. She is not sure that other women will join her in change.

Her indecisiveness stems from the two parts of her strength. First, the professional success and financial security of the upper-class woman puts her at odds with the lower-class woman. Both will more often choose to stand with their class than with their sex. Second, the Englishwoman's cheekiness is only cheekiness. She still views herself as a "girl" whose strength is not great enough to attack the massive male Establishment, and whose rights aren't worth very much anyway.

Although the Woman's Group on Public Welfare lists over one hundred national women's organizations operating in Great Britain, the majority of these have their roots in charity and service organizations which still have only peripheral involvement in women's causes.[18] The current Women's Movement sprang out of the student activist campaigns of sixty-eight when women found they still had only second-class status; i.e., they were good enough to carry banners and make coffee but not good enough to give speeches and make policy. American female visitors played a proselytizing role. Women workers also became more active, and by 1969 the Movement could boast a major women's labor strike for equal pay at the British Ford plant—an action that would have been unthinkable even two years before.

Today, however, Women's Liberation groups in England still have no national office, no central means of communication and generally accepted priorities. This lack of national organization reflects the varied needs of women in unions, women who want nursery places for their children and/ or women who need equal pay and equal rights across the board, but it also causes friction and redundant efforts. The first worldwide Women's Liber ation festival scheduled to take place on the Isle of Man was canceled. Why? Because "the response was not encouraging and local support wasn't good."[19]

4

Working in a Man's Castle

The English have a name for the woman who spends a
great deal of time and energy on her environment—house-proud. Although
few people will admit to using the adjective sneeringly, everyone resents a
woman who puts her possessions above everything else. The comment,
"Oh, she's a bit house-proud, isn't she?" carries all the approbation of
saying, "She's a bit hoity-toity, isn't she?"

The British like having their homes "rumpled and hotchpotch." They
like having children who come in for tea covered with mud. They like having a carpet that can withstand the tramping of boots recently returned from
a walk on the moors. Husbands in the Civil Service or the army may be
meticulously neat, but they don't want a wife who demands that her sense
of order rule the household. A timetable regimen like that of the French
ménagère or the German *Hausfrau* is abhorred.

This attitude is partially due to the fact that the home is considered the
man's castle. Fifty-five percent of English dwellings are owner-occupied,

thanks to the oldest home-mortgage system in the world. Until the late sixties, mortgages could be financed only on the husband's wages, and most often it is he who takes responsibility for modernizing the house. American television comedies parody the wife in jeans, harping at her husband to help her paint the kitchen. United Kingdom comedies parody the husband in overalls harping at the wife to stop knitting and help him paper the sitting room.

Housework itself is considered a "nothing" job, once the decorating has been done and the furniture has been bought. The house is small, after all, and staffed with all the antislavery devices of two continents. The point is "A woman shouldn't have to work."

The exterior of most city and suburban homes is a precise replica of its neighbor—groupistic and uniform. Only the gardens burst with color and originality. But again, the garden is traditionally the man's turf—his place to grow roses and escape The Daily Slog.

The household ordinarily revolves around the television set. If you can't afford $25 for a used one, you simply rent a set from the neighborhood lending store. The English are involved in television more than their counterparts on the Continent, because the programs are more interesting and varied. It's not uncommon for an English couple to admit they haven't been out for two months because every evening there's been some program that they've wanted to watch. As in the United States, friends may be invited over for a snack and to watch a particular program, and people who drop in unexpectedly are likely to be shoved into a corner until Alf Garnett has finished his Bunkerisms for the evening.

England has more hours of daytime television than the Continent and most United Kingdom day programs are informative documentaries or lesson programs connected with children's schools. These and a multitude of weekly women's magazines fill the day for many lonely housewives.

Loneliness and boredom are the biggest problems of the newly married woman who doesn't work outside the home. Although the custom of dropping in on one's new neighbor is stronger in England than in any other European country, many neighbors are still rigidly reserved. The highest neighborly commendation is "they keep to themselves." New neighbors are looked on more as possible sources of rose ruining than of friendships. Garden-flat occupants jealously guard their plots of green. The war that ensues between them and people with children can be grotesque.

English cities, based on the conglomerate-of-villages principle, are particularly pleasant for shopping. Supermarkets, discount warehouses, shopping centers and even bulk buying through the mail are possibilities, but popping into the local greengrocer's for fresh vegetables and into the local bakery for bread persists. Stores are small, the owner knows the clients and everybody is informally introduced over the rising price of tomatoes. Such friendships, however, rarely lead to invitations to someone else's home, or to friendships between the husbands. This happens only when both men find themselves working on the same hobby, or happen to bump into each other at the same pub. The husband then often brings his new friend into the home.

Widening the family social circle is the man's prerogative. "I never thought about it," wives will comment. "Yes, John is the one who suggests we invite somebody new over. Once in a while I'll take the initiative when we have a party, but I'd feel strange introducing our neighbors down the street to him at dinner. I mean, *I* like her well enough, but that doesn't mean our husbands would get on, does it?"

Once the guests have arrived, sex-segregation traditions mean that the English hostess is cut off from conversations on politics or business or power in general. Instead, she and the other ladies retire after dinner while the men settle down for serious conversation over cigars and the second glass of port or brandy. This practice has largely disappeared among younger couples, but Barbara Cartland, England's Amy Vanderbilt, still allows fifteen minutes for the ritual,[20] an amount considered inadequate in the political and executive business circles where the most important conversations are held among the men after the ladies have "retired."

Cut off from expressing herself freely in a formal social context, the Englishwoman is denied entry to another traditional female province—the kitchen. Although English cooking is no longer limited to canned spaghetti and instant coffee, with many Englishwomen baking their own bread and making their own preserves (just as many sew their own throw pillows and curtains), there is a general complaint that nobody cares about cuisine. The English husband is a meat, bread and potatoes man. "He doesn't care what he has as long as it's the same thing every night," one career woman told me. "Not that I mind. I used to make up batches of steak and kidney that would feed us out of the freezer for a month, but then I found out Birds Eye meat pies satisfied him, and now I just keep weekly supplies of those on hand. A gourmet husband would be a bit difficult, anyway, wouldn't he?"

As the French Government was discreetly informed when Queen Elizabeth II went visiting in 1972, thirteen-course banquets are not necessary. The queen prefers simple meals in the Buckingham Palace style, consisting of a "beginning, a middle and a pudding."[21]

Yet another means of self-expression in the household—acting as comptroller of the finances—is also closed to the Englishwoman. Unlike the French or Italian wife, Mrs. Blogg is not the one to pay the bills or make the contract with the gas or electric company. In fact, if she tries, she must have her husband's signature or pay a bond of fifteen pounds. Legally, the wife has no right to see her husband's tax returns, although he is required to sign hers.

English law is adamant on nearly every point. The man is breadwinner and owns the home. When buying a new house one must be particularly careful to register it under both names. Otherwise the husband has every right to borrow against it or sell it without so much as mentioning the fact to his wife or giving her any of the proceeds.

Political tempers flare on the issue of whether to pay state child allowances to the mother of a family or to incorporate them into a tax rebate for the husband. Whatever a woman saves out of the housekeeping money is only half hers and half the goods she buys with it belong to the husband. If a woman doesn't contribute regularly to the joint bank account, it is considered to be entirely the husband's. If a woman needs a loan to start a business, bank managers often require her husband's signature on the application form, even though she finances and staffs the venture on her own. This has sometimes been required even when the woman was legally separated or divorced.

If all these avenues of self-expression are closed to the Englishwoman, how does she keep from going mad? The first solution lies in socializing with other women. Dropping into the local "caf" for a cup of tea or into the pub to have a glass of sherry with female relations, friends or working companions is a major activity. The Englishwoman is also at ease talking with men, despite the after-dinner, separate-sex tradition. She is not at all loath to getting into arguments over anything from politics to sexuality with men she knows well. She is less assertive than her husband in a group where she doesn't know people, but otherwise she is much more at ease in expressing her opinions than her American counterpart.

The other main area where she is effective is in the use of her household allowance. With a tight weekly budget for which she is accountable to her husband, the Englishwoman is the most price-conscious consumer in the West. She spends hours every week making sure she has bought the cheapest butter, going across town to take advantage of a children's shoe sale, ferreting out the tiny hole-in-the-wall supplier of wholesale toilet paper. When something like the sugar shortage happens, people on the streets can be heard muttering either, "Do you know who's got sugar?" or "You can get sugar at Tesco's if you hurry!"

When she's not bargain hunting, the Englishwoman is often playing Bingo or figuring up the football pools. In 1973, two women, Doris Binfield and a Mrs. X of Nottingham, jointly won $1.28 million in the soccer pools. It was said to be the world record. Meanwhile, Britain leads the world in the amount spent per adult on Bingo and other forms of betting, nearly $25 per adult,[22] a figure that reflects the national obsession with trying to make one's finances go further.

Lastly, the upper-class woman spends a good deal of her time in charity work. This does not always directly involve money. Often it concerns direct services such as driving old people around on visits or making toys for underprivileged children, or working for the hundreds of animal shelters.

The important questions are, "Do these activities give women satisfaction and status?" and "Why aren't there more Pankhursts in the seventies?"

The ultimate answer lies deep in class schism and the degradation of the workingman. If work is something one has to do, a daily punishment for being born into the wrong class, then work does not provide satisfaction and self-esteem. The simple pleasure of being taken care of becomes very important. As giggling teen-agers told a *Nova* interviewer, "Well, the husband has to do the work, doesn't he?" A career as child-wife, with a man taking the hard knocks, is enticing. Even if it means never being taken seriously. Even if it means meager wages for those who don't marry.

If a woman gets bored at home, she can always return to the working world. Temp circuits cry out for her, or she can join the ranks of women in industry and sales. A man doesn't have this freedom, and it is doubtful that he ever will. The question of whether or not the majority of women should relinquish this freedom in the face of the rising probability that they won't have a man to take care of them all their lives is important, but it is still largely academic in England.

5

Motherhood in Nanny Land

The English birthrate peaked in 1964, and then started downhill at a speed equivalent to the rising rate of women entering the labor force. By 1972, the English were having fewer babies than during the thirties.[23] It would appear that the attractions of motherhood in the United Kingdom are quickly yielding to the lure of the pay envelope and the "breed less, breathe easier" maxim. But the picture is not as clear-cut as all that. As we have seen, the Englishwoman's opportunities in employment are not extensive. A woman who chooses a career suffers social pressure. Means of expression in the home also have low status, leaving only clubs, charities and Bingo as a competitive means of self-expression. Motherhood continues to hold its own as a viable career alternative.

There are many signs that this is the case. One of the most curious is that England is the only country where baby-snatching excites national interest. Sometime, somewhere in other countries, someone *must* snatch a baby from its buggy while it is parked in a front yard or outside a shop. One sees babies elsewhere, ripe for snatching. But if it happens, nobody knows about it. In England each snatch is a national emergency, accompanied by blazing headlines, psychiatrists appearing on television and exclamations of sympathy and horror for the mother, the baby and the baby snatcher herself.

Although the incidence of baby-snatching is increasing, the actual number of cases is tiny and the psychological profile of the culprit hardly threatening: a nubile, teen-age girl, with no thoughts of ransom—only insecure and looking for someone to love and depend on her. Sometimes she does it to bind herself closer to her boyfriend or young husband. Not the sort of individual to shake a nation if that nation were not extremely preoccupied with the importance of motherhood. Where does the baby-sitter fit into the history of nanny land?

Over a hundred and fifty years ago the joys of motherhood lost out to the trend toward a leisurely living style. By the turn of the century, motherhood as a trade profession was passé. Nobody who was anybody did it anymore. It was, after all, a form of physical work—not only intolerable for the Privileged but distasteful to the People, as well. One had heirs, of course. One had to continue having heirs. But at the moment of partum, one turned this product over to Nurse or Nanny.

The Professional Mother existed in many countries during Queen Victoria's time. Upper-class women in Italy and France, as well as in England, used the *au pair* system to make motherhood a half-day occupation. In England, however, the middle class as well as the upper class strongly believed that child care was a revolting occupation. Another difference was that, in England, Nanny somehow managed to become a uniquely powerful phenomenon, the household tyrant.

During the first part of this century, Nanny evolved from Jane Eyre's gentle governess, afraid to ask for a second crust of bread, to the snappy Mary Poppins, who frightened Mrs. Banks out of her admittedly limited senses with the mere hint of leaving. This evolution was simple. Nanny became a tyrant *because* she was so popular. In Jane Eyre's time, there were only a few families who offered employment. Fifty years later, a good Nanny was as valuable as a good executive secretary is today. The family was willing to do practically anything to keep her.

There were two problems inherent in the system, and it is fascinating to see which one caused the demise of the Nanny.[24] The most glaring was the plight of the displaced mother. "I had an absolutely super Nanny," an Englishwoman will say. "Never saw much of Mother. She always seemed to be a bit ill, poor thing."

Of course she was ill. That's what everybody expected of a lady. With her hypochondria and opium addiction, her years of teas and weekending, the displaced mother could not, obviously, oust Nanny from the household. Nanny's departure was accompanied by many weak cries from the drawing room of, "How shall I ever manage?" In a life devoted to doing absolutely nothing, coping with heirs appeared an impossible task.

It was the second problem that brought about the disappearance of Nanny, and even this might not have succeeded without World War II. The second problem was Nanny's status. Despite the fact that she was treasured wherever she went, despite her unique role as the only person allowed into the gulf that separates adult from child, Nanny knew that nobody who had other options would take the job. When the war came along and job markets opened up in hundreds of fields previously closed to women, Nanny was tempted. She had always been strongly motivated by a sense of duty, and industry was now thought to be the place where patriotic duty lay. Somewhere along the line she also tired of being a nickname in another family's snapshot album, and decided in favor of her own husband and her own heirs. As the strong character in the system, she was the one who set about creating her own demise, leaving behind her a trail of nostalgic children's stories about one of the few consistently self-propelled single women in literature.

Nanny did not succeed in systematically disenfranchising the English mother alone. She did not, after all, care for children all their lives. At age five, boys were traditionally shipped off to boarding school. The girls often lived in the nursery until later, but they were expected to become full-time members of their sex/age group by age eleven or thirteen.

Boarding school has always held a notorious place in English life, as will be seen when we focus on childhood. True, it was more expensive than a servant, so that fewer individuals were personally influenced by it. Still the mystique surrounding boarding school seeped through society, and Enid Blyton's tales of Malory Towers days were vastly more popular with little girls who never left home than with the girls who actually attended the schools. As far as the English mother was concerned, it was one more piece of evidence that professionals could raise her children better than she could.

The Victorians believed that placing the child in an isolated peer group under a severe but rigidly impartial disciplinarian was the only way to civilize the child. This could be done by the governess (the word itself is self-explanatory), but total physical separation from the home was the preferred method. The earlier a child was exposed to the hardening process of structured group living, the better the child would be able to meet the hardening responsibilities of adulthood. Living with Mother, on the contrary, had a weakening effect, because mothers were prone to emotional coddling.

At the same time, in the non-U sector of English society, Mother developed a mystique nearly as strong as that of the Italian mamma. Children in these families flock around the strong central figure of Mum. She gives them something to eat—even if she has to go without. She protects them from attack; she tells them what is right and wrong. Magnificent Mum is alive and well in mining communities, on the soccer field, on the construction site and in the underworld.[25] In London, if you call a plumber or a removal man, he arrives with a couple of brothers to do the job. "We've got the most business because we've got the biggest family," one builder announced proudly. "Each one o' me brothers has his specialty, and me mum takes care of the phone and the schedule." It is this class, where the mother counts, that produces the Baby-Snatching Instant Mum.

The status of the upper-class mother underwent change in the middle of this century when it was discovered that children suffered long-term mental and emotional retardation when deprived of their parents. This discovery, which hardly caused a ripple in countries that had believed in the deprivation effect all along, was articulated by Dr. John Bowlby, whose studies in conjunction with the Tavistock Institute centered on juvenile delinquents —primarily children who had been separated from their parents during the blitz years. He concluded that the propensity of children toward delinquency and associated emotional problems was directly related to their having been separated from their mothers, particularly if the separation took place during their formative first five years.

Subsequent child psychologists have labeled Bowlby's work as simplistic, and he himself has modified his beliefs, but the original effect on his theories on government planning was profound. It was decided that the mother's place was with her child. Job-enticement programs were scrapped, since they would sap the very roots of society. The Victorian practice of awarding children to the father after a divorce was reversed. All mothers were good because their children needed them and them alone. Motherhood had regained its prestige. England's birthrate did not rise with the same alacrity as America's during the 1950s, but it did rise, and women who had worked all through the war went back home to take care of the brood. Queen Elizabeth and her husband produced four heirs and all was right with the world.

The argument between the Nanny and the Bowlby philosophies is still alive today, and a synthesis is emerging. The ideal now is to give children complete attention through infancy, and then plunge them into a peer group under the guidance of a professional paraparent. Boys are still sometimes sent off to boarding school by age seven, but for both sexes the desirable time to make the break is now thirteen. Oddly enough, after formal schooling is finished and the individual has firmly cemented a relationship with the sex/age peer group, teen-agers usually return home. They stay there, often paying rent out of the money they make at their first job, until they themselves marry and qualify for a mortgage or a council flat.

Now that we've examined the status of motherhood in England, what does the experience actually involve for the average mother?

In the initial stages of a relationship, birth control is considered the male responsibility. The resistance of young girls throughout Western society to the implication of scheming involved with the Pill or other forms of contraception is particularly strong in England. "It's like meeting your boyfriend with your nightie on, isn't it?" commented one teen-ager. Boys interviewed by the Opinion Research Center in March 1972, all knew about contraceptives, and most knew they could obtain condoms at barbershops, garages and in the men's room in many pubs. A few said they would go to a drugstore or a doctor.[26] Next to condoms, the Pill is the most popular method of contraception, followed by the diaphragm and other female contraceptives. Coitus interruptus is not considered by most young people, but apparently continues to be practiced among middle-aged people. The entire country recognizes and accepts vasectomy. The operation received publicity in the sixties, and in 1970 a retired grocer was describing his own experience and advocating the value of the operation for sexual happiness in marriage.

At that time, a *Sunday Times* reporter noted that everybody in the office sniggered a little at the interview and the grocer refused to give his name. Two years later, Michael Parkinson, a well-known television talk-show host, put an end to coyness in the lead interview of British *Cosmopolitan's* first issue. The story of Parkinson's vasectomy quickly took on legendary proportions. By 1974, when *The Sunday Times* was running a half-page feature on nine more vasectomy victors, ranging from Rev. Alan Whittle to concrete worker Tony Robb,[27] questions like, "Has it dropped off yet?" had become such clichés nobody seemed much worried anymore.

All the interviewees, however, had fathered more than one child. The Family Planning Association does not feel it is likely that a childless man—particularly if he's unmarried—will get a vasectomy in England. The operation was put on the National Health plan first in a London borough in January 1973, and now is available free everywhere. Privately it costs $60 in a clinic. By the mid-seventies, F.P.A. clinics alone were performing over ten thousand vasectomies a year.

The image of the knowledgeable young male and the ultimately prepared older man, however, represents only a small part of the overall picture. The primary responsibility for pregnancy still lies with the female. Although the boy may swagger about with a condom in his wallet, he feels little concern for "a bird who gets herself pregnant." Once a relationship begins she is the one who goes to the clinic to face the stares at her ring finger and find out about contraception.[28]

Ten years after the introduction of the Pill and the organization of the Family Planning Association, the number of illegitimate births and abortions has decreased. There are now approximately 60,000 illegitimate births annually—compared to nearly 70,000 in 1967—and the number of abortions seems to be stabilizing at around 115,000, not counting the approximately 50,000 performed on foreign women and an estimated additional 25,000 illegitimate abortions. According to a study done by Margaret Bone in 1973, this leaves approximately 50,000 unwanted births, but only a tiny percentage of this figure is put up for adoption. Under Bowlby's influence, social workers usually counsel keeping the child, and society still believes so strongly in the bond between mother and child that even children suffering from battered-baby syndrome are often automatically returned home.

Pregnancy follows the Northern European and American pattern of regular visits to the doctor, exercise and breathing classes and regular vitamin dosages. Women generally feel that pregnancy is "only natural" and that therefore they should "carry on without a fuss." Midwives are popular in England, as in the rest of Europe, and women report a special closeness with these professionals that makes the experience relaxed and enjoyable.

Childbirth at home occurs more often in England than in most other Western countries, but the procedure is being phased out. "Safety must come first" is cited as the official reason. It was found, after a hospital strike in Ashton-under-Lyne, that of the sixty-five mothers who had their babies at home, 72 percent chose to have their next child at home as well. Other studies indicate that nine out of ten women prefer to have every baby except the first at home. Furthermore, the safety argument is being challenged, since it has been shown that babies of normal weight have a better chance of survival if they are born at home where they are not exposed to hospital viruses. This would indicate that the traditional English practice of hospitalizing only women with problem pregnancies is most medically sound.[29]

Mothers complain that obstetrics wards are cold, unsympathetic and disagreeable places to spend their first forty-eight hours with their new baby. "I was ordered about from the moment I arrived," one disgruntled woman said. "Nobody has any feelings for you as a person or even as an intelligent part of the team that is supposed to be all working for one goal—the delivery of a baby. They plonk you in bed with an enema and a pubic shave like you were so much meat, and shoo your husband out as quickly as possible unless he's really firm about it. Once they wheel you into the delivery room, they shoot you with a spinal or jam the gas mask down. A lot of women I talked to had wanted natural childbirth, but they weren't given a chance to say so. With my second baby, I made sure I had a doctor who let me go through with it and then gave me the baby to hold right up next to me, but I could see the nurse thought that was a bad idea. She kept cautioning me not to breathe on it or jolt it and the like. As if we hadn't been jolting together up the hospital steps not twelve hours earlier."

Mothers who take advantage of the facilities for unmarried women at the Mother and Baby Homes emerge even more bitter. The original purpose of the homes was to provide women with a place to stay during the latter part of their pregnancies and for a short while thereafter, but with convent rules and a severe staff they became so unpopular they hardly exist today. Considering the fact that there were places for nearly twelve thousand in the 1960s,[30] this is a tragic loss of facilities, but unwed mothers prefer to find a room for rent or join a commune rather than submit to these rigid establishments.

Being an unwed mother has been popularized in England by such famous women as Vanessa Redgrave, Bernadette Devlin and Mia Farrow. Today, however, only Vanessa Redgrave remains steadfastly single. English society no longer throws women into the madhouse for conceiving children outside the bonds of marriage, as it did fifty years ago,[31] but the pressures to conform are still very strong.

Until 1972, nursery facilities in England lagged behind those of every other industrialized country except the United States. In that year, the Education Minister, who was then Margaret Thatcher, proposed a national network of nursery schools for three- and four-year-olds. The program's limited implementation has been due as much to the falling birthrate, which somewhat eased demands on primary school, as to official effort. The educational authorities believe that there will be a place for every three-year-old "whose parents want him to attend" by the school year beginning in 1977. Unfortunately for working mothers, these schools are half-day affairs and close during the Christmas, Easter and summer holidays. Arrangements for lunches are made, however, to give children of poverty-level families a regular free meal.

Taking matters into their own hands, mothers in cities have organized play groups with a rotation system of parent participation. These have accommodated over a hundred thousand children.

Children are sent to school at an earlier age in England than in any other Western country except France. If they reach their fifth birthday by the first day of any of the three annual school terms, they start school. This is the point at which society begins to take over the child's upbringing, and Mother is left either to produce another child or to find another occupation.

What has Mother been doing during those vital first five years? According to Dr. John Gibbens, whose book, *The Care of Children from One to Five,* has enjoyed steady popularity since 1936, "Many mothers are apt to think that the first year of life is the most difficult, that once a child has reached his first birthday there is no need to worry anymore. He will be able to fend for himself. To my mind this view is mistaken. [In the first year it] is the growth of the body that you are witnessing. But with the coming of his second year you have to deal with something quite different—the growth and development of the emotions, the intellect, the child's spirit, his knowledge of right and wrong, his sense of dependence and independence . . . this is far from easy . . . there is no question of that—I am old-fashioned enough to believe that the finest task for a woman is the making of a happy home, the bearing of children, and the bringing-up of children so they may have a good start in life. . . . Young children really need the constant companionship of their mothers, and feel all at sea if they are brought up by other women."[32]

Gibbens is concrete in his advice. He is talking to mothers exclusively. Fathers can help occasionally with stern commands to "go to sleep immediately," but Gibbens does not mention other fatherly responsibilities. He comments casually that no child should be given threats to "wait until your father comes home," arguing that such discipline is unfair because it keeps the child on tenterhooks and may lead to a fear of the father.

Discipline is strictly mother's affair, like washing nappies or spoon-feeding the child. Gibbens' image of the mother is an individual who is firm but also friendly. He describes her efforts at character building as nothing less than "the creation of a masterpiece." He disapproves of thumb-sucking and is emphatically opposed to the "detestable" practice of giving a baby a pacifier, warning that it will rot the infant's top, front four teeth.

He is remorseless about children over age two who refuse to give up their bottles or who suck their blanket or bits of cloth. He advises staging an accident so that the offending item falls into the fire. "It may be difficult not to smile at his look of utter consternation, but anyway, you go on to say how sorry you are, but never mind; he's getting too big for [such habits anyway]. I have never known this bit of acting to fail—the child accepts it with a perfectly good grace."[33]

Gibbens is equally stern on the subject of bedtime, but more flexible on toilet training and feeding. Masturbation is passed over as unimportant at this age and "easily treated" by giving the child more exercise through nursery school or a holiday on a farm. Don't make the child feel guilty. Be sure to answer all questions about where babies come from honestly but without too much detail.

The child is considered malleable, possessing certain inherent strengths and weaknesses which the mother should recognize and accept as soon as possible. All babies are not born equal. "However good the soil, a wild daffodil cannot become a King Alfred flower, a carthorse will not become a racehorse." It is the mother's duty to make the child accept this.

The mother's role as the one who shapes the next generation is a strongly appealing one, reinforced in many ways by society. Career women will repeatedly say they gave up work during their children's first five years. Some say so proudly. Others only comment mildly that they hope their daughters will have good state nursery facilities to help with the job. R. K. Kemdall, in a series of studies of university graduates in the early seventies, found that over two-thirds of all professional women who dropped out of the labor force did so to look after their children. "Women in Society," a report presented to the Margate Society in 1972, also pointed out that it took a very rebellious and self-confident person to articulate a decision against having children.

That same year in London, Elaine Morgan published *The Descent of Woman,* an anthropological polemic tracing human pre-history from the female point of view. Her conclusions are important to women in many fields, but her chapter on "What Women Want" is particularly relevant here. Arguing that women must make society understand the importance of the mother and the obligation to support her profession systematically, she adds:

"What [women] will no longer have any right to do, once 'accident' is altogether ruled out and every child is the result of conscious choice, is to give birth to it and then shortly afterwards start raising the cry of 'Will no one for Pete's sake come and take this kid off my back?' . . . We must face the moral consequence, which is that motherhood will be an option, not an imperative; that anyone who thinks the price too high needn't take up the option; and from that point on, where children are concerned, more inexorably than ever before, the buck stops here. On the distaff side. If we try to dodge that, we lose all credibility."[34]

Morgan advocates that a mother be supported by organized society, or by a husband who also wants children, or by herself through a seesaw technique of formal work some years, motherhood others.

In a sense, her idea is an outgrowth of the Nanny concept, but her Professional Mother of the future has built-in features like a womb and a supportive husband and/or society. Implicitly, Morgan is upholding the concept that all women need to have children. "The buck stops . . . on the distaff side." Her very choice of the word distaff emphasizes woman's maternal nature. Morgan goes on to conclude that once reluctant mothers opt out of procreation, the daughters of future generations will all be natural "broodies fizzing with estrogen." The idea conjures up visions of lines of ladies outside the Baby Licensing Bureaus, or the granting of a Baby License as Grand Prize to the winner of the Miss World Contest.[35]

6

Growing Up Cheeky

From the beginning, English girls lead very separate lives from their brothers. On the surface this hardly seems true. What about all those fictional troops of English sister-and-brother teams? What about the unisex bands of teen-agers wearing the same costumes and hairstyles, sporting asexual nicknames and worshiping androgynous pop stars?

While it is true that English girls are encouraged to punch back on the school ground and are given a physical training as rigorous as that of the boys, they are treated quite differently emotionally. This starts during infancy, when the boy is supposedly favored by Mum while the girl belongs to Daddy. Mothers and fathers play with "their" children differently— Mum praises her son's independence, gives him a hug when he's hurt himself before shooing him out to play with the other children. Dad is present only in concentrated doses. He is less sympathetic to his daughter's scrapes and tears but encourages her rebelliousness, even her disapproval of him. A popular television commercial concludes with a zoom focus on a tiny daughter telling her clown father seriously, "I don't think that's funny" in an adorable little lisp.

Girls are supposed to be well-spoken and by nature more civilized than boys. Discipline—a word one hears in the first ten minutes of every Parent-Teacher's Meeting—rarely refers to girls. Mum takes over formulating personalities as children grow older. Mum is thought to have a mystical understanding of her female offspring that will bind them together through thick and thin, even if the family is upper class, and the child's life is actually spent with Nanny. The father can bitterly blame his daughter's rebellion on her Oxford education, bad company and lack of discipline. The mother is silent, for her guilt is knowing that the bond between her and her own flesh and blood has been broken.

As in France and Italy, the event that most clearly separates humans from animals—i.e., when the child begins to speak—is a very important one in the life of an English girl. Unlike the Latins, however, the English firmly approve of animals.

"I can understand landlords having rules against children," commented one reader of *The Sunday Times*. "But to deny my dog a roof over its head is downright uncivilized."

"Well, I think it's right for Swedish authorities to interfere if someone is mistreating a dog," an English professional woman said. "But they have no right whatsoever to interfere with disciplining children." Rather taken aback at her own statement, she thought for a minute, then added, "Well, I suppose, if there is a case of obvious brutality or neglect, but to investigate a family who administers a good spanking is ridiculous. A dog that cries on the other hand . . . after all, a dog can't talk, can it?"

England is the world's most animal-conscious nation. In families with both pets and children, the older children have full responsibility for their animals' feeding and grooming. Toddlers are allowed to play with the dog and/or cat and are taught to be gentle, kind and loving. "Don't hit the dog" is a far more stringent command than "Don't hit your brother or sister." Otherwise, as we shall see, the child's developing world of words becomes the chief means of expressing acculturation into the civilized adult society.

The child's life changes radically at five, upon entering "real school" and becoming suddenly a responsible individual. School behavior is important to parents and so is learning. Boys will be boys, and a certain amount of rowdiness is expected from them, but girls are expected to adapt quickly. Girls are not ordinarily caned as boys still are in many primary and secondary schools, despite the 1973 Inner London Education Authority's ban against corporal punishment. A very few teachers will still cane girls up to age eleven, but such treatment is rare. Parents, who would not consider protesting a teacher's bruising the palms or the backsides of their son, will be outraged if their daughter comes home crying. A boy's rowdiness must be curbed by physical force, but a girl poses no real threat, and therefore deserves no real punishment. Instead she is simply subjected to ridicule or shame.

The Victorian I-am-never-wrong father has disappeared to some extent. The upper-class father quite often opts out of his role entirely . . . or passes through his daughter's life only in flashes, with indulgent "Well done" accolades for a triumphant school year or thunderous "I'm cutting off your allowance" threats for a breach of etiquette. Lower-class fathers still feel responsibility, and can become violently disappointed when daughters don't live up to the paternal image of them.

The girl looks up to her mother for day-to-day instructions on manners. These are constantly reiterated and often quite complex. In the lower class, manners rest on the "don't make a fuss" principle, while in the upper, the antifuss precept is elaborated into an arduous set of rules about dress, posture, conduct and language. Barbara Cartland, in her popular *Book of Etiquette,* notes that the first words a baby learns to say are "Mummy" and "Daddy," and among the next six will be "please," "thank you" and "good-bye." She admonishes a school class to stand and address the teacher formally and expects a child to thank the cook for a good meal. Cartland further insists that while at boarding school, children should write thank-you letters to their parents for holidays, Christmas and birthday presents and parties.[36]

Language is crucial to the English. Accents and local dialects immediately reveal an individual's social class, and mothers are particularly proud of children who are "well-spoken." This is one of the major reasons for sending a child to an independent fee-paying school. Children who are articulate in the right way have a guaranteed entrée to the channels of power as adults.

Language is used not only to define who is educated, but also to give a girl her first sense of herself. She is silly or bright. She is sweet or cheeky.

Oddly, the importance of the ability to reason well verbally is not incorporated into parental discipline. English children are not encouraged to find out "why" they must not play with knives or take the grocer's apples. They are simply told "no." Disobedient children can be scolded or told, "Mummy doesn't love bad little girls," but they are given few explanations for parental rules.

It is fascinating to note how words are used to cope with emotional problems. By isolating an issue they divorce a person from the brunt of pain. In a long interview with five of the women who served as maids of honor at Elizabeth II's coronation, all of them slipped into calling themselves "one" or "you" when talking of crises in their lives. A widow said, for instance, "Having had this interest as well as running a large farm has helped one a little in the past year when one has lost both one's husband and one's father within a month of each other."[37]

"One" does not let oneself be carried away by emotions—whether one goes to a Malory Towers boarding school or a State Prison. Girls at the first institution are made to feel ashamed for any "first-night sniffing," while women at the second tell each other, "Might as well laugh as cry." After all, why create a fuss?

Crying is totally taboo for men, who feel vastly superior to women who break down. The English male feels that emotion should be strictly controlled, and he may turn violently on someone who is "moaning and sniveling." Women are more sympathetic, but still condescending. Emotions are a luxury one can indulge only when alone . . . or if one happens to be among the one in every six Englishwomen who is receiving care for mental disorder. (The ratio for men is one in nine.)

English children are separated more forcibly from their parents than any others in the West—not only by being placed in the nursery if they happen to come from a family with money (Bridget Dugdale lived in "the children's quarters"—an extra house next door to her parents), or by being made to start school at least a year earlier than children in other countries, or by being shipped off to boarding school, but in a hundred little ways. Children do not eat dinner with their parents. The young ones have tea around 5:30 or 6:00 P.M., give Daddy a perfunctory kiss when he arrives home from work and are banished to bed by 8:00 when the adults have their meal.

In the working-class home that does not have a staggered eating schedule, children are often required to be silent through the meal. More casual households isolate the grown-ups from the children by a wall of television programs that prevents any conversation until long past the children's bedtime. The pub—that cornerstone of adult group life—has traditionally been closed to children.

Liberalizing the law that leaves the kiddies parked at the Laundromat or on the sidewalk outside the pub door has been extremely difficult. The brewers don't want to sell soda pop and lose some of their beer business. The publicans don't want kids overrunning their establishments. The male patrons think it is bad enough that women have invaded and prettified the "saloons" so that "a man don't feel comfortable to do his drinking."

The basis for such isolation is quite simple, and concerns the English belief that children are evil. People may not feel this directly about their own offspring. They express their fears about their own children by trying to protect them from the taint of others in another social class. But, in their hearts, the English believe that the child is not to be trusted. The Victorian belief lingers that the only way to mold children into responsible adults who will know their place inside their social group is to put them through the harsh "boot camp" rituals of the schools. As W. H. Auden has said, "Every child deserves as much neurosis as it can stand."[38]

The concept is made crystal clear in literature. A *Lord of the Flies* descent into blind bestiality awaits any child who strays from civilized discipline. The movie *If* showed that children who are allowed the slightest leeway will destroy society with *Clockwork Orange* thoroughness.

Belief in the innate badness of the child also explains the regimentation in the schools. Corporal punishment is only the most visible expression of a rigid disciplinary system designed to whip a band of savages into a crack team of civilized young adults. These control measures are primarily emotional. "Fagging," for example, is a concerted emotional effort to break down a newcomer's individuality. Winston Churchill's school agonies are well documented. So are John Stuart Mill's. Notorious headmasters maintained their power by means of regular floggings. Supposedly such dictators are relics of the past, but scandals still occur.

Boys, with their burden of primal evil, bear the brunt of these grim experiences. But upper-class girls are not exempt. Boarding schools are equally proud of their ability to toughen the young female. Girls like those depicted in the Malory Towers books are not only disdainful toward "first-night-sniffers" suffering from homesickness. They also stoically march back into lacrosse games with bent and bruised ankles accompanied by admiring cries of, "Hooray for your determination!" from their games' mistress and comments of, "It won't do the foot any harm—probably do it good."

Others are not so ecstatic. Journalist Judith Stone wrote, "I went to boarding school when I was five, and I've regretted it ever since. There were some good things . . . two friends . . . the ability to eat institutional food. But there remains a haunting sense of having been acutely unhappy as a child."

She outlines the problem: when one can't go home at night, there is no safety valve, no escape from school bullies, no place of security and privacy and no one to help sort out real from imaginary injustices. There is the extreme awkwardness of beginning menstruation in a place where one is expected to bathe with roommates and undress in front of them. Stone's own letters to her family are all stilted and reserved. When anticipating a birthday visit, she writes, "Could you possibly send me a box of chocolates so it gets here on Wednesday or Thursday. . . . If you have a present for me, could you possibly bring it down with you as I like opening it with you?" Stone's mother wrote twice a week and visited once in every three, but Judith asks, "Please, could you come more often?" She felt she had no home. Having spent so much time away, her parents' house was alien and friendless.[39]

In other countries, such a Draconian way of life inside children's boarding schools would affect only a minute portion of society, but in England the regimen of child repression extends to most of the fee-paying day schools and to many of the state schools as well. Permissiveness disappeared with the sixties. The Inner London Education Authority has been the only one in the country to outlaw caning. Ignoring the experience of the rest of Europe where caning has been banned, English pedagogues conjure up specters of American Hell's Angels as soon as any such proposal is presented.

This is the country where the policeman does not carry a gun because to do so would encourage counterviolence. But when it comes to children, such concepts are simply ignored. It's no wonder that when Dr. David Shaffer of the Institute of Psychiatry in London conducted a study of the children under fourteen who had committed suicide, he found that the crucial factor involved a discipline crisis in which children had disappointed their parents by their lack of academic success.[40]

Rigorous school rituals and tests of strength operate with girls the same way as they do with boys. Women speak with nostalgia of their ability to overcome the hardships that were manufactured for them, the predawn sports practice and the horsehair blankets. They forget the pain and remember the triumph and the teamwork. They tend to react with the same grim determination when facing adversity in later life, a quality that makes them superb at carrying on, but not so good at rethinking, improvising and innovating. They are unsympathetic to emotional holocausts, tending to believe that fresh air and rigorous exercise will conquer all beasts. They prefer women who are bossy over women who are "sticky sweet humble."

The training accounts for the "tweed and oxford" quality of the older upper-class women, the feats of female daring on mountains and oceans and deserts, the "chum" ability to rough it with a man. It combines with cheekiness to make for female success in politics and business and the

IRA. It explains the curious combination of determination and foot dragging that marks the ordinary British worker, who will move mountains to overcome adversity and bring work to a dead stop at the first whiff of unfairness. It underlies the perverse English pleasure in hardship—the joy in announcing that Depression is at hand and everyone must show mettle, as is evident in all current economic assessments from the queen's speech on down.

Physical training may account for another trait that is especially developed in Englishwomen—the love of horses. Psychologists throughout the western world have speculated on the female attraction to horseback riding, but it is in England that the activity reaches the point of being a national fetish. The majority of the 1.75 million people who ride in England are female. Women founded and continue to own and operate the Sadon Saddlery Company, one of the most successful equipment firms in the country. Elizabeth II spent her adolescence with horses. Princess Anne met her husband on the jumping circuit, and celebrated her wedding with a horseshoe-shaped cake. A few years ago, *The Sunday Times* ran a four-part series on pony ownership for children, in which the little girl was supposed to ask her father for the money, equipment and grooming tips and her mother for advice on training etiquette and ways to make friends with animals.

The emphasis on sport and physical confrontation undoubtedly plays an important part in the English horsewoman mystique, but it is intriguing to speculate on the trait more broadly. The similarity between riding and the sexual act has often been noted. What is discussed less frequently is the similarity between riding and marriage. The horsewoman utilizes a gentle and repetitive touch to force a much stronger animal to obey her. She uses sweets and cajoling words. She gives him creature comforts and love. He responds by carrying her around on his back and loving her. No other activity open to the girl child so clearly explains to her the art of using her wiles, love and habit of good manners to manipulate another much bigger creature.

The training carries over into the Englishwoman's reaction to male society, her desire to maintain decorum, her ability to be firm with men and ultimately her reluctance to join Liberation groups. Since she has a method that works, she is appalled at the "fussy" and "strident" attacks of the Liberationist.

Group awareness, as we have already noted, begins earliest among the upper class, where the child spends even its infancy in the nursery, receiving liberal daily reminders of the difference between the chiid and the adult. The child's world is inhabited by sisters and brothers and their Group Leader—Nanny or the *au pair* girl.

Children in other classes are also separated from their family at a young age—some forced into play groups, some simply shunted out on the streets. Girls, with their civilized cuteness, are not as isolated from their mother as boys are from both parents.

By the age of five, the cleft between adult and child is complete, and society sets about isolating other peer groups. First, the child is cut off from older children. Schools have strict rules that children over age seven may not play with the little ones. Big brothers are scornful of younger children and particularly of younger sisters. Only a big sister may be expected to help with the little ones.

The next group partitioning is sexual. A century ago, single-sex schools were the norm in every Western country except the United States. Today, all countries except England are consciously moving away from them. The tradition, having experienced a period of disfavor with intellectuals, is now on the rise again because parents insist that discipline and education are better in single-sex schools.

While nursery and infant schools are largely coed, the single sex syndrome sets in at primary level. At this stage parents budgeting for fee-paying schools will often choose to send their sons to a boys' school, but leave their daughters behind.[41]

Peer-group segregation reaches massive proportions at age eleven. The child entering secondary school is made to understand that the move is a very important one. In the first place, facilities are totally separate from those used by younger children. The buildings are usually at different locations and no sports grounds or classrooms are shared. The school is much larger than the "small, local primary school." More important, secondary school has the reputation for being much more difficult and strict.

The English have nearly phased out the much-hated eleven-plus exams, which at one time determined whether or not a child would be able to continue studies leading to white-collar employment or would be streamed into classes leading to manual apprenticeship jobs. This has eased some of the intense anxiety felt by preadolescents trying desperately to live up to their parents' academic hopes and making or breaking their futures in one super test of braininess.

The stress has not totally disappeared, however. To enter secondary school, the eleven-year-old must maneuver a course somewhat more complicated and traumatic than the American college-acceptance procedure. First, the parents must inform education authorities of their choice among the secondary schools in the area. School records are sent to the first preferences. If the child is accepted by one of the "right" schools, great relief! If not, the family loses status. A battle often ensues between educational authorities and parents, with the child being kept out of school entirely as the ultimate form of protest.

It is at the secondary-school level, as the child arrives at the age of budding individuality, that society insists on the most clear-cut uniformity. Quite literally. Uniforms for all children, both in class and in sports are mandatory. It is thought that this gives them a sense of belonging, and blurs class distinctions between those with fancy clothes and those without. Then, too, it solves the early-morning confusion over what to wear.

The uniforms themselves are bland. Jackets, jumpers and skirts. Two neutral colors contrasted with either red, green or blue. Boys no longer wear short pants (except to private primary schools and a few ultraconservative fee-paying secondaries), but girls often wear ties. The overall tone is muted and male.

Secondary students often commute on city buses, and one school tribe then confronts another in public places. Theoretically, this test demonstrates who is best-behaved. One of the articulated advantages of school uniforms is that the public can constantly gauge the effectiveness of each school's discipline. But the students are involved in their own status games. The ones in the "right schools" play up their superiority, but the others, having no means to better themselves, make the most of being noxious. Interestingly, this rarely dissolves into tests of strength. Fear of being kicked out of school or out of their group is too strong for that. Instead, students show off by smoking and cursing.

Over two-thirds of the secondary schools are single-sex institutions. Most parents of girls seem to favor the segregation. Those who do not will only admit, "Well, I suppose it's a good idea for girls and boys to have opportunities to meet. But the primary thing is to get them to learn. As long as that can be done at mixed [co-ed] schools, I'm not against it. . . ." A lurking fear of the uncivilized boys is always present.

In practice, sex-segregated education appears to have serious drawbacks. Boys' school graduates are notoriously beset with emotional problems. Girls' school students are not as thoroughly prepared academically as science-lab facilities in particular lag behind those in boys' schools. Career councillors for girls don't recommend competitive fields, pushing secretarial training instead, "just to be sure." Results of this attitude were clearly defined when the International Association for the Evaluation of Education Achievement did its exhaustive study of 258,000 pupils in twenty countries. In its report presented at Stockholm in May 1973, it stated that girls fall behind boys in their performance and general interest in science, particularly in physics and applied science, but that these differences are reduced by coeducation.

The average British girl leaves school and steps into adulthood at age sixteen—the youngest in any Western country except Italy. Like other Europeans, she does not think of a driver's license as the symbol of independence. Instead, her goals are getting a job or boyfriend. Despite her preference for exotic clothes, her "bird" image and her lack of self-esteem, teen-age unemployment figures indicate that she is far better able to cope with the job step than her brother. Generally speaking, she lives up to society's belief in her ability to become civilized.

It is important to discuss the rites of passage into adulthood for boys as well as those for girls because the difference is explicit. The overwhelming majority of both sexes have always entered employment as soon as legally permissible. By the time they are eighteen, over 90 percent are already looking for work. In comparison, only 55 percent of the same age are entering the job market in the United States.

Even in this initial stage, however, the job holds little status. Girls immediately classify themselves as Temps. Boys see their work life stretching ahead of them in perpetual drudgery. Many feel trapped by the system, and many refuse to take their places at the oars. Social workers often complain that young males do nothing but hang around youth clubs and destroy other people's property.

The girls, on the other hand, have it better. Not only do they find work more easily, but the jobs themselves have a more positive image: the sexy shop girl, the fabulous secretary, the down-to-earth industry worker. Such young women rarely seem to find their jobs interesting. What they do seem to get out of them is the freedom to spend their own money on whatever they want. Some manage to break away from home and live completely on their own, a more difficult feat to achieve in England than in the United States. Others haven't made the break yet, but feel they are making headway toward that point. Most important, unlike the boys, they don't feel trapped. They are using the system, instead of being used by it. And when a girl tires of the game, she "can always find a man to look after her."

This invariably turns out to be the central point, the hub of a girl's plans for the future—having "her" wedding, settling down with her husband in a little flat, working until the first baby comes along. The flat and the babies are important, but most important is the husband. Most girls have very clear-cut ideas about wanting someone with whom they can share their lives, not just someone to give them security and a socially acceptable way of life.

7

Teammates and Antiteammates

    "Women," said Germaine Greer, "have very little idea how much men hate them."[42]

    "Your husband is a kind, loving provider. What more could you ask?" Scottish Widow Fund asked the readers of *Woman's Own,* before answering, "A tax-free income if he should die unexpectedly."

    The classic sexual archenemies. Misogamy versus avarice. Is that all there is to female-male relationships in England? Is that why so many famous men and not a few famous women have publicly turned away from heterosexuality? Are the nightly battles of "Bless This House," "Till Death Do Us Part," "Man About the House" and all the other English-family television comedies simple reflections of the prevailing reality? Is every home poisoned at the core, and the world's worse curse the live-in mother-in-law?

    It can't be. There are too many English marriages where people genuinely seem happy with each other. They treat each other with respect, and are not as likely as Americans to expect perfection. "I think most people get married," a friend said, "because they need somebody they can trust—somebody they can unscrew their wooden leg with, and sit by the fire and be content with."

How does this relationship develop? The observer is initially struck by the English girl's earthy acceptance of sexuality, a trait that develops early in her life and continues throughout adolescence, whether or not she attends a single-sex school. Five-year-olds jumping rope chant, "Oh, little Dutch girl, dressed in blue, here are the things you must do. Bow to the queen, salute to the king. Pull down your knickers for the football team." Older girls exchange rude jokes about their boyfriend's sexual prowess. Covers of *19*, England's equivalent of *Ingenue* magazine, flaunt full frontal photographs of erotic cancan dancers with red ruffles framing see-through lace panties. Young television heroines archly warn their mothers about wily next-door neighbors. Flocks of nubile teen-agers descend on the male strip shows featured in a few pubs.

Formal sex education in the schools, however, has not advanced much beyond the "Don't get into trouble" stage, if the clients of Grapevine, a London sex-counseling service, can be believed. Although booklets and educational films are available, few schools make use of them. A general policy has not been stated, but most school administrators feel that "such things" are best left to a few words in girls' physical education and tech (home-ec) classes. Since parents also tend to be circumspect, most adolescents learn about sex from books, television and each other.

The biggest game during the ebullient blooming years may be sexual, but English adolescents have not been prepared to participate. Having grown up in single-sex groups, their sexual encounters are fraught with the excess electricity of the unknown. Girls with brothers are besieged by girl-friends asking questions about what men are like—as if brothers have been confidants during the years of social separation. Places to meet each other are limited strongly by the fact that society still does not condone the young, self-generated romance. Within the last few years, city pubs with dance bands and discotheques have become places where singles can meet. The scene is not as predatory as the singles bars in America because the pub regulars give depth to the group and the crowd tends to be younger and more optimistic.

Then, too, the moment of decision comes early. At 11:30 P.M., the publican goes around announcing "Time, Ladies and Gentlemen." Everybody downs a last drink and suddenly the decision to join or separate has to be made. The girls are usually in favor of joining; the boys are unsure, but strut about cursing to all their male companions as a way of letting everybody know they're in control of the situation. They also tend to be defensive and even cruel with girls, whom they see as antagonists intent on forcing them into the system. The girls, knowing what they want and having the approval of society behind them, try to be patient and subservient long enough to bring the boys under their lead.

The invitation to fish 'n' chips or to coffee at one's bed-sitter is what matters. The invitation indicates interest. It does not, despite the reputation of swinging London, necessarily include bed and breakfast. Much has been written in England about the decline in morals since the introduction of the Pill in 1962, or since the lifting of the ban on *Lady Chatterley's Lover* in 1960, but it appears that the change is more verbal than real. When Geoffrey Gorer, the English social anthropologist, did his latest study, *Sex and Marriage in England Today,* in 1971, he found that 26 percent of the men and 63 percent of the women had not had intercourse until marriage.[43] Two years later, when the Opinion Research Centre was again asking more or less the same question, 43 percent of English women maintained that premarital virginity was important. Men were 79 percent in favor of premarital sex, but the majority from all age groups limited permissiveness to couples who were formally engaged. Only one man in five, under the age of twenty-five, was in favor of sex "for the fun of it."[44]

If the couple do "get involved," it's usually at their own or a friend's bed-sitter. "We went over to Mandy's for coffee and to listen to some more music, you know. And then Mandy and Jacob decided to go out and have a pizza, and we stayed behind. . . ."

Courtship rites can be freewheeling because early employment gives the English teenager the longest period of financial self-sufficiency of any woman in the West—six years until marriage at age twenty-two. More often than not, she still lives at home with Mum, but she feels as independent as the American college woman.

The major portion of her independent energy is spent on that most controllable element of the sexual rituals—the costumes worn. This is the girl who made Mary Quant and reshaped the international dress industry. Before the 1960s and the miniskirt, she literally had nothing to wear. With only a few job opportunities and starvation wages, she made do as best she could, graduating from her school jacket and skirt to the traditional twin sets and tweeds. Quant made a revolution with her reasonable prices, her classlessness and—most of all—her fun-loving femininity.

The boys brought about a similar revolution. They were the first to wear long hair. They found tailors who were willing to cut suits to fit young,

slim bodies for a price they could afford. Carnaby Street became more famous than Savile Row. The boys, too, insisted on being properly attired
for the all-important courtship games.

Officially, "engagement" in England means publishing the banns just as
it does in Catholic countries. If finances permit, the girl is given a dia-
mond. Unofficially, the announcement may be simply an offhand statement
to the parents, and/or the more serious trip to the Family Planning office for
the Pill. But these are the cold, practical details. The decision to become
life teammates, in England, is very much an emotional one. Time and
again, couples will say, "It was just like an explosion between us." "I
couldn't seem to think about anything else but her." "He fit my fantasy
man . . . I mean, just perfectly." Couples profiled through in-depth interviews in Drusilla Beyfus' *The English Marriage*[45] regularly commented
on the fact that they knew they were in love "in the first three minutes,"
"after we'd been together weeks," and so on. It is this mystical ideal of
the Perfect Partner who suddenly materializes on one's doorstep that makes
people reluctant to mobilize sex education, reluctant to be prepared for an
affair with contraceptives and reluctant to "sleep around." Sex is serious,
a sacred ritual that marks breaking with childhood and launching on a new
partnership.

Once relatives and friends of a couple know about their engagement, the
couple may move into his place if he has one. In a few homes the girl's parents may turn a blind eye to her boyfriend's staying in her room for several
hours or even spending the night there. The two may travel together. The
majority, however, do not live together full time until they marry and have
the traditional honeymoon.

Until the housing supply eased somewhat in the sixties, a couple often
moved into the wife's parents' home.[46] Today the overwhelming majority
plan to move into their own place, even if it's only a tiny bed-sitter with the
bathtub under the kitchen table, the gas and electricity operating via coin
meter boxes and the refrigerator on the landing next to the communal bathroom, to be shared with four other couples, also newlywed. In the first
glow of teamwork, this idyllic poverty can be wonderful fun and funny,
particularly if one is good at that dry brand of humor cultivated by the English.

Marriage itself, however, has a dark reputation. Not only is it the basis
for 90 percent of the jibes on BBC comedies, but it has been portrayed by
writers from Shakespeare to Joyce as a union for mutual destruction. In the
past, the writers were mainly male, and their major complaint concerned
the ravenous female. As social commentator, Jack Trevor Story, explains,

the word among his friends was "If you go out with a grown-up woman, she'll suck all your insides out."[47]

Today, as women writers articulate their stand, matrimony still comes out badly. Marriage enervates and withers, according to writers like Penelope Gilliatt, Doris Lessing and Penelope Mortimer. Marriage is a font of poison, according to the Women's Liberation leaders like Eva Figes, Germaine Greer and Juliette Mitchell. Marriage is bound up with a primal rape scene so imbedded in our subconscious that we, of all female primates, have lost our cyclical mating drive, according to anthropologist Elaine Morgan.[48]

Both male and female writers accuse women of being the main proponents of marriage. They differ only on which partner *exploits* the system.

England's divorce rate has been spiraling since the beginning of the sixties. This is due in part to the Reform Divorce Act, passed in 1969, which made no-fault proceedings possible if a couple had been separated by mutual agreement for more than two years, if the one instigating the divorce had been deserted for two years, or if one party wanted a divorce after five years of separation. Otherwise, adultery is still the primary grounds for divorce, although "unreasonable" behavior can sometimes be considered. Unreasonable means "grave and weighty" physical or mental cruelty. Beatings are unreasonable, but, according to women's rights authorities, Anna Coote and Tess Gill, the odd blow during an argument is not. Refusing to have children, sodomy, bestiality, mentally unbalanced behavior or drunkenness can all be called "unreasonable," but a man's preferring his men friends, his club, his newspapers, his games, his hobbies or, indeed, his own society to association with his wife—that can be called "the reasonable wear and tear of married life."[49]

Then, too, the rising divorce rate may reflect the rising expectations of marriage partners. With the stabilizing influence of welfare and a more affluent national economy has come a trend toward an emotion-based relationship. The minor dissatisfactions of communication have taken on major importance, particularly for wives. Professor Geoffrey Gorer underlines this in his 1971 discussion of the "symmetrical" marriage where the wife wants a husband with whom to share leisure activities. In the twenty years since his first study, he found that three times as many women have come to feel that a man who habitually "goes out on his own" causes damage to a marriage. These wives put "selfishness and inconsiderateness" at the top of their list of husbandly faults.

On the other hand, Gorer discovered that husbands still tend to think that marriage problems center around finances. They no longer bemoan having to live with in-laws. Their chief complaints about their wives are "nagging and extravagance." This chauvinistic mentality is particularly common in mining towns where a man gains status by cunning dodges to avoid giving his wife her household allowance. It's the syndrome behind habitual Saturday night arguments, and the bitter entrenchment of the marriage partners. The husband wants to spend his money with his "mates" so that he can be "one o' the lads."[50] The use of the terms themselves spell out the situation. He wants his childhood partners. He was raised to play on a single-sex team and that's where he still feels most comfortable—whether he goes to the pub or the club. The wife may well be more at ease visiting her mother or attending a charity affair with her chums. Neither one of them subscribes completely to the notion of total marital togetherness.

Both marriage partners agree that sexual loyalty is all-important. Gorer found that 92 percent of his respondents felt that fidelity was fundamental in marriage. Women stated emphatically, "Faithfulness is what marriage is to me." Both sexes condemned adulterers as "disgusting, terrible, unforgivable, cheap, poor character, rotten, stupid, callow, a bit of an idiot." They felt that a man might foolishly stray sometimes, but an adulterous wife should be "shot," "kicked out of the house" or "given a good hiding." In addition, adultery was nearly always cited as a major factor in causing separation and /or divorce.

In spite of the rising rate of divorce and the passionate belief in sexual exclusivity, there is still strong evidence that one involved in the actual situation will be tolerant. Take the wife of a prominent executive. When asked about her husband and a Playboy Bunny, she remarked matter-of-factly, "It's not pleasant to hear secondhand that your husband is living it up with a Bunny girl in London. I shall be demanding an explanation." When Lord Lambton's publicized affair with a call girl forced him to resign from Heath's cabinet, his wife snapped, "How these silly rumors of divorce started I really don't know. They are utterly ridiculous. I stand by him."

Women's-page columnists support such attitudes. Anne Edwards of the *Sunday Express* comments, for example: "Most wives have got their husbands pretty well sized up, have weighed to the last ounce the disadvantages and compensations of having him around, and it is they who in the end decide the terms. . . . A clever woman makes damn sure that in return for the bargain she gets her own way 90 percent of the time, safe in the knowledge that the one thought which never enters his arrogant head is that she probably doesn't really care all that much about him any more anyway."[51] Marje Proops, England's Dear Abby, is not as hardheaded, but she does recommend that a wife should forgive an adulterous husband and try to change her own ways in order to keep him.[52]

Tolerance and willingness to "give another chance" cuts across classes. Comic-strip antihero Andy Capp and his wife, Flo, both have a roving eye and are proud of it. "Intimate Strangers," the television series about a professional couple, portrayed an incident in which the wife was unfaithful; in the end, the couple came through to more love and deeper understanding.

Perhaps an adaptation of the open marriage is not as farfetched as it seems at first. If we look at these cases closely, we see a realistic acceptance of "passing fancy" affairs, and equally realistic attempts to "sort out matters" if the extramarital involvement goes beyond that.

At this point, one stops to inquire whatever happened to the spinster? After all, as Nanny she had a widespread and romantic tradition. Florence Nightingale virtually founded a single woman's industry. Daisy Bates and the other Victorian women explorers were world-renowned. A hundred years ago, England was the major country where the single woman possessed not only status but mystique. She was sometimes despised, but she was also romanticized as a self-reliant individual with a magical umbrella or an enchanted bedknob, free to go wherever she pleased.

Today, the image has lost much of its appeal. TV commentators carp that they don't want another chance to speculate whether Greer wears knickers or not. Figes and Mitchell are classified as dried-up warmongers, Redgrave as "a bit daft." The pull into teamwork is too strong. Without a family around her, a woman is as weak as a prime minister with no Cabinet and no party backing.

Single women still exist. Since there is a surplus of men in England, their existence is largely a matter of choice. Deirdre McSharry, who has worked as a journalist and editor in both the United States and the United Kingdom, points out the importance of this. "In America, every now and then, you'd get to the office and there'd be one of these great weepy holocausts. The morning-after-the-row scene. Here, you just don't have that. Single women aren't frantically trying to latch onto somebody."

Statistically speaking, however, most of them do latch onto a steady profession. Like Nanny and Miss Nightingale, they go into a service profession, such as the government, the Health Service, or the army, where equal pay with men is guaranteed, and automatic job advancement is secure. In addition, such posts offer the emotional rewards of community service, always a big motivating force in England.

Their routine of living is simple. Single women find other women to share housing. They go for outings and develop cultural interests. "I've got my own way of doing things, and I don't want to change it for any-body," they insist with eccentric pride. When they take time to reflect, however, they are often bitter about their lot in society. A secretary in sub-urban Finchley complained about "the amount of money they take from my pay check. Old-age benefits are something else, of course. But why should we have to pay for schools and school lunches and child medicine and child dentistry and youth clubs and all the rest? We didn't burden so-ciety with any children. Why do they put the tax burden on us?"

Some of these women enter into Lesbian relationships. Their choice is easier in England than in many countries for several reasons. First, with a childhood spent in the company of other girls—sometimes with a girls'-boarding-school background—the choice is more likely to come up. Sec-ond, in intellectual circles, there is a respected tradition of Lesbianism and bisexuality. Third, Lesbians do not suffer severe social sanction even in less-sophisticated circles.

It is said that no law was passed against Lesbians during the last century because Queen Victoria refused to believe that women were involved in "such things." In any event, the law forbidding male homosexuality was struck from the books in the mid-sixties. Any sex act is now permissible in a private place between consenting adults.

Drag shows and female impersonators have become popular, led by the redoubtable Danny La Rue, who has been a hit for years, and has per-formed for the queen. Audiences at La Rue's performances tend to be mid-dle-aged, non-Londoners and 90 percent female. His show includes song and dance, but the main attraction is the sexual-innuendo joke. "Isn't he a rude one?" members of the audience chuckle, but no one takes offense. Ribaldry is freely applauded by all ages.

Sexual eccentricity—the more exotic the better—is brandished by the pop stars. Mick Jagger and Bianca, David Bowie and Angie, the couples stare out of their publicity photographs looking like epicene twins. Elton John with his platform shoes, his incredible clothes and his absolutely un-precedented glasses, flashes advertisements for androgyny. Even staid companies like Tonik Mohair Fabrics have taken up the theme of deca-dence in full-page color ads portraying a narcissistic couple draped across an opulent couch and surrounded by ferns and finery.

Bizarre sexuality has long been accepted among English intellectuals. Biographies of the famous, like those of the tormented and suicide-prone Virginia Woolf, the bisexual Vita Sackville-West, the urbane Somerset Maugham or the iconoclastic Oscar Wilde have all illustrated this trend and concomitant tolerance.

Today's graduates of single-sex schools also learn sexual responses torturously late. Not during adolescence, when every step one takes in any direction is unsure, but later, when social graces should have become automatic. Off balance, some develop unusual sex rituals. The rest understand and tolerate their behavior. This is accepted by the general public as well because single-sex adolescence is so nearly universal.

The English public loves to know about decadence. It gasps at the stories of the bottom-spanking ex-mayor of Chelsea, who reportedly invited girls to "help on a Thames yacht." It laps up stories about Profumo and Lambton and their lush parties and voluptuous call girls, and has a good giggle over pointed questions put to important people about their private lives.

When Margaret Laing was researching her book, *Edward Heath: Prime Minister*,[53] she got "a frosty silence" in response to the question why had he never married. She concludes that after being jilted by a girl with whom he was deeply in love (he kept her photograph by his bed for thirteen years), Heath never wanted to try again. This would certainly be in keeping with Heath's determined nature, but the important point was the reaction of the majority of the people, who enjoyed the speculation. They rather liked having a P.M. with a mysterious, perhaps exotic side to him. Americans today would probably elect a woman to the Presidency before an unmarried man.

The English taste for sexual nonconformity, however, does not extend into the majority of private lives. Two years ago, Gallup was commissioned by the London *Daily Telegraph* to do a poll on the most-admired woman and man. "My wife" placed second among the husbands (Queen Elizabeth was first) and "my husband" ranked fifth among the wives. The replies befit a country that made the martyred Roman priest, Saint Valentine, into the patron of love at first sight. Not only is a larger percentage of the English population married now than in the past, but in spite of the rising divorce rate, statistics point to happiness in marriage. Wives and husbands live significantly longer than unmarried people, and are less susceptible to insanity, acts of violence and cancer. England is the only Western European country where the female suicide rate has declined during the past fifteen years. The married Englishwoman is the least likely of her peers to do away with herself.

Several public marriages illustrate how well British matrimony works. Take the complicated union of Mary Quant and Alexander Plunket Greene, or that of Jean Muir and Harry Lockert. Both women are the biggest breadwinners and the best-known members of their families. Both men devote themselves to managing their wives' careers. And both couples appear able to enjoy themselves unselfconsciously, to laugh together easily or have a good row without guilt.

These same elements may be found in the most conventional marriage on any street in England. If the pair is able to overcome fidelity to the childhood single-sex teams, the partnership often works miraculously. They're chums, working and fighting on equal terms. They feel free to snarl at each other the moment something goes wrong, and sort it out as pragmatically as possible. The important thing is that such couples know how to make their team function, and they're willing to work to keep it functioning. They don't ask for perfection. More and more, they ask for understanding and sharing. Respect seems taken for granted. The secret is that they are sure of their sexual role.

Today, Bernadette Devlin is married. So is Michael Caine. After years of denouncing matrimony, these famous singles yielded to the pressure to get their home team together. As a friend expresses it, "You finally decide you're bloody well going to let everybody know you're *proud* of your warm bed and your kids and your giving each other life."

When I first started investigating the Englishwoman, I asked the editors of several women's magazines to describe their readers. To a woman, they agreed that the Englishwoman is not domestic; she has wide general interests and is blunt about sexuality. They felt their readers are happy to be women. Just like Dilys Powell.

The Englishwoman has her problems, of course. Motherhood, for the ideal, two-child family, is only a short-term occupation. A husband may be more tied to his childhood single-sex team than to his wife. A woman who doesn't choose a professional career but is compelled to go back to work feels off balance. All working women suffer from their second-string status in relation to the primary position of men as the "real breadwinner."

But the Englishwoman has reached a sense of satisfaction through the renewal of the importance of motherhood and her status inside the traditional wife-husband team. Her rigorous physical training, her cheekiness and her sense of humor contribute to her self-confidence. Her disregard for the work ethic makes her value her freedom to escape The Daily Slog. She doesn't expect perfection, nor does she believe that men have it better. In short, she knows how to carry on, enjoying the life she has made for herself.

Part Two

The Italian Woman—

Matriarchy in Motion

1

Mamma's Responsibilities, Mamma's Status

        A great deal has been written about the poor, downtrodden Italian woman. What Anglo-Saxon writers in the past have tended to ignore is the reason for her burden. She is supporting the oldest and most firmly established matriarchy in the Western world.

    Take the commonly cited point that traditionally adultery was a crime for the woman but not for the man. The basis for this law was very simple. The woman was responsible for the family unit—the structure on which all Italy firmly rested. To threaten it was criminal. The man—an untrustworthy, flighty soul—did not have a similar responsibility. Mamma would forgive him.

    Ernst Bernhardt, a noted German psychologist who has lived and practiced in Italy for over twenty years, calls the Italian woman the Great Mediterranean Mamma, and traces the history of her matriarchy back beyond the Romans to the Etruscans. He contends that after the Romans rolled over their enemies in 266 B.C., they imposed a patriarchy lasting for nearly

75

a thousand years. By the end of that period, the cult of the Mother had welled up around the wheels of the conquerors and reinundated the country. Italy has been a matriarchy ever since, he believes, except for a brief period under Mussolini.[1]

For centuries Italy was swept by invasions. While men were away fighting in impressment armies, the women took complete responsibility for the society. Mamma ran the family. Mamma raised sons to feed the armies. Mamma and the family formed the only solid rock in the continual chaos of regimes and counterregimes, juntas, Papal States and city kingdoms.

The pattern is still clear-cut today, particularly in the South, where the population is made up of grass widows and young children. Just as the Renaissance popes bestowed titles and land only on their real allies, i.e., their blood relations, the modern family feels a primary, and very deep responsibility for all its members. A black sheep is protected and pulled out of trouble, regardless of the cost. As a young matron, in the process of selling a valuable painting that had been in the family for centuries, explained "Clelio is bankrupt, so we have to raise the money to keep his villa and servants. Otherwise, he'll never have the *bella figura* [good appearance] necessary to win another contract."

Even for such a simple matter as obtaining the official identity card needed to register for a pension plan, my maid had to leave Rome, where she had lived for the past forty years, and go back to the town where she was born. No one except a relative could sign the affidavit acknowledging her identity.

In preparing to become the cornerstone of this family-oriented society, the Italian girl has one goal—to be *una ragazza seria* (a serious girl). "Serious" is an important Latin adjective. In both Italian and French, it indicates a wide range of characteristics, each involving self-discipline and self-cultivation. The *ragazza seria* strives to be level-headed, respectable, capable. Her strength is continuity and stability.

Her rewards will be status and responsibility. Although she is known as the "Angel of the Hearth," the Italian woman controls the *cassa* as well as the *casa*. The *cassa* is the till, and Mamma is firmly enthroned there, counting out the money in every family-owned shop of the country.

The status and responsibility of matriarchy are just as evident in the churches. Mamma—represented by the commanding figure in Michelangelo's *Pietà*—is both the Mother Church and the Madonna.

Female dominance is apparent even in the language. While a man introduces his wife as *la mia signora* (my patroness), a wife simply presents *il mio marito* (my husband). Husbands rarely present their wives with the corresponding word *moglia* (wife), and wives never introduce their spouses as *il mio signore* (my patron).

The formal pronoun for "you"—for either the man or the woman—is *Lei,* which is also the pronoun for "she." In other words, when one wants to show respect, one uses the female form: "I do hope She (You) enjoyed the dinner, sir." Throughout Italian history, power groups have always been thought of as feminine; i.e., *La Signoria,* the councils that ruled the city states, and *La Carboneria,* the rebels who backed Garibaldi. Even the most important rules of social behavior—those involving *la bella figura*—are grammatically expressed in the feminine form, and reflect a tradition of feminine values.

Since World War II, the legal status of Italian women has undergone enormous changes. June 1946 marked the first national election with women's suffrage. When the Constitution was adopted two years later, it specifically stated that women are fully equal with men. Subsequent governments have passed supportive equal-employment and equal-opportunity legislation.

Because of constitutional equality, the law that made adultery a crime only for the wife was invalidated by the Italian Constitutional Court in the 1960s. The early seventies saw legalization of divorce and birth control. In 1975, the court ruled that abortion is legal for women whose physical or mental health is in "serious" danger.

Simultaneously Mamma has been forced to accept the different values of the North European countries. With industrialization, the viability of sprawling families has been threatened. Industry attempts to break the mother's hold over her sons with promises of money and modernity. Films and television present American, German, English and Scandinavian ways of life as more exciting and exotic. The modernization of Mamma has not been a totally rewarding experience.

2

The Heritage of Matriarchy

Our knowledge of the power of the Etruscan woman is limited. We have never been able to decipher the words that decorate the rims of Etruscan pottery and the elegant black and terra cotta designs that are abundant in their tombs. The pictures that dominate these decorations often show women being waited upon by members of both sexes, or a ruling couple seated side by side in apparent equality. A popular motif is that of the woman bestowing a gift on a man kneeling before her.

Whereas the Etruscans built their empire mainly on diplomacy and trade, the Romans relied on the sword. Even so, women held high rank in the Roman patrician class. Their influence inside their families was formidable, and they often ruled the nation through a son's minority or manipulated the world through their husbands.

Agrippina, the infamous wife of Claudius, who poisoned her husband in order to raise her son, Nero, to the throne, is the best-known of these women; but there are others, including Messalina and Valentinian's widow.

78

The Roman goddesses, the key female archetypes during this era, were the all-important overseers of the human condition and display a great variety of temperament.

Diana, the goddess of the chase, is believed to have been the most important diety the pre-Roman tribes brought with them from their northern homelands. As these nomads spread into the fertile land of the Italian peninsula, Ceres, the goddess of earth and plenty, rose to power, though Diana's influence with travelers, diviners and astrologers continued to be vitally important.

Venus, a relative newcomer to the mythology, is often credited with having designated the holy site where Rome's first settlers built their city.

It was not until the city was well under way that Jupiter came to rule the Roman goddesses and gods. Unlike Diana, he did not rule alone. At his side was Juno, his consort, who epitomized all female characteristics and served as the patroness of women, birth, marriage and death. Together, Jupiter and Juno were protectors of the national wealth—she because the Roman wife traditionally looked after household finances, he because of the man's duty to oversee property.

Of the twelve major Roman deities, six were women—Juno, Diana, Venus, Ceres, Minerva and Vesta. Minerva, the Roman counterpart of Athena, was not as highly esteemed as her Greek sister, but the annual festival held in her honor to celebrate the arts and trade was one of the most sumptuous holidays on the Roman calender. Vesta, from her simple origin as the virgin guardian of the hearth who was worshiped at every family meal, developed into the protectress of the national hearth. A fabulous temple was built in her honor, peopled by the vestal virgins, awesome women who were consulted before all major decisions of state.

Despite these formidable role models, Roman women themselves did not hold political power directly. The Roman code of laws gave the paterfamilias literal "property" rights over all the members of his household, and for a long period of time he had the right to have his wife executed, even if he was alone in suspecting her of adultery.

In 534, less than a century after the fall of the Roman Empire, the first queen came to rule in her own right. Amalasuntha reigned over Neopolis (Naples), a region that preceded the great city-state empires of later Italian history. Countess Matilda of Tuscany was the most powerful feudatory in central Italy during the eleventh century. She was followed by two Joannas, who ruled Naples from 1343 to 1380 and from 1414 to 1435, respectively.

Queen Joanna I was an intense and powerful woman. She murdered her first husband and married twice thereafter, but none of her husbands was able to wrest power from her. Childless, she adopted two sons, and played them against each other to ward off any opposition to her own power. Meanwhile, she discovered Boccaccio, encouraging his rich and bawdy work, as well as that of others in her court who showed artistic and musical ability. The seeds that were to lead to the Italian Renaissance had begun to sprout.

The court of Joanna II was also marked by intrigues, assassinations and quarrels among adopted heirs. Unlike her grandmother, who is believed to have been assassinated by one of her vindictive sons, the second Joanna seems to have died from natural causes.

As the city-states gained power and cultural status, highborn women came to play an important role in the arts. During the fourteenth and fifteenth centuries, Italian universities opened their doors to women (the university concept began in Italy), and in 1678, Elena Lucrezia Cornaro Piscopia became the first woman in the Western world to receive a university degree. Padua awarded her a doctorate of philosophy when the Pope rejected her application for a doctorate in theology despite her elegant discourses in Greek and Latin.

As the Renaissance flowered, women painters achieved distinction. Sofonisba Anguissola, the eldest of six artist sisters, was a widely acclaimed peer of Michelangelo. Among her paintings, *Three Sisters Playing Chess* was particularly important, since it was the first to portray people involved in everyday activities.[2]

The archetype of the Lady was born and flourished in the 1300s. There was Beatrice, the ethereal, virtuous, perfect but unobtainable who inspired Dante Alighieri in his *Divine Comedy,* and the beautiful but disdainful Laura who haunted the sonnets of Petrarch. Courts of Love were established, one of them ruled by Laura. Like those already thriving in France, their purpose was to decree the principles of chivalry and applaud those knights who upheld the proper virtues. Aristocratic men devoted themselves to the jousting tournaments and the Crusades.

The Ladies were sporting with the pages and developing the arts. Intrigue was everywhere. Both sexes manipulated lovers of both sexes like so many pieces on a chessboard. The Tuscan court of Madame Royale Maria Christina, the Milanese court of Caterina Sforza, the Ferrara court of Lucrezia Borgia, the French court of Caterina de Medici and later of Maria de Medici, all were rife with Machiavellis, Casanovas, Cagliostros and Lorenzas.

Stronger, however, than Beatrice or Laura was the consummate Lady of all time, Maria, or Mary. First designated as Holy and Truly the Mother of God by the Council of Ephesus in 431, Maria held the position of Honorable Intercedent with Christ during the era of the Crusades. By the time of the Council of Trent in Trento (1545–1563) her special position—higher than all the saints and angels in heaven—had become one of the key focal points in the struggle between the Churches of England and Rome.

Maria played an incalculable part in the lives of the common people, who never participated in the aristocratic and chivalrous world of Beatrice and Laura. In Maria's wake came the female saints—Clara of Assisi, Caterina of Siena, Lucrezia of Siracusa—women who won the devotion of the masses by truly adhering to the very intricate, highly moral code espoused by their aristocratic sisters. The predominant feature of the saints was their absolute adherence to virginity.

Such immeasurably powerful Lady archetypes naturally generated antitheses. Among the highborn, there were the heroic viragins, who performed feats of strength and skill on the battlefield. Sisters to the Warrior Woman of the North, little is known of their story in Latin countries, where the Lady dominates the history books. Only the story of Bradamante, which runs through Ariosto's *Orlando Furioso* epic, gives details about the extent of their prowess in Italy.

Mary's negative counterpart is well known in history. She is the Witch, the woman of evil, the daughter of the temptress, Eve. She has as much power to lead the world to destruction as Mary has to lead it to salvation. The first papal bull indicting her was declared by Innocente VIII in 1482. Over the next three hundred years, nearly 400,000 people were put to terrible deaths. The majority were women—old, young, aristocratic or peasant women. Most vulnerable was the prostitute. With no man to attest to her value, she worked under the ancient curse of profligacy and the contemporary curse of venereal disease, and fled as best she could from the long staff of the Inquisition.

Influences from northern Protestantism during the 1800s dissipated the imposing power of both Maria and the Witch. The Italian woman, as mother of the court and mistress of its intrigues, also lost status as the Courts of Love dissolved.

Napoleon's ideal of order pervaded the country. The patriotic soldier, not as easily bought off as the mercenary or as dedicated to the *bella figura* as the knight, began to play the dominating role. Armies closed borders and looted art treasures. War, the deadly, bloody, male test of physical strength, became the only route to success.

Following the unification of Italy in 1871, Queen Margherita promoted female education in all fields, and sponsored the Royal Institute of Higher Learning for Women in Rome. Contessa Adriana Zon Marcello began rebuilding the Italian lace-making industry. The craftswomen unionized into the Association of Italian Feminine Industries. Women's groups and women's newspapers sprang up around the country.

The first woman to receive a doctorate of medicine from the University of Rome (1894) was Maria Montessori. Working first as an assistant at the Psychiatric Clinic, then as a lecturer of anthropology, she was appointed director of a children's hospital and by 1900, had set up her own school for subnormal children, the Scuola Ortofrenica. Seven years later she established the Cora dei Bambini, where she began using her unique methods of child training.

Women's rights were being redefined outside Italy's cultural centers. In 1897, a Sardinian girl of fifteen published her first book, *Sangue Sardo (Sardinian Blood)*. Despite censorship and reprobation for her vivid portrayal of village life (the people of Nuoro did not believe a woman should write, much less a child of fifteen), the girl went on to finish her schooling, and to write over thirty novels as well as four volumes of short stories. In 1926, Grazia Deledda became the second woman to be awarded the Nobel Prize for Literature with her *La Fuga in Egitto (Flight Into Egypt)*.

In 1925, Italian women won the right to vote in municipal elections. It was the last step forward for Le Feministe Italiane. Mussolini, his sights set on a return to the glories of ancient Rome, made vast revisions in the legal code and firmly reinstated the paterfamilias concept. Universal suffrage was not achieved until the 1946 Constitution, but throughout World War II, Italian women, trained in hardship and intrigue, formed an important part of the Resistance. The stage was set for the Oriana Fallacis, the Natalia Ginsburgs, the Lina Wertmüllers and the Dacia Marainis of today.

3

Mothers as Lovers

Italian patterns of courtship begin to manifest themselves before adolescence. Daredevil ten-year-old boys snatch kisses from disdainful girls, only to be severely reprimanded by ever-vigilant mothers. The ritual that will be repeated throughout life is already apparent.

In the cities, groups of girls as young as thirteen undulate along the street every afternoon in tight pants or flowing skirts. They slice through flocks of whistling, catcalling boys—walking quickly, self-consciously hoping to appear casual.

Dating, per se, begins at a later age in Italy than it does in other Western European countries, and the most common practice is for several sixteen- and seventeen-year-old girls to group together with their respective boy-friends. As elsewhere in Europe, one must be eighteen to have a driver's license, so the group either travels by bus (the countryside is also served by hourly buses), or walks.

The time they can spend together is short. Girls are allowed out of the house only between 4:00 and 9:00 P.M. Parents who permit a girl to go out alone *nella notte* (after dark) are few. As a result, the Piper and other rock-music clubs open at four in the afternoon—as do the movie houses and the strip shows.

An extensive study of women and contemporary mores, conducted by Shell Oil in the early seventies, indicated that the great majority of parents refused to allow either their daughters or their sons to stay out as late at night as they wish until they are in their twenties. A number of parents went so far as to say that this privilege should never be granted, regardless of age. They were particularly protective toward their daughters, but 3.8 percent also felt that sons, even over the age of twenty-five or married, should always have a curfew.[3]

By his early twenties, a man must have a car. A Fiat 500 costs $1000 new or $200 used. It is a required status symbol that proves the man is capable of earning enough to support a family. I've known Italian women who've forced their daughters to stop dating university graduates when they discovered the young men had no cars. In each case, they felt such a *ragazzo* (boy) wasn't worth their daughter's time.

The majority of women become engaged between the ages of twenty and twenty-five. Their *fidanzato* (fiancé) is ordinarily two years older. The engagement period averages two years, but can last ten years and even longer.[4]

Even during this period of intense involvement, a couple must respect curfews. A twenty-six-year-old secretary gave a typical description of what she and her *fidanzato* do: "I don't have any family in Rome, so I live in a women's dormitory run by nuns. Armando and I have been engaged for seven years—ever since I came here, in fact. I have to be in the dormitory by nine on weekdays and by ten on Friday and Saturday. Neither Armando nor I get off work until seven, but since we're in the same office, it's easy to go for a bite to eat and then maybe a walk or a cup of coffee in the piazza. Weekends, we sometimes go to the theater—neither of us likes opera. And we see a lot of films."

Parties, even for couples who are engaged, are often sex-segregated. As soon as the music stops, men head for their male friends, while the women drift toward female groups in the corner. The older university crowd is often more sexually integrated, but couples there do not split up and talk to others of the opposite sex.

Sexual *rapporti* (relations) are highly controversial. Women still write sad letters to magazine columnists saying they lost their first *fidanzato* because they "ceded" to him, and they lost their second because they confessed about the first. A well-known psychologist conducted a survey recently among a group of male student activists, and found that 90 percent of them still wanted to marry a virgin.[5]

The remaining 10 percent is vociferous and their views are well publicized. They believe in the concept of the "free couple" in which both members enjoy whatever sex life they want. Or they insist that, if they must endure a long engagement, they should be free to have sexual relations before marriage for sanity's sake.

Considering the prevailing conservative attitudes, society's treatment of young lovers is surprising. Traveling through the country, a couple can register in the same room at a hotel as *fidanzati* and no one will raise an eyebrow, except in Sicily. Small hotels in cities will take in couples for the afternoon. The courts have recently ruled that a car with windows "steamed over or otherwise curtained off" constitutes a private residence, and police have no right to investigate what is happening inside.

Most of this acceptance has been granted in the past ten years, and is an outgrowth of a new attitude toward extramarital sex. Whether or not this will be followed by across-the-board tolerance of premarital sex is not certain.

Marriage is a magnificent affair. Lucrezia Love, a Texas woman who married an Italian film producer, described the city-hall ceremony. For pomp and circumstance, it outdid most Fifth Avenue church occasions:

"My *fidanzato* and I were both late. We arrived together, as this is the custom. There was a doorman to open the car door, and a red carpet up to the magistrate's office.

"Inside, everything was done in red. Red velvet drapes covered one wall. There were deep red Oriental rugs. In the center of the room were a pair of huge, high-backed, red velvet chairs for us. The magistrate, wearing a ceremonial *bandiere* [ribbon] across his chest, stood behind an enormous carved desk. Off on one side, a tiny old man wrote out the records by hand."

Marriage contracts are common, although many women consider the practice old-fashioned. (This trend is beginning to reverse itself among feminists.) A simple contract is signed by each during the mandatory civil part of the ceremony. In it the man assumes financial responsibility for his wife, their children and both his and her parents, while the woman promises to carry out all financial duties the husband cannot fulfill.[6]

If the husband for any reason is—or becomes—physically incapacitated, the wife may follow an ordinary legal procedure to have herself declared *capo di famiglia* (head of household). With this, she gains family bonuses and the ability to sign for the family on all legal documents. She also assumes financial responsibility for her spouse, their children and their parents.

The wedding night in Southern Italy is still often accompanied by great ceremony. The bride brings with her a *corredo* (trousseau)—consisting of sheets of satin or lace-trimmed linen costing $100 and more; delicate, hand-embroidered pillowcases to match; hand-shirred, floor-length night shifts with long sleeves, high collars and buttons in the back. The Sicilian wedding night can still mean the bloody towel hung in the window by the mother of the bride the next morning. The "cult of the bed," it's called.

Mario Puzo in *The Godfather* gives a succulent description of the values of the freshly awakened virgin. His Michaele encounters in his young, innocent wife an eager, passionate woman. Today's statistics indicate that the majority of young husbands are closer to those bitterly described by the Prince in *Il Gattopardo (The Leopard)*, "I've contented myself with a woman, who, in bed, makes the sign of the cross before every embrace, and who, after, at the moment of highest emotion, doesn't know anything more to say than 'Gesú Maria!' When we were married—that is, when you were sixteen—all that exalted me. But now [I'm sick of it]. . . . Seven children I've had with you—seven! And I've never seen your belly button!"

From Rome northward, total innocence on the part of the bride is not considered necessarily desirable, but the ideal of virginity is maintained for two reasons. First, it is a guarantee against illegal, extramarital children. Second, virginity is considered a recognizable, physical "badge" that a woman is *seria*—level-headed, far-seeing and self-disciplined.

Concern for virginity is carried to the extreme in the widely accepted Sicilian practice of a "repair marriage" for a woman who has been abducted and raped. In 1966, when Franca Viola became the first woman in Sicily's history to refuse such a marriage and sent her rapist to prison instead, she was threatened by the Mafia, and her father's orchard was burned. There have been only a handful of other challenges to the custom, and the abductions continue. (Some of the "repair marriages," of course, are arranged by the young couple as a way of circumventing parental disapproval.)

These marriages illustrate one area where women have lost out in the matriarchal system. Since a raped woman may become pregnant, the law not only forgives her rapist so that he may form a family, but it insists that the woman bow to him as well. The custom is totally at variance with the American shotgun wedding, where the woman (the supplicant) gets pregnant so that society will force the man (the power) to marry her. In Sicily, the man (the supplicant) threatens the woman (the power) with dishonor so that society will force *her* to marry *him*.

If you speak with an Italian woman, she's likely to tell you that marriage is bliss . . . for the first year. A husband surprises his wife with perfume and flowers. He brings her lace underwear and elegant clothes and is patient with burned dinners.

Her status within the community changes. Before marriage, particularly in the South, she was always chaperoned. Meeting girlfriends was discouraged and absolutely forbidden *nella notte*. Even the hour of *passeggiata* (the evening walk) had to be taken in the close-linked family group.

Passeggiata in the hundreds of little towns up and down the Italian peninsula comes with the sunset, when the sky turns a panne-velvet pink. The main piazza looks off over the sea, or commands a view of nearby vine fields and mountains. As the sun sets, the square fills rapidly with people. They walk in groups—girls with their mothers and sisters, boys in flocks of four to ten, men, arms linked with business partners. They sweep up and down, talking animatedly among themselves. The newlywed couple arrives on this scene like the king and queen of the chessboard. Flanked with relatives and friends from both sides of the family, they are special, set apart.

After marriage, a woman becomes *una signora*—an adult. No longer a prisoner of her virginity, she can go out of the house alone. She is free to visit her married women friends. She can shop whenever she pleases. She has responsibility; her entire family includes her in the decision-making conferences.

An Italian woman can also obtain this respect through age. A spinster arrives at independence around age thirty-five—that is, some fifteen years after her married sister. The Italian spinster has many advantages over her Anglo-Saxon counterpart. She is not frowned upon, but is honored in the family council. She contributes to the family coffers, lends a hand in the household and is considered a help rather than a burden to the sister she ordinarily lives with.

Money is the newlywed couple's biggest problem, and in Italy this is often alleviated by living with in-laws. Intriguingly, latest surveys indicate that this solution works quite well—when they live with the bride's parents. Nearly a third of the Shell respondents felt that conflicts with the husband's family was a major source of trouble in marriage, while only 8.5 percent worried about discord with the wife's parents.[7]

By the end of the first year, the couple has ordinarily reverted to the prematrimonial social pattern. The married woman spends most of her time in the society of other women. The link with her mother is never broken, and most observe a daily ritual of conferences in person—or by telephone if necessary. Their discussions of family relationships, family conflicts and family purchases are vital, for only family advice is considered valid in these matters.

When the Italian woman is not with her mother, she is with her sisters, her girlfriends or her maid. Conversation in these interfemale relationships is personal and concerned with family problems. University graduates rarely discuss "men's things"—politics and business—just as their mothers and grandmothers avoided discussing war.

The women have coffee together at midmorning, tea together at 3:00 P.M., aperitifs together at 6:00 P.M. They shop together, and seldom buy so much as a blouse unless they have consulted each other. They shout across the street or the courtyard, apparently enjoying the noise and the gossip as a proof of existence.

In a *passeggiata,* the married woman again walks with the women and her husband links arms with his male friends. If she and her husband go to the theater or the opera together, only he discusses it afterward. She talks about children, domestic help and winter versus summer resorts.

She returns to her *seria* clothes. Usually she is pregnant, but even if she isn't, she is no longer interested in the tight pants and the flowing skirts. Her husband no longer brings flowers and perfume.

Neither partner, however, feels particularly short-changed by this metamorphosis. Italians believe that loss of the initial excitement in marriage is simply natural—regrettable, perhaps, but to be expected. Nearly 50 percent say that their union is a success, and a further 43.7 percent state stoically that their marriage is *come gli altri* (like the others).[8]

The partners look on each other as natural allies who will go through eternity together. Ideally they make most decisions together, and the purchase of big items—the refrigerator, the color TV, the drapes—is often attended by in-laws from both sides of the family. Deciding on a home, unless it is a gift from the bride's parents, is reserved for the couple alone. The husband often decides on the purchase of a new car by himself. The wife, in a surprising number of families, decides which political party to vote for.[9]

The most striking contrast with the English marital pattern, however, is in the Italian management of family funds. Of the 1414 couples from all parts of the country who were queried in 1973, 37.8 percent declared that the husband hands his pay over to his wife, who pays all the bills and either gives him a fixed sum of money or doles it out *volta in volta* (piecemeal) when he needs something. A second large group—37.3 percent—puts funds in a communal place (checking accounts are not common in either England or Italy), where both the husband and the wife can take out what is necessary for their expenses. Only 15.3 percent of the husbands keep the money, pay the bills and give the wife an allowance or the *volta in volta* payments.[10] Predictably, the husband's control of money is strongest in the industrial northwest, where the wife's *seria* image as the keystone of the family has been most eroded.

Most foreign men think of the Italian woman as the Earth Mother—the warm, passionate, hot-honey soul of nature. Italian sex magazines play up a different image. Nudes do not have the *Playboy* girl-next-door aura; Italian models look hard, professionally sensual, as calculating as cats.

Today, even this image of the smoldering Italian woman is being discredited. Some 60 percent of all husbands complain that their wives are frigid with a *noblesse-oblige* approach to sex. Filmgoers laugh at the plight of the husband locked out of the bedroom because he doesn't earn enough money to support more children. A young, newlywed actress recently gave the advantage of marrying money as: "The freedom to refuse one's husband because he can afford to buy sex somewhere else."

A few wives admit that their own inhibitions are at fault. Others retort that sex isn't important or that their relationships with their husbands are hopeless. But the majority blame their husbands for being poor lovers. A popular Italian magazine found that one in four couples never has any foreplay whatsoever. Eight percent of the wives received only a few kisses before making love. One out of five over age forty-three reported that they and their husbands had given up on all sex relations.[11]

Professor Giuseppe Cattaneo, a leading sexologist, feels that both the woman's inhibition and the man's abruptness contribute to the problem. "We mustn't forget," he comments, "that coitus interruptus is still a widespread form of birth control—as is total abstinence."

However, he sees psychological factors as the main culprits. "Italian women often marry a 'baby' to satisfy their maternal urges. Meanwhile, the men mistakenly perpetuate the myth of the Latin Lover. When [a man] doesn't succeed as a sexual superman, both [partners] are confused and guilty. Italians must realize that they have to *work* at sex and have the maturity to accept a degree of failure."[12]

To quell frustration, extramarital love affairs have long been part of the Italian marriage pattern. In 1828, Longfellow wrote his brother Stephen from Rome:

"There seems to be no kind of shame attached to the dissoluteness of manners. Whenever I go to the principal street of the city at the hour for promenade, I see a lady of the highest tone, who has a rich, young banker as her *cecisbeo* [gigolo], driving in her carriage, with her daughter, her husband and herself. However, there are many families of manners and morals as uncorrupted as ours."[13]

In the past, only aristocratic women could afford to flaunt their dalliances. The ordinary wife, adhering to her *seria* responsibilities, concerned herself with her household duties, children and women friends. Together, women marched through life, arms linked, eyes straight ahead, male approaches bouncing off them like firecrackers off a tank.

At one time, all of Italy recognized what is now considered "the Sicilian practice"—the right of one spouse to assassinate the other if she or he commits adultery. In the traditional scene, the husband returns home unexpectedly, finds his wife in bed with another man, lunges to the bureau drawer where he keeps a pistol, shoots his wife (who is considered the major offender) and then takes off after the other man. After the second execution, he turns himself over to local authorities, full of contrition, and is given a five-year sentence for second-degree murder "committed under temporary insanity." According to newspaper reports, this archaic retribution still happens in Sicily on the average of ten or twelve times a year.

In approximately one out of every four of those cases, there is an interesting variation—the avenger is the wife. It is not like Texas, however, where only the man is protected by "the unwritten law";[14] the wronged Sicilian wife is ordinarily shown the same leniency by the courts as the husband.

Prostitution is another traditional answer to marital sex problems. Authorities estimate there are one million women on the streets—or one for every dozen adult females. Because of the three-hour lunch break, midday is often the time prostitutes are busiest. The *bella di giorno* (beauty of the day) is so popular she is considered to be a major reason for the reluctance of business to institute an eight-hour workday.

Lunch hours also offer opportunities for the housewife to pick up extra money. During a crackdown on three houses of prostitution in Milan, the chief of police stated that investigations were going ahead very slowly and delicately so that wives would not be "inconveniently forced to reveal the particulars of their occupations" to their husbands.

A Christian Democrat senator, Signora Lina Merlin, proposed the 1957 law that officially closed all houses of prostitution. Women working on a free-lance basis, however, were not declared illegal. A common criticism of the Merlin law is that it does away with the regular checkups that were required for all women who worked in houses. The Polizia di Buoncostume (literally the Goodcostume or Goodcustom Police) do check a woman's papers, however, and if she doesn't have a current medical certificate, she often spends several nights in jail. The law does not require that a specific charge be brought against her for this kind of harassment.

The Merlin law also states that "if something under a woman's skirt shows," she is guilty of "enticement." During the era of the miniskirt, several tourists were jailed for five days on this charge. The court requires that police give detailed descriptions as to color, lace and specific flower adornment of the unmentionable "something" beneath the woman's skirt.

Middle-class women are still reluctant to acknowledge the likelihood that half the people having affairs are other men's wives. "I'm perfectly willing to admit that Giuseppe has strayed once or twice," a wife will say, as she packs her bags for the summer holidays, "but myself? Well, the only kind of woman who sleeps with anyone but her husband must be a woman of the streets."

But it is in just the kind of resort where she spends June, July, August and part of September that the cruising older woman, so well known in Italian folklore, is most prominent. Every summer Italian women flock to the beaches and mountain towns with their children to get away from the heat and "unhealthy air" of the cities. Except during August, when four out of five Italian businesses close down, husbands are only weekend guests.

Local garage mechanics in these holiday spots are bloated with Casanovaism. Beach conversations among women who know each other well may include explicit discussions about how various men perform in bed. *L'Italiana* is not a romantic. She does not waste time dreaming of the Utopian lover-husband. For a large number of women in the middle and upper classes, the solution to sexual frustration is to take a lover. And usually the woman is sensible enough not to insist on an exclusive contract with either Romeo or Marco.

As the law now reads, neither she nor her husband can be taken to court except when there is an "indecent exhibition of a relationship." In other words, as long as a woman doesn't bring her lover into the conjugal home, or take him out to dinner with her son, she is behaving reasonably and lawfully and does not threaten the family.

The middle-class Italian woman dresses to emphasize her underlying sexuality. On her compact body, she wears snuggly fitting clothes. Her figure tends to remain solidly round; she belongs in a Raffaello painting and not in a fashion magazine.

The miniskirt was never successful in Italy, but pants and the midiskirt caught on immediately. They fit with the *seria* image. The all-time favorite is a sweater and a skirt hemmed to exactly one inch below the knee. Demure, but snug. Heels are always worn with any outfit; no Italian woman wants to walk like a man.

Her face, a smooth, heavy-pored surface, is nourished by the olive oil in her food and does not wrinkle easily. The average Italian woman wears less makeup than any other woman in Europe,[15] but those who do wear it enjoy it immensely. Eyes are outlined in blue. False eyelashes are popular. The mouth is emphasized in the latest shades. Her hair is thick and easily waved. She visits the hairdresser once a week for a complicated, cotton-candy concoction, and wears a protective net to bed the next seven nights.

Accessories include a single strand of pearls, and quite often a scarf tied loosely around the neck. Fur trimming or fur coats (particularly leopard) are popular.

The overall effect—the heels, nylons, snug clothes and fur coats—is a specific formula of discreet sensuality.

As taboos against discussing sex crumbled in the mid-sixties, Italian newspapers and magazines began publishing articles on the subject. Psychologists talked about the problems of frigidity and marital insecurity. Gynecologists expounded on sex-related physical problems.

Playmen, a careful copy of *Playboy,* appeared on the stands, and became an immediate money-maker. Published by Signora Adeline Tattoli, the blonde mother of three, *Playmen* was the company's second foray into the sex-magazine field. First had been the much cruder *Men.* Both sold out on the newsstands within hours. They had to. The day after they hit the stands, remaining copies were always confiscated by the Polizia di Buoncostume under Code 528 and Code 725. The two magazines have been indicted more than three hundred times, but neither has ever been convicted.

General-interest magazines struck another gold mine. In the fall of 1968, *Tempo*—Italy's equivalent of *Look*—introduced the first installment of a serialized sex encyclopedia. It was inserted in the magazine inside a hermetically sealed polyester bag, with a red flag warning all mothers. The text of the trumpeted insert was as dry as a 1922 primer on gynecology, and the illustrations were poorly printed reproductions of famous paintings like Titian's *Sacred and Profane Love.*

Modern media merchandising being what it is, another encyclopedia series evolved within a few weeks. This one was also encased in polyester, but the text was closer to the Hegelers' *ABZ of Love,* and the illustrations included line drawings of copulating wooden mannequins—still stiff, but certainly explicit.

This encyclopedia not only advertised its forbidden contents, it also featured a male and female nude photograph on the cover.

The nudes were mother and son.

Inadvertently, the encyclopedia had pointed to the strong Oedipal undertones that run through Italian social life. Italy has a long history of prominent homosexuals and bisexuals—Michelangelo and Da Vinci among other documented historical personalities.

On the whole, Italian society supports and accepts homosexuals more easily than any country in Northern Europe. The strong mother-son relationship is considered highly admirable. School systems encourage a boy whom Anglo-Saxons would oust as a "sissy." The tradition of men dressing like women at carnivals or fiestas is far older than today's acceptance of women in pants.

Homosexuality is not illegal. Police do not harass homosexuals, or haunt the public urinals. Just before the tourist season, the Polizia di Buoncostume make raids on the Colosseum, the Sant' Angelo bridge and other famous landmarks to pick up a few of the most blatant transvestites for several days"'questioning." Otherwise the police leave them more or less alone.

As a result of this tolerance, the Italian homosexual is rarely as bitter as his American counterpart. He is also less likely to marry for the sake of appearances, thus sparing many people misery.

The Lesbian, in contrast, has never enjoyed open social tolerance. The *seria* precept made it nearly impossible for a woman to be accepted in this role. An affair with another man might disrupt her family, but an affair with a woman would, it was believed, destroy her viability as a mother. From time to time, newsstands now carry political tracts by Lesbian feminists who are currently trying to change that belief, but so far there is little evidence that the general public has been affected. Homosexual actors have always been treated gently by the press, but when French film star Maria Schneider openly declared her sexual preferences while working in Rome, she was immediately attacked by newspapers and magazines calling for her deportation.

It was predicted that the legalization of divorce would wreak havoc on centuries-old social patterns. "Our way of life is based on the eternal character of the family," it was pointed out. "While it is true that some (presumably wayward husbands) suffer under the old system, many others (presumably abandoned wives and children) would suffer if divorce was legalized."

This argument would have been acceptable if there had not been an increasing number of *fuori legale* (outside the law) families. These consisted of people who had formed a permanent second union after a disastrous first marriage. Without divorce, these couples had no legal status whatsoever, and could be prosecuted for bigamy.

The woman's existence inside such a union was particularly difficult. She had no right to financial support or to a share of goods or property. The children were considered bastards. Although they could bear their father's name if he formally recognized them as his, their rights to inheritance were practically nonexistent. In the late sixties, when legalization of divorce was being hotly contested, it was estimated that over a million Italians were members of such *fuori legale* families.

In December 1970, divorce was legalized. Within months the infuriated Catholic Church had secured the five hundred thousand signatures necessary to force a national referendum, but the flood of divorce petitions that both sides had predicted never came. During the first three years that divorce was available, only 92,188 couples filed. Of the 66,641 decrees that were granted, more than half had been initiated the first year. By 1973, the number of petitions had dropped to 15,301—or one for every twelve marriages.[16]

These statistics played an important part in the 1974 national referendum as to whether or not the country should retain the law. Pro-divorce forces pounced on the clear indication that Italian social mores had not been disrupted. The law was upheld by a solid 59.1 percent of the vote.

Today petition for divorce will be considered by the court when (1) a consenting couple has been legally separated at least five years, (2) a consenting couple has proof of a *de facto* separation of at least six years, or (3) one member of a dissenting couple can offer proof of a legal separation for at least seven years. There have been very few cases where a divorce has been granted to a member of a dissenting couple when children under the age of fifteen are concerned.

Alimony is awarded only in the case of a "wronged" party. It can be (and has been) paid by the wife as well as the husband. Since alimony cases involve a lot of paper work, couples often choose out-of-court cash settlements preceding a mutual-consent petition. Alimony itself can be paid either as a lump sum or on a monthly basis. The lump-sum settlement is popular because it avoids future collection problems.

Divorce is still considered only in the last resort. The wife-husband bond remains the sacrosanct base of society; imperfections are still tolerated.

4

Mothers as Mothers

The mother-child relationship permeates every aspect of emotional life in Italy. Television ads solemnly intone, "Working with children is life's most important task—with children you work with the future." Italian rock singers bring out several songs a year about "Mammina" and "Cara Mamma" and "Bella Mamma." Over half the Shell respondents felt that "Motherhood is the principal thing in life for the woman, and she must dedicate herself to it entirely, accepting whatever sacrifices necessary."[17]

On a "trauma scale" similar to the one developed by Thomas Holms in Washington, D.C., the Italian woman placed the death of her son at the very top of the list.[18] The American listed the death of her husband first and the death of a child a poor fifth—after divorce, separation and incarceration.

Fully aware of the importance of this close-knit bond, the Italian popular press always takes note when the mothers of famous people die. Obituaries offer everything from discursive condolences to the bereaved son, to long mood pieces on the life of the mother. When the mother of Giuliano Salvatore, a notorious Sicilian bandit, died, Rome's leading columnist used the occasion to reminisce for a full page about how she herself had gone through her son's funeral the previous year.

Italy has a low rate of suicide, but those who throw themselves out of windows or off bridges (the most common methods; as the use of guns is rare) are usually young men or old women. Their desperation arises from feelings of uselessness or from having been abandoned by their families; their final message is invariably addressed to *"Cara Mamma"* (Dear Mama) or *"Cara Figlio"* (Dear Son).

The rare variation on this pattern—when a mother or father with small children commits suicide—illustrates again the Italian mother's "ownership" of her offspring. Only the Italian mother takes her children with her as she leaps in front of an oncoming train or plunges from her tenth-floor balcony. Such mothers have not abused their children or attacked them in fits of violent discipline, as is so often the case in Northern European and American infanticide. They take their children with them simply because they regard the children as part of themselves—better off dead than struggling through life alone.

Despite all the emphasis on motherhood, however, the Italian woman is not a baby-making machine. The annual birthrate in Liguria is only 12.6 per thousand inhabitants. In Tuscany and Umbria, it is only 13.5. These rates are commensurate with that of West Germany, which currently has the world's lowest rate of 11.3.

Italy's national birthrate is 16.3, slightly above the present United States figure, but until 1972, the Italian rate was lower than ours. Since World War II, the Italian birthrate has been significantly lower than those of the other European Catholic countries, and half that of Catholic Mexico, Peru or Venezuela.

How has this been accomplished?

Looking through Italian magazines and newspapers, one finds a few articles explaining birth-control methods, but the only devices available over the counter are the condom and a clock with two small disks that appear on alternating fortnights. If set according to instructions, the fertile period will come up green, the nonfertile, red—it's a Catholic clock.

Legal prohibition against selling birth-control devices or distributing birth-control information was lifted in 1970, but a woman must still be financially comfortable to afford the Pill. The cost of a month's supply can feed a family of four for a day. However, the moral inhibition against the

Pill is not so strong as one would think. "Those foreigners," young matrons were prone to say after Pope Paul issued his Humanae Vitae encyclical, "those Dutch and American bishops and their fighting over the Pill! In Italy, we leave Il Papa [the Pope] to his talking, and we go ahead and take *La Pillola*."

In 1961, the most popular form of birth control in rural areas, according to a University of Perugia survey, was coitus interruptus. At that time, it was the method used by 98 percent of the people polled.

The cross-country respondents in the Shell study twelve years later reported that coitus interruptus was still being used by 53.2 percent of the couples who were practicing birth control, with the largest number being over forty-six or between sixteen and twenty-five. The rhythm method was the next most popular one, with 43.7 percent reporting its usage. The condom was next, 27.2 percent; the Pill was fourth, with 22.2 percent. Diaphragms, douches and vaginal foams were used, but mainly by the woman above age thirty-six.

Intrauterine devices are practically unknown in Italy. Anal intercourse, which was once enthusiastically described to me by the mother of one as *"il mètodo suprèmo,"* is apparently widespread, but has not been investigated statistically. Vasectomy or tubal ligation is illegal, and—although discussed in magazine articles—treated with great disapproval by the medical hierarchy.

In reality it is not birth-control precautions that keep the Italian birthrate down, but abortion.

Before 1975, when the Constitutional Court legalized abortion in cases where the mother's mental or physical health is in serious danger, abortion for any reason was illegal in Italy. Even then, however, doctors across the country believed that there was at least one abortion for every live birth. Some estimated a rate of one million a year.[19]

Luigi de Marchi, the head of the Italian Association for Demographic Education (a name adopted before it was legal to plan parenthood), says Italy should build a monument to the abortionist. "She's saved the country. If it weren't for her, Italy would now have a population of about 70 million. The Church and State would suffocate with a population that size. Our system lives on its own violations."

Most abortions are performed on married women who already have children and cannot afford more. Family economic welfare is considered more important than Church morality. Fees for the operation run between $32 in small towns to $500 for what is euphemistically called an "exploratory operation" in a respectable city clinic. Authorities estimate that abortionists make over $100 million a year, and kill as many as twenty thousand women.[20] Still, there are only a few prosecutions of abortionists each year—perhaps because their patients are also liable to a stiff jail sentence.

Because of the high value placed on virginity, the unmarried girl rarely faces an abortion. If she does find herself pregnant and abandoned by her *fidanzato*, however, her family prefers to arrange an abortion for her. Often she will be disinherited if she goes ahead with having the child, for this aberration from the traditional family pattern is considered obscene. Even today, a father can have his unmarried daughter thrown in jail for becoming pregnant.

Being an unwed mother is more difficult in Italy than in any other Western European country. The woman receives no family support. Keeping the child with her is financially impossible unless she has a well-paid position in the city, for social services are not extended to her. Giving the child up for adoption means consigning it to a national-orphanage limbo that makes Dickens' almshouses look cheerful. The plight of the unwed mother is one of the worst problems in Italy, despite the courageous fights of women like Anna Magnani, who have at least made it possible to discuss the issue.

Inside the family, the birth of a baby calls for great celebration. During a woman's nine months' pregnancy she is treated like a fragile flower. She's given seats on buses and pushed to the head of the line in supermarkets and banks. She's stuffed with chocolates and vitamins. Mother and mother-in-law do her housework. Strangers come up to her on the street, pat her swelling abdomen and give her blessings.

Only the upper-class women do exercises and practice weight control. For everyone else, pregnancy is a period of total indulgence.

No Italian woman is enthusiastic about natural childbirth, or about having her husband present during birth. The general aim is to "get through them with the least effort possible." Childbirth is considered a form of physical labor and, as such, demeaning and distasteful.

Hospital visiting hours are never observed in the maternity ward. Colorful parties of well-wishers arrive at any time of the day or night carrying baskets of flowers and fruits, lace layettes and bottles of liquor or champagne. When I had my baby, our American friends tried to hide their bottles. When we asked the nurse for glasses, she took one look at the bulges under several coats and said, "Would you like to put that on ice, or will ice cubes do?"

The return home from the hospital is a red-letter event. The mother-in-law hangs a bow over the street door—a pink one for a girl, a blue one for a boy. When Signora Celia Campara, the wife of a Sardinian bandit with a $16,000 price on his head, bears a child, announcements are more complex. Father is informed by a pistol-shot salute if it's a girl or rifle salute if it's a boy.

There is one more postnatal *festa* to anticipate—the christening party. The new mother can invite as many people as she wants, and her mother takes care of all the arrangements. As soon as everybody has arrived, the baby is put to bed and *la mammina* becomes queen of the occasion.

Wealthy women can still hire a *balia* to wet-nurse their babies during the first year. This is particularly important, mothers explain, for a baby with an allergy to cow's milk. The *balia* invariably comes from the farm country north of Rome. Only these women, it is believed, possess the centuries of training and the natural physique to breast-feed for months. Italians have patience with world affairs, but personal problems tend to set them into squalls of rage. Anyone who can be patient and produce milk consistently is considered a marvel.

The *balia* is paid a liberal $320 a month, plus wardrobe, room and board. She is allowed to rest most of the day, and her only duties are caring for the infant. Her total cost runs to $5000 a year. Considering the fact that 74 percent of Italian families have an income of less than $3500, she has reason to be placid.

After the *balia* comes the governess. At the turn of the century, Italians preferred German women, but now their first choice is an English Nanny. An *au pair* girl from abroad, who lives with the family while studying, presents a problem. Although she has the snob appeal of being able to teach the child a foreign language, she is considered flighty and irresponsible. No Italian woman wants to expose her husband to daily doses of an English or Swedish girl, but Americans and Australians have a better reputation. English-speaking Swiss and Japanese girls are a premium.

Last choice on the *bella figura* list is the Italian girl, who is thought to be unreliable and without linguistic talent. If she is not a relative, she is likely to be despised more than the maid, made to do more work and be paid less. Unskilled and unprotected by the law, she is the downtrodden Cinderella of many households.

Nurseries are under great pressure to expand and modernize. The state has long had a system of *nidi* (nests) which operates in conjunction with state-aided orphanages.

These nurseries will take babies as young as two weeks, and care for them from 6:00 A.M. till 6:00 P.M. while the mother works. Cost, including meals, is free in needy cases, and only a few cents a day for those who can pay.

In the North, where adult family members often work in Switzerland, there are *nidi* that care for children around the clock, except on weekends. The Swiss refuse to allow the children to enter Switzerland, because they don't want any possibility of the workers becoming immigrants.[21]

These institutions are a source of easy, illegal money for the ruling Christian Democrat party, however. One of Rome's former mayors is under indictment for siphoning off nearly $50,000 from the orphan and *nidi* funds with the help of a friendly vegetable wholesaler who was supplying the kitchens. When Luciano Infelisi, a Rome prefect, opened a new investigation, he found children sleeping in unheated rooms, wearing rags, forbidden to play and being fed bread, pasta and rotting vegetables. Discipline was strict and medieval punishments common.

Obviously, such institutions are considered the last resort for the workingwoman with children. Still, they do exist, and the government is trying to clean them up.

Montessori nurseries are available for the children of parents who can afford to pay an average of $80 a month. Although these offer only half-day care, they accept children as young as eleven months, and undertake the messy tasks of diaper training and teaching a child to eat with utensils. The former is accomplished through peer pressure. Children are not allowed to wear plastic pants. If they make a puddle, nobody criticizes; the child is simply changed quickly. A morning of wearing the same pair of pants one started with, however, is a great achievement observed by all the rest of the two-year-olds.

One Montessori school in northern Rome is experimenting with a "creative environment" for the newborn. Babies are placed in a room that is freely visited by older children, just as in a family. The baby learns from the two-year-old, while the toddlers benefit from observing struggles that they themselves have gone through.

Children in this school are allowed more freedom than in other Italian Montessori nurseries, which generally dislike the permissive reputation they have abroad. The school has a "fight room" where children settle their differences. Bullies who take away other children's toys are never reprimanded by anyone except the other children. The youngsters learn only by imitation, and teachers always speak in a deliberately low, musical voice. These pupils appear unusually even-tempered and creative. The headmistress says that the "free family" atmosphere has restored several emotionally disturbed children to stability.

Authorities estimate there are 2.5 million in the three- to six-year-old age group. Two million of these are attending nursery school.[22] Of these, fully a million and a half are in parochial establishments. There is a saying that children are dominated by Mamma until she turns the job over to men in skirts.

Whether operated by a man in skirts or a woman, the nursery school is one of the most important influences in shaping the gregarious Italian. From birth onward, the child is part of a group.

The tradition of keeping the baby in the same room with its parents until the first birthday is not always a sign of poor housing. Parents feel that an infant will be lonely in a room by itself. Again, as children begin to explore the world around them, their mothers, their big sisters, their grandmothers, their governesses are always with them—not to stifle their independence, but to shield them from desolation.

It is natural for such children to fit quickly into the scheduled life of a nursery school. There they learn to sit for three hours at a stretch with only a piece of paper and a crayon to entertain them. All the children are doing the same thing, and the teacher talks to them constantly.

The girl who shares a bedroom with a sibling throughout childhood, and may share a desk throughout her school years, is as much at home in an adult group as any Western European woman. She has no need for a large amount of personal territory to buffer her from others. She walks with her arm tightly linked to those of her women friends and hovers toward her companions over tiny tables in the piazza coffee bar, where they talk with flamboyant gestures, occasionally touching each other's arms or shoulders to emphasize agreement.

Sunning in the piazza with the baby carriage is a regular occupation for young mothers who do not have someone to look after the child. Italians, like other Europeans, are great believers in fresh air, and the piazza is the only place where these inveterate city dwellers can be outside and at the same time enjoy each other's company.

At home, babies are rarely allowed to crawl around freely, but are kept in bed with their pacifiers securely in place. During the first year, mothers spend a large amount of time playing kootchy-koo and peekaboo games. The "got-your-nose" game, where mothers pretend to snatch the child's nose away, is often switched to "got-your-penis."

As soon as the child can talk, a change takes place. Not a sudden metamorphosis, it manifests itself throughout the second and third year as a child's baby words grow into sentences and finally into expressions of independence. From that time onward, the mother rarely takes the child out for its own sake. She takes the four-year-old along with her, of course, when she goes visiting or shopping. Sometimes this entails a stop in the piazza to talk with her friends. But simply going to a park to let the child play—no. If she has someone paid to baby-sit, the sitter will take the child out. Otherwise, the father entertains the children on weekends.

The mother does not play games or act the playmate. If one sees a woman playing *tutti-giù-per-terra* (ring-around-the-rosy) or *la campana* (hopscotch) with children in the piazza, she is always a foreigner. When the whole family is out on *passeggiata,* the child runs to *Papà* when she wants to show off her new ability to skip rope . . . and to Mamma when she has hurt herself.

What has happened is simple. As soon as children are old enough to talk, they become "human" and recognize their mothers as "human." At that point, mothers feel the obligation to become *seria*. They do not stoop to the child's level, but immediately promote the child to theirs. The child becomes Mamma's companion and must listen to Mamma's problems, family gossip and the latest events in intrafamily feuds.

The man is the one who fusses over everyone's new baby, while his wife stands back, solemnly acknowledging the new mother's responsibility. The father is the child's playmate. He buys the extravagant toys and plays the ally in pretend games. He teases the children and tells them fairy tales as well as teaching boxing, horseback riding, skiing and soccer. While he's enjoying the children, mother is stolidly dealing with *casa* and *cassa*.

Discipline is also Mother's responsibility and the most common punishment is scolding. What incites her wrath? Disrespect toward adults, indifference toward household schedules or getting dirty.

In order to win praise from *Mamma* and *Nonna* (grandmother) and teacher, the children must keep their shoes immaculately polished and their white blouses white. In Italy there are no adherents to the English belief that "the happy child is usually a dirty child" or to the cheerful English acceptance of twisted ankles and scraped noses. The principle is to protect children from physical stress as much as possible, and it applies to both sexes. In a society supporting the matriarch, physical competition is downgraded.

The child's role in the interplay of discipline is to cry and show verbal contrition as quickly as possible. Children are not sent to their rooms to think things over alone. The Italian training program is the exact opposite of that utilized by the Swedes, who control children with "significant silence." In order to clear the slate, the Italian child must do penance and receive absolution from Mamma.

By age six, 98 percent of Italian children are in school, but in the country they begin leaving by age eleven to go to work.[23] Legally, however, children are supposed to attend school until age fourteen, and approximately half the students continue into the *scuola superiore,* which does not finish until age nineteen, but is vital for obtaining white-collar positions.

Schools are chronically overcrowded. Children attend in double and sometimes triple shifts. Books are outdated and handed down from sister to brother to sister. Emphasis is placed on rote learning of the classics. Practical experience in chemistry or biology is curtailed by inadequate lab facilities. Gym classes are sometimes held in alleyways and there are few extracurricular activities.[24]

On the surface, the reason would seem to be a simple lack of financing, but there is a subconscious motivating factor, and it is consistent with dominance of the female sensibility. *L'Italiana* wants no part of physical competition, so physical activity is ignored by the simple expedient of neglecting funds for lab and gym facilities. One never finds a high school paying for a basketball court at the expense of hiring a new language teacher.

Italy has been the first European country to back parents' participation in school boards enthusiastically. (Programs were initiated first in Scandinavia, but met with little public interest.) The first Italian boards were elected in February 1975, with a full 66 percent of the parents taking the trouble to vote. They were joined by 67 percent of the students electing their representatives and 90 percent of the teachers electing theirs.[25]

Mamma can talk with the teacher about specific problems on the fifteenth and thirtieth of every month. Contact on a personal level is usually guarded, because the Italian parent—unlike the French and the German—always takes the child's side.

Once Mamma collects her brood at the school gate after their five-hour shift is finished, the school's influence stops. For the majority of the child's waking hours, the companion is Mamma. Children are rarely called upon to do chores. Instead, they learn to spend hours quietly reading, playing with dolls or crayons or talking to Mamma. Some active boys may be enrolled at a local sports club at a nominal cost, but the quieter children of both sexes do not indulge in this practice.

If children are allowed outside, they are accompanied by Mamma, *Nonna* or aunt. Girls are kept on a particularly tight rein. Playing on the street carries the stigma of lower-class neighborhoods, and Italian cities have few parks. The child is not entirely discouraged from having friends her own age, but they take a back seat to the family. Even an expedition to buy baby brother's shoes means that a little girl must leave her friends and accompany her parents and siblings.

Nor do children have pets. Mamma might have a status lapdog. *Papà* may have a hunting dog. The homosexual can be seen strolling the piazza with a pair of Neapolitan mastiffs. The little girl does not need a dog to learn how to be a mother—she practices with baby brother. And she does not need a companion. She has Mamma.

Italian children enjoy one freedom not given to Anglo-Saxon children. They are allowed to stay up until eleven, twelve, one o'clock at night. That, after all, is the time to enjoy some of the best hours of family fellowship.

Fights with peers reflect the taboo against physical activity. Small children are never allowed to hit each other. Shouting/screaming matches are the natural substitute. As children grow older, they still rarely get into fistfights. An argument that disintegrates into a physical confrontation is conducted by the far more feminine means of open-hand slapping. Teenagers play soccer, where hands do not touch the ball, and emphasis is on speed and agility, in contrast to United States style football or English rugby, where blind bravery and brute force are applauded.

Until age eleven, both girls and boys wear school smocks which are outgrowths of the pervasive feminine influence. They are puff-sleeved, full-skirted and are completed by a large, floppy bow under the chin. Boys usually wear short pants hidden underneath, and are difficult to distinguish from the girls.

Teen-agers, since the late sixties, have taken to protest marches and group demonstrations, demanding that funds already allocated for bigger schools and better facilities be spent. They have also insisted that the state do away with the eleven-year-old cutoff exams that stream children either toward or away from university studies. Authorities have agreed in principle to all of these claims, but have been slow and erratic in implementing them.

Students are also pressuring for sex education. Courses are currently being taught in Perugia and Venice, but when Dr. Ennio Oliva tried to institute a six-lesson series in a Rome junior high school, he ran into trouble. He had the approval of 158 of the 161 parents involved, but the project was reported in the press and he was fired. The best sex-education courses in

Rome now are thought to be the marriage-preparation lectures offered by several Church parishes.[26]

Parts of the Italian school system are very progressive. Italy may trailblaze with the staggered schedule; i.e., some classes continue through summer holidays and then cease for three months in the winter, so that facilities are utilized throughout the year. There are also official plans to enlarge the summer-camp program for underprivileged children to include holiday accommodations for their mothers. By law, all employees must have at least twenty days of paid vacation every year, but thousands of working mothers cannot afford to get away from home.

5

Mother Grows Up

       A childhood dominated by Mother produces adult attitudes that differ significantly from those in patriarchal societies.

One of the most obvious is the Italian view of the law. It has been pointed out repeatedly that Italians do not respect the law. Everyone in the country plays the tax-evasion game, and the big names in industry and property development play it on a grand scale. Nobody pays any attention to No Parking signs and speed regulations. Cities are ringed by postwar buildings, of which 56 percent are located on land originally intended by city planners for parks.[27]

To the ordinary Italian citizen there are justifications for this casual attitude. Historically, laws were imposed by patriarchal invaders. The terms "civil disobedience" and "passive resistance" are rarely heard in Italy, but the attitudes they signify have been known for centuries.

Second, obedience to the law suffers because the Latin conceives of law as immutable. At first this seems paradoxical, but a closer look reveals its logic. Since laws were handed down either by foreign rulers or the Church, no ordinary citizen had any chance of changing them. The governing bodies themselves were obligated to the immutability of their proclamations. At the top, the way to deal with law was not to change it outright, but to "reinterpret" it—a process which is still the only one officially accepted by the Church. Ordinary Italians deal with the immutable law the same way they deal with immutable time. They ignore it or they get around it.

Italians never confront. If they are accused of infringing on one of the myriad and often conflicting laws that bulge the files in the Palazzo di Giustizia, they argue for a few minutes, and then become contrite. Ordinarily, the human manifestation of justice forgives them. In psychological terms, the matriarchal society is geared to lavishing love on the prodigal with human failings.

The most pervasive reason for disregarding the law, however, is that the law's obligations conflict with the basic belief in putting the family first. Luigi Barzini, the noted Italian journalist, explains this very clearly: "Anarchy in Italy is not simply a way of life, a spontaneous condition of society, a natural development; it is also the deliberate product of man's will, the fruit of his choice; it has been assiduously cultivated and strengthened down the centuries. The strength of the family is not only, therefore, the bulwark against disorder, but at the same time one of its principal causes. It has actively fomented chaos in many ways, especially by rendering useless the development of strong political institutions."[28]

The essential simplicity of this belief was illustrated to me when every morning for an entire year I met a car driving along a one-way street in the wrong direction. Since the street was also used by the police en route to their central station, the car was often stopped. The driver would explain that he was taking his boy to school, and unfortunately he lived at the wrong end of the block (the school was about three-quarters of the way up the street). Only once did he get a ticket, and no one suggested that he should make the boy, who appeared to be about ten, walk from the corner.

The picture of the Italian vis-à-vis the law changes abruptly when one looks at the pattern of violence. According to the latest United Nations comparative statistics, Italy ranks second lowest in homicide rates of any Western European country, with Norway, another family-oriented society, only a few points below.[29] Italian incidences of rape, armed robbery and mugging have always been low, and senseless vandalism of public telephone booths or other public facilities are practically unknown.

It is obvious that the ideals taught in childhood have survived. Overt scrapes with the law besmirch the family *bella figura*. Such behavior is considered vulgar and stupid. Italians do not glorify the notion of "showing you're man enough to conquer others." They try to solve conflicts by persuasion and avoid trouble by using their wits.

The adult Italian male would feel totally out of his element trying to mug someone—as much as a female does in other societies, where she has been told that enforcing her will physically is simply "not the thing to do." The Italian is not averse to participating in the clever heist, the guileful kidnaping (where the victim is most often a grown man) or the quick purse snatching, but happily for society he is not violently destructive.

Runaway teen-agers are also rare—although some cases do exist. The steady, nationwide rate had been running eighty per month, but recently there has been a significant change. Until the seventies, 60 percent of the runaways were boys. Now 60 percent are girls,[30] and they tend not to return home. The boys go back to Mamma after a few days, but the girls— determined and serious as ever—make their own way. Police claim that all too often they find a pimp who is quite willing to help.

The only pronounced serious-crime pattern is group violence, today usually committed in the context of political conflict. Throughout history Italy has known attacks by enraged mobs. The roots of this crowd violence are deeply entwined with feelings of frustration about the immutable law, but it is fascinating to note how Italian groupist orientation is reflected even in the area of violence. Italians always scoff at reports of solitary assassins in the United States. When a mad sculptor attacked Michelangelo's *Pietà* in 1974, the Italian newspapers dropped their conspiracy theories ("Anarchists?" "Artists' League?") only when they found the man was a foreigner.

Aversion to physical confrontation has its disadvantages. The influential *Il Corriere della Sera* has editorialized that Momism is the cause of Italy's poor showings in the Olympics. As the paper explained, Italy, with her overdoses of galoshes and woolen underwear, will never raise a batch of hardy athletes. What it didn't mention was that Italy glides brilliantly on the international soccer fields and across international bridge tables.

The Italian is also often an unsuccessful soldier. He has been accused of desertion under fire and lack of discipline. What is involved?

The Italian cannot keep his mind from reacting to what his body is doing. If an act strikes him as wrong or impractical, he stops. The soldier who deserted the battlefield may easily have belonged to one of the thousands of Italian families who sheltered Jews during the last war. Italians are not cowards—they simply do not obey orders blindly.

The place where the Italian upbringing has a distinct advantage is at the international-business bargaining table.[31] There the battle of wits and the verbal arguments practiced so assiduously in childhood come in handy. Fiat used its wiles to set up a vast international network of plants in Austria, Spain, Africa and South America, and was awarded a coveted $800 million contract with Russia. Zanuzzi is the largest manufacturer of household appliances in Europe, and is appreciated from Scandinavia to Spain for its reasonable prices and simple repair systems. In the recent world economic crisis, Italy amazed the international banking community by sliding dangerously toward collapse, and then smoothly righting herself within six months by a rigorous internal control of spending and by vigorous exporting successes.

The dominance of women in Italian society has also contributed to the continued interest in religion. Ninety-nine percent of all Italians are baptized, married and buried in Catholic ceremonies. Habitual religious observation, however, is far more likely to be a woman's preoccupation than a man's. Nearly half the women attend church regularly on Sundays and saint's days, and 14.2 percent also go during the week.[32]

To the questions of why people attend church and why a destitute woman will put money in the offering box, two answers are repeated. Women go to church because they feel luxuriously at home—even in the baroque caverns of Saint Peter's. They feel that some small part of all the majesty belongs to them. The wizened old lady in black, sitting quietly beside the Michelangelo, a shaft of sunlight coming through the stained glass to wreath her face, is not uncomfortable. She knows no one will bother her no matter how long she sits there. Wrapped in her history and religion, she prays for her own and her family's absolution.

The Church offers abundant human contact. A very real voice from the confessional gives penance and absolution. Congregations casually tolerate groups that choose to gossip during a ceremony, or arrive and depart as they please.

God is thought of in human terms. In Sciacca, Sicily, for example, the people take the Christ statue to the cool mountains for the summer, feeling that He should have a vacation from the heat like everybody else.

The most important contact, of course, is Mary, Holy Mother of God. In Rome, itself, there are forty-four churches dedicated to Maria . . . and fewer than a half dozen dedicated to Christ. Pictures of Maria not only decorate the night tables beside many beds, but they turn up in unexpected places—on the walls behind the desks of city officials, over the cash register at a used-car dealer's.

The Church has not eradicated the Italian belief in magic, signs of which are scattered through the Italian culture. Sexual undertones are often blatant; villages celebrate numerous fertility saints' days, including one where giant towers of reeds are burned to honor the sprouting of the wheat. Shops hang the phallic, red *corno* (horn) in doorways to ward off the Devil, and both sexes often wear *corno* charms on permanent necklaces, bracelets or watchbands. A Neapolitan woman will ask a man from outside her family to bring her a kilo of salt on New Year's Day so that she can scatter it about the house. When it is swept up, it is believed to take all the evil of the past year away with it. Superstitious women sometimes approach men asking to touch their genitals in order to counteract an evil omen.

There are several laws against black magic. One that has been enforced recently is against *plagio*—the theft of a soul. In the early seventies, university professor Aldo Braibanti was denounced by the mothers of two male students who had been living with him. He was convicted of *plagio* because the mothers were able to prove that their sons' personalities had altered radically during their stay with him. Braibanti was sentenced to nine years in jail.[33]

Death, like other rituals of Italy, is accompanied by appropriate fanfare. Hospitals send patients home to spend their last days and die in the arms of the family, rather than under the impersonal auspices of medical science.

A woman often spends years planning her final trip to *il posto mio* (my place). Funerals are marked by huge floral wreaths, a solemn service and an elegant hearse. The traditional family still has the crystal-sided carriage drawn by eight, black-plumed, inkblot horses. Cemeteries are jumbles of elegant tombstones.

As in other countries that have witnessed the health revolution of the last century, the woman lives longer than her husband and usually presides at his funeral. Dressed in black, adorned only with a strand of pearls, the wife goes through the ordeal sustained by the constant help of her female relatives. Dealing with the undertakers, closing the house and making arrangements to move in with her daughter or daughter-in-law, the Italian woman remains calm and competent.

The graveside scene is in marked contrast. The wife collapses against an understanding son. It is a moment for weeping and lamenting. There was little respect in Italy for Jacqueline Kennedy's graveside composure after the assassination. "How could a person be so cold?" people asked.

Tolerance is not a virtue in Italy—it's a natural trait as inherent as breathing. A woman cannot force her will on others, so she must abide differences without trying to conquer them. Italian society is based on a live-and-let-live psychology. Refusing to believe in perfection, Italians therefore refuse to indict imperfection.

Unfortunately, tolerance of imperfection goes hand in hand with indifference to misfortune. If the entire country belonged to one big family, Italy would be the perfect society, but there are those who have somehow fallen outside the nest. Welfare is at a bare minimum. Low-income housing is practically nonexistent. Even earthquake victims, who make front-page news, are given no more than makeshift refugee camps to live in until somehow someone in the family manages to make a life somewhere else.

No one suffers more than the children who through some mischance fall into the state orphanages. These *figli di nessuno* (children of nobody) carry the stigma of being abandoned, of not belonging to a natural family group which traditionally shares the burden of any nieces or nephews in dire straights. Lacking "natural" protection, they are branded as the offspring of unfeeling monsters.

Everything in the system works against an abandoned child being adopted. Certain that the power of blood ties will make any mother—even the one who deserts a nameless baby at a church door—inevitably reclaim her child, authorities erect innumerable obstacles to declaring an infant "adoptable."

It is also thought necessary to have an iron-clad guarantee that the child can never compete with any natural-born offspring of the adopting couple. Until 1967, when Signora Maria Pia del Canton and ten other women members of Parliament successfully instituted new legislation, adoption was illegal unless the adopting parents were over forty-five and childless.

The state system of orphanages, ONMI (Organizzazione Nazionale di Maternità ed Infanzia—National Organization of Motherhood and Childhood), is supported by per capita subsidies, so it is to the institution's advantage to keep the children. ONMI officials are currently under indictment for allegedly operating with two lists—a long one for the government and a short one for the adoption agencies.

To date, 200,000 children have been declared adoptable, and some 300,000 couples are on adoption-agency waiting lists. Placements, however, are proceeding at a rate of only 2700 children a year.[34]

The last characteristic of adult Italian society that we must examine at this point is vitally important: it is the Italian woman's satisfaction with being female. This was evident in all age groups and in all parts of the country in the Shell survey.

The interviewers asked women to rate their reactions to the "female facts of life" on a scale from pleasurable to unpleasurable.

Slightly more than 50 percent marked the onset of menstruation as pleasurable, 26.4 marked it unpleasurable, 23.5 didn't know. Becoming pregnant was marked pleasurable by 79.1 percent, unpleasurable by 5 percent and don't know by 15.9 percent.

Pregnancy itself was pleasurable to only 56.3 percent, but 89.5 percent enjoyed the birth of the first child and 76.2 percent enjoyed breast-feeding (compared to 74.3 percent who found the first months of marriage pleasurable).

Of all the experiences on the list, only the menopause received more than a third unpleasurable votes—59.4 percent, with 34.1 percent who didn't know and 6.5 percent who found it pleasurable.

The ways they rated what they feared were also revealing. The greatest fear, marked as important by 62.9 percent of the respondents, was of bearing a deformed child. A close second was the fear of being left alone in life. The thing least feared was pregnancy, but just above that was the fear of being assaulted. Another problem low on the list was the fear of growing old.[35]

A number of respondents indicated that women feel themselves decidedly superior to men, and the man's second-sex status often shows up in ordinary social situations. In a sudden crisis, where a pedestrian is struck by a car or someone collapses on the sidewalk, it is always the woman who rushes to help while the men stand back, looking helpless. A man may be sent by the woman to telephone for an ambulance or a man may drive the victim to the hospital, but it is the woman who organizes the rescue.

It is the man who most often exhibits social unease. In conversation, the man is the one affected by chronic stuttering. He is also far more likely to be subject to nervous twitches, and will often dust off the sleeve of a friend (of either sex) while conversing. Walking down the street, he nervously adjusts his genitals—remembering, it's said, the childhood game of "got your penis."

He is concerned with the way he dresses and he plays the peacock. He wears the brightest clothes of any male in the industrial world, and uses the most flamboyant beauty products from hair dye to youth injections.

It is important to point out that, despite all this, *il signore* visibly enjoys his life. He is uninhibited about breaking into song on the street. Sitting at the neighborhood café, having his espresso with friends, he comments *"Che bella la vita!"* ("How beautiful is life!"), and everyone agrees. His moves to other countries in search of work are always considered temporary, for he never loses his conviction that life in Italy is the best there is. His belief is backed by statistics. He has a longer life-span than a man in many of the Western European countries, and cardiologists have found that the probability of his suffering a fatal heart attack between the ages of forty-five and fifty-four is one-third that of the American male.[36]

The first thing a foreign woman notices about the Italian male is his avid advances toward practically every female he sees. He thinks of the accessible woman (in contrast to inaccessible Mamma) as a different species, a visitor from another world.

But the aggressive Italian is a *papagallo* (parrot), not a wolf. He is rarely violent. Instead, he pinches, whistles or comments, *"Che belle gambe ne hai!"* ("What beautiful legs you've got!"). He stops to ask directions, the time, to point out a lost coat button or to remark on how handsome your dog is, how exceptionally well-behaved your children are. He does this audaciously, certain in his belief that every woman, particularly every foreign woman, is a passionate fire just waiting to be ignited.

The plain fact is that frequently he is right. Many women come to Italy whenever they have two weeks free, because the Italian male accepts female passion openly, and eagerly. Not even the Frenchman offers such an unencumbered, guilt-free approach to an affair.

Take Fabrizio, a blue-eyed, dark-haired Italian with a physical zest that sends off sexual impulses at the rate of six a second. He works in the film industry and wears tailored shirts and tight pants that show off his build. He's not the *pappagallo* who harasses you on the street, but his sex appeal is insistent.

Fabrizio says he was introduced to sex ten years ago in his midteens by his aunt. His mother was the formidable tyrant of the *cassa* in his father's shop, but his aunt (the wife of his mother's brother) was relaxed and friendly.

Fabrizio now dates foreign women. He speaks English fluently and commands enough German and French to get along well in bed. He doesn't like to juggle more than one girl at a time, and he doesn't think of himself as promiscuous.

He says he likes English, American and Swedish women the best. They're the most fun to be with and they have the most imagination in bed. Who's at the top of the list? Well, maybe Swedish women. Americans are always making him do dishes, and the English just don't seem to learn how to use a bidet. He dislikes women who aren't fastidious.

And what does he think about the Italian woman?

"The Italian woman? I don't think about the Italian woman." Fabrizio looks around for a minute, then points at the Chianti bottle on the table. "The Italian woman is like that bottle. I may use her when I want to, but I don't think about her"—a rather graphic summary of the female-male relationship in Italy. Beyond the physical level, it is often completely hollow. The man's heart belongs to his mother, his head belongs to his male friends—Anna gets the genitals. The arrangement is considered quite acceptable as long as the woman's heart belongs to her children and her head belongs to her women friends.

The dynamics of the interplay between sexes, even in moments of extreme stress, is intrinsically different from its Anglo-Saxon counterpart. The Italian woman rarely cries; she weeps. And she weeps only in sorrow, when there is a confrontation that touches the family. Crying over a stray cat dead in the streets, the hopelessness of a traffic jam or the gas being turned off because someone forgot to pay the bill is unknown. An American male swells up and becomes protective at the sight of tears, but the Italian wilts and becomes submissive. It brings back memories of Mamma. His reaction is conditioned by the dramatic family emotional scene, where the man is invariably in the wrong, and the best thing he can do is repent and arouse the protective forgiveness of Mamma.

The man is not only considered guilty until proven innocent in the home situation; he is usually outnumbered. Both his mother and his mother-in-law will ordinarily band together with his wife. Although he may win the day's battle where there has been a monumental outburst of anger on all sides, he does not expect to control the family in the patriarchal sense. Inside the Italian family, the man is always "the Other," an outsider who must prove his value daily in order to be allowed to participate.

6

Mother as Homemaker

           Housework rates little glory in Italy, perhaps because it involves physical effort. Nevertheless, it is a major time consumer, and deserves some attention.

Ninety-six percent of Italians live in apartments, unlike Northern Europeans, who prefer separate houses. Even farm families prefer to live in villages rather than on the open land. The Etruscans invented the apartment building, and the concept of group living has been gladly accepted by every generation since.

Over half the population owns its own co-op apartment. If financially possible, the bride's parents give an apartment as their gift to the newlyweds. The bride then registers ownership of the property in her maiden name and retains the right to any profits that come from it if she rents or sells it. It is an eternally intact dowery. It is also a hedge against the future for the mother of the bride, for there is the implication that she should always have the right to live there in her old age.

Ground floors are considered undesirable—passersby can look in. All accessible windows are heavily barred. The ground-floor entrance door is a massive *portone* of oak or ironwork, which is closed every night at nine sharp—one of the most punctual events in Italy. Carved into it is a dwarf door through which one can creep out or bring in guests.

The private door to the apartment is also heavily barricaded. In the United States heavy police locks have only recently become popular but every Italian dwelling has always had doors that could withstand an army. There are floor anchors, ten-inch-long key bolts, peepholes and throw braces. The same holds true for any door leading to a terrace.

Once inside, the first room is a secluded entrance hall, furnished only with a hard wooden bench for waiting. The Italian would be horrified at the thought of ushering a visitor directly into her home. A connecting hall, with doors on either side, leads away from the entrance. The layout is designed so that a guest can easily be conducted to a sitting room without seeing any other part of the house. The floors are cold, smooth marble tiles or terrazzo stone, only occasionally relieved by a throw rug.

Behind the "public room" is a maze of interconnecting halls. In upper- and middle-class homes, these are used by the maid. In lower-class homes, they are used by the women of the household when they are doing demeaning physical work. The entire household is kept scrupulously clean, but fancy decoration is considered necessary only in the sitting room.

The dining room is used for welcoming in lower-class homes, but usually only coffee, liquors or sandwiches are offered. "Come for dinner" is a rare invitation, unless a woman has servants to prepare and serve the meal. Instead, when the family wants to entertain, they use the communal house—the piazza. There, they invite the group to their favorite restaurant, where everybody—including Mamma—can relax and enjoy the occasion.

Further buried in the upper-class apartment are the family's private rooms. Friends are rarely taken on "come see our new bedroom suite" tours. When visiting the sumptuous Sophia Loren-Carlo Ponti villa, one is shown the impressive entrance with the curved white-marble staircase leading up to the main part of the house, as well as several sitting rooms and a rococo dining room. Sometimes, one is also conducted through the third-floor modern salon, Sophia's study and Sophia's bedroom, but there one stops. Ponti's rooms, the children's rooms and the servants' quarters are off limits.

In short, the layout of the Italian home is like a topographical map of *L'Italiana*'s psyche. Set inside a city apartment building, the individual apartment is designed to be separate. Doors are heavily guarded. Voluptuous, decorative curves are carved in stone. *Bella figura* public rooms are served by hidden halls. The inner rooms are plain and practical.

The woman's day does not necessarily begin with the family breakfast. Fare is ordinarily light—a cup of strong, black espresso and perhaps a roll or a doughnut. Old-fashioned families sometimes fix a coffee-and-milk soup with pieces of bread floating in it. Many take breakfast at the corner coffee bar.

It is mandatory that children be taken to school at nine o'clock, even if they are twelve years old and the school is only a block away. Only about 50 percent of their escorts are mothers, however. The rest are mainly fathers, but there are a few governesses and grandmothers.

Office workers and store clerks must be at their posts by 9:30 or 10:00 A.M. Middle management often doesn't arrive until 11:30 or noon, but they then work—after a lunch break from 1:00 to 4:00— until 8:00 or 9:00 P.M. Supper at 10:00 P.M. is common.

One of the most enjoyable tasks of the housewife is shopping. Italians worship fresh food, and most women shop at least once a day. Bread will not keep crusty from lunch to suppertime, and going out twice or even three times a day is not usual.

Forays in search of the perfect orange are not difficult. Most apartment buildings have shops on the ground floor, and what one's own building doesn't have can usually be found across the street. *L'Italiana* uses the occasion as an opportunity to flirt with the shopkeeper, to act out her frustrations and aggressions and relax. It is also a sort of emotional mirror. She knows what form she's in by her ten-thirty encounter with the butcher. So does the butcher. The day is made up of these human triumphs and failures.

Back home, the housekeeper carefully sheds her street clothes and hangs them up. Her shoes are brushed and shelved, and she dons her housecoat and house slippers. In poor neighborhoods, women may run out to the bakery in housecoats, but this is not done in middle- and upper-class districts, where house clothes are strictly indoor wear. No woman of any class ever appears in public wearing curlers. The rest of her appearance may sometimes be a bit disheveled, but never her hair.

The woman frequently has help with the housecleaning. Live-in maids cost $350 a month, plus room and board and clothing, and they are difficult to find. The daily maid has taken her place at a maximum of $300 a month for six hours a day, six days a week. If there is no maid, there is often a live-in mother-in-law or an unmarried sister to help with the chores. A survey in 1973 indicated that not only did the mother-in-law help with the housework in the majority of Italian households, but she did *all* the work in 24 percent of the homes. [37]

Not all household tasks are modernized. Floors need daily mopping and polishing—a backbreaking chore, even with the popular Italian electric floor polisher. Most ironing is done with lead-heavy irons, which are non-thermostat affairs. Even now, only one iron in every four to be found in the stores is a steam-thermostat type.

On the other hand, refrigerators are far more common and important in Italy than elsewhere in Europe. The courts have ruled it illegal to impound a family's refrigerator under bankruptcy proceedings. It has been added to the list of vital necessities that cannot be taken away, including one's clothes, the kitchen stove, table and chairs and the beds.

The ordinary Italian family also has a good washing machine (two-tub washers, which are still sold in England, are not seen here), a food blender and a hot-water heater—sometimes only for the bathroom. Dishwashing is physical work, not considered as important as the pampering bath. Electricity is expensive, so stoves are usually gas. Some are equipped with a combination gas/electric system to facilitate preparation of long-simmering sauces on one back burner.

Major appliances cost approximately $150 apiece, are cleverly made and do not require expensive repairs. Available on time payments, they are bought throughout the country. American-style built-in kitchen cabinets have been widely available only since the mid-sixties (this is true throughout most of Europe), and are in great demand.

Lawn care and gardening do not enter the Italian woman's schedule. No one has more than a few potted plants on the balcony, unless they can afford a gardener. The grow-it-yourself movement involves too much physical effort to be popular.

L'Italiana is the original instant cook. Italian cooking has a fabulous savor, but it is not usually due to hours spent slaving over the stove. The major meal is the dinner, served between 1:00 and 2:30 P.M. It consists of a pasta course, meat, salad, bread and wine. There may be a dessert, but ordinarily the meal is concluded with fruit, cheese and espresso.

Pasta has been a mother's-helper meal for centuries. She puts the sauce together in the morning and lets it simmer. At mealtime, she boils water and tosses in the spaghetti. Presto! She doesn't even have to defrost.

The main course is usually veal cutlets, which can be breaded ahead of time and pan-fried quickly at the last minute. Variety is achieved with cheese, anchovy or tomato sauce topping.

Markets sell fresh-cut tossed-salad greens every day. These require only oil and vinegar. Fresh-cut mixed soup vegetables are also available. In many areas, bread and wine are delivered to the door—or, more precisely, to the basket hanging on the rope that the housewife lowers out the window when the merchant calls up to her. In Sicily, markets sell precooked vegetables, steaming hot and ready for the table.

Dessert is always bought at the *pasticceria* (bakery shop). I have never eaten a homemade dessert in an Italian household. Cakes and pies are not particularly appreciated anyway, because they are difficult to make with the hard winter-wheat flour available. The best ones consist mainly of whipped cream and chocolate or chestnut paste.

Italians are faithful to their own cooking. Rome is an international capital, but there are only half a dozen foreign restaurants, and these are supported mostly by foreign residents and tourists. The Italian is content with the traditional *ristorante* or *trattoria*.

The mystique of the meal lies not only in the food. As in France, eating is a ritual that brings the family together, to laugh, sing and talk over family problems. *Il pranzo* is a touchstone of existence and one rarely sees an Italian film—even all-male adventure tales—without the traditional meal scene.

Eating out in the evening stretches into the late hours, and leads to poor theater attendance. No one would think of rushing *il pranzo* for such an insignificant thing as professional entertainment. Participation theater among the animated relatives and friends gathered at the dinner table is more important.

7

Mother as a Career Woman

The Italian woman won the vote and explicit constitutional equality almost as easily as the American woman put through the 1964 Equal Pay and Opportunities Act. *L'Italiana* first voted nationally in the plebiscite that took place after World War II. Article III of the Constitution, which was subsequently accepted in 1948, states that "All citizens have equal social dignity and are equal before the law, regardless of sex, race, language, religion, political opinions or personal and social conditions."

Article IV states, "The Republic recognizes all citizens' right to work, and promotes the conditions that render this right effective."

Italian law also guarantees equal voting rights, equal pay and equal eligibility for public office.

La signora is covered by special protective statutes as an employee—she is not to work at night; she cannot do heavy or dangerous work; she cannot be fired for marriage or pregnancy. If she becomes pregnant while working, she is entitled to four months' leave with pay—one month prior to birth, three months after. An additional month can be taken at half pay. If she is breast-feeding, she has an hour of paid time in the morning and an hour in the afternoon in which to feed the child. Any firm employing more than thirty-five women is required to have a free nursery on the premises for children.

As *capo di familia* the husband is granted family bonuses, health insurance, travel allowances and so on. The working wife does not receive these, since she is not assumed to be supporting a family. As already noted, however, it is legally possible for her to assume the *capo di familia* benefits (and responsibilities) if her husband is incapacitated in any way or if she is a widow.

April 1975 saw further revisions by Parliament in the family laws. The wife now has an equal say in where the family lives and in how the children should be educated. She can also travel abroad without her husband's written permission.

She has, however, always had the right to retain her maiden name. For legal purposes, in fact, a woman's maiden name is required. That is the way she is recorded on official lists from hospital rosters to police blotters. The family's electric, gas and telephone contracts are often signed by the wife, using her maiden name, and even the home—particularly if it forms part of her dowry—can be held in her maiden name alone.

Whether or not a woman is married, she may keep her own bank account, and she can retain the proceeds from her own transactions if they do not involve conjugal finances. Wealthy women have kept entire fortunes out of their husband's reach in this way, although this right may be abrogated by the 1975 family legislation.

Either the wife or the husband may take the respective spouse to court for refusing to perform the conjugal act. Several such cases, on the part of both wives and husbands, are heard in Italian courts each year. The average jail sentence for the offense is one month.[38]

Although the legal position of the woman in Italy looks impressively solid, authorities rarely fulfill their pledges to her or anyone else.

For solutions to emotional, economic or social problems, a woman can turn to the dozens of state-aided moral-defense leagues. There are leagues for young maidens, wives, mothers and homeless elderly women. There is even the Comitato Italiano di Difesa Morale e Sociale della Donna, which was formed specifically to help prostitutes resume normal life.

These institutions, however, are encumbered by enormous bureaucracies (and frequently with graft), and are rarely much help to the woman in serious trouble. Sometimes, in fights with landlords or employers, *L' Italiana* can get help from the local Communist Party. (This service is unique in Italy, and a mainstay of Communist popularity.) Sometimes newspapers will publicize her plight. Raising money from private donations for a child's expensive, life-saving operation is a favorite newspaper project.

But currently the most help is to be found through the Women's Liberation organizations which have been in operation since 1960, when the Italian Women's Union was reformed. Today, there are at least six large groups, of which the Unione della Donne Italiane (UDI) is still the best-known. Including the Christian Democrat Centro Italiano Femminile, the movement estimates that it has over five million members. They publish several magazines, all of which are nationally distributed, though they do not have large readerships.

The groups have formed a loose alliance, and since the late sixties have organized joint demonstrations on divorce, child-care programs, distribution of birth-control devices and abortion clinics. In general, they do not advocate reform so much as the enforcement of laws already on the books. They point out that employers are not offering equal opportunities nor paying equal wages. They decry the fact that out of the dozens of state ministries employing over thirty thousand women in Rome itself, only two have the legally required day nurseries. The women's groups pressure unions to insist on management compliance with the statute of equal opportunity for job advancement.

Another cause that has brought the women striding down the Via Nazionale, their militant baby buggies festooned with posters, is the outcry against the corrupt ONMI orphan and child care agency. UDI has been particularly active in campaigning to reform the institution because it wants to use the orphanage facilities for regular day-care centers. They point out that ONMI buildings are often left empty, with equipment gathering dust in forgotten corners, and children being jammed into the private apartment of an overworked baby-sitter, while orphans are not permitted to mingle with outsiders. They want to change the ONMI management, integrate day students with the orphans so that all can use the facilities and pay teachers from their own ranks to look after the children.

In Italy the woman who leaves the home to work has more than progressive (albeit sporadically applied) legislation behind her; she also receives impressive social support. The tradition of the live-in mother-in-law and the character of long-simmered sauces combined with quick-fix pasta and cutlets make both housework and cooking particularly conducive to working. If a woman is one of the hundreds of thousands of government or municipal white-collar workers across the country, her work hours extend from 8:00 A.M. to 2:00 P.M.—a schedule that leaves her totally free in the afternoon to take care of the children and the home. Pirelli, Italy's giant tire and rubber company, has also experimented with half-day work for women. Those with a conventional workday profit from the long lunch hour if they work close to home.

Although none of these support systems function perfectly, it is still surprising to see how thoroughly the pervasive status of the family has undermined what could be a strong female-work-force pattern. Italy has the lowest rate of working women of any country we are studying. It reached its ebb during the sixties, when only one out of four workers was a woman.[39] According to the Unione delle Donne Italiane, one million women left their jobs during the 1967–69 period alone. This, in a country where, during the fifties, women made up nearly half the work force.

To an extent, the increase of women workers in the fifties was only one response to a recovering economy where the male work force was still decimated by war losses. As younger people of both sexes came into the picture, the women tended to drop out—sometimes upon marriage, almost always at the birth of their first child. But their motivation for quitting went deeper than the simple advent of new responsibilities.

In Italy, as in England, the status one derives from one's job—that amorphous concept often cataloged under the term the Work Ethic—is low. For centuries Italians have been locked into rigid caste systems where no one was free to choose his or her work. Men did what their fathers had done, just as women imitated their mothers. The idea that either of them enjoyed "freedom *to* work" never occurred to anyone; status was firmly tied to "freedom *from* work." With rising affluence, women quit in droves—particularly in blue-collar areas which involved the much-hated physical activity.

Even more important to the Italian woman than the lack of status in her work, however, was the lure of the alternative. When a woman quit her job, she could occupy herself completely with the focal point of life—the family. Seated at the heart of her society, she was secure in the knowledge that everyone's first allegiance went not to The Job, The Cause or The State, but to her and The Family.

The day came, however, when industrialization arrived from England, Germany and the United States. Set up along patriarchal lines, it demanded specialization from the individual and dispersal of the family. Giuseppe went to Germany to work on heavy machinery. Maria went to Milan to work as a secretary for Pirelli. Rogero and Vito stayed in Sicily, but became distributors for Scala soap products, and no longer tended the family orange grove. A woman's children often lived in worlds where a commandeering, strong, possessive mamma was a threat rather than a protection.

Many women have responded to this situation by once more going to work outside the home. Of these, a significant number think of their occupations as permanent and have no desire to quit. A pan-EEC survey, however, indicated that the majority of Italian working women still do so because of economic necessity.[40] As for the problem of "housework boredom" so often decried by Anglo-Saxons, Italian women in the Shell survey listed it as a poor tenth among their reasons for working.

The young middle-class woman who goes out to work today is likely to follow the tradition of the woman behind the *cassa*—the difference is that she is not taking care of the till in the family grocery store, but manages her own chic boutique. A "little shop" has become as much a *de rigueur* graduation gift for her as the year abroad has been for the American girl.

Doors are open to her in other careers as well. She is not barred in any way from medicine, law, engineering or architecture schools. Neither is she excluded from the important career-related organizations like the Italian equivalent of the AMA or trade unions.

Although schooling is state-subsidized through the university level, advanced study becomes a financial problem for a woman if she does not live in a city, since there is practically no student housing on campuses (college dormitories are almost exclusively an American institution), and even the dormitories run by nuns average over $100 a month. This, combined with the high cost of books in technical fields, makes higher education difficult, even though nearly 70 percent of parents want their daughters to have an education equal to that of their sons.

An important change is brewing among the young, however. Over half of them now insist that an education is their first goal in life. Twenty years ago, it is believed only one girl in every six wanted to go through school. The rest wanted to get married.[41] In the last ten years Italy has seen the greatest increase in university attendance of any European country, and women have been the biggest contributors to that expansion.

The woman who is educated and wants a professional career faces the traditional problem of becoming established: society believes that the workingwoman takes bread away from a family. A woman doctor, therefore, calmly accepts waiting three years longer to obtain a hospital staff position (important as a basis for her practice) than does her male colleague even though he finished at the same medical school, with the same qualifications, at the same time.

Once she acquires all her credentials, however, the professional woman assumes authority easily. Her conservative clothes, her *seria* manners, her confident way of speaking, all make her easily accepted among her peers of both sexes. She is not forced to give up the freedom to play different roles in order to be dignified because being dignified is the only role she's ever learned to play. Personally, she may suffer the same problem as the man in patriarchal societies, because she is expected to be *seria* no matter what her real personality is, but professionally she gains from the tradition of responsible women.

Beverly Pepper, a well-known American sculptress who creates gigantic pieces in metal, explains this in day-to-day terms. In Italy, she is *la maestra*. She is friends with the steelworkers who weld and polish her work, but they never question her decisions or forget to do jobs for her because "a woman's work can't be important." When she works in American steel plants, on the other hand, it's, "Hi, Bev. Where'd you go last night?" The casual approach undermines authority.

Another important distinction of the Italian professional woman is the manner in which she is addressed. Take a newspaper story on Elisa Lissi, Rome's watchdog of buried ruins. Lissi is often in the news, since she has the power to halt construction when there is an important archaeological find such as the ancient mosaic floor discovered during the digging of foundations for the new City of Justice complex. Lissi oversees the excavation of the treasure before work can resume. She has her doctorate in archaeology and is married. In references to her, she is Dotoressa Lissi, La Lissi or simply Lissi. Both in conversation and in official reports, Italians not only commonly drop marital status, but often do away with the sexual designations as well.

Career women in Italy are acting as train engineers and airline pilots and masons. The Ucciardone Prison in Palermo—the notorious "rock" that holds the Mafia convicts—has a woman as second in command. Women are mayors of provincial towns and senators in the capital. Rome city council has four women members, and a woman is city planning commissioner. There are women fashion photographers, industrialists, surgeons and judges.

Italy does not have any Bonnie Parkers. The women do not kill in cold blood (and the men do so only infrequently). She has no female armed robbers, no Bridget Rose Dugdales, no Ulrika Meinhofs. The very idea is an insult to the *seria* image.

Perhaps because she has so long undermined the principles of politics and because she still despises politicians, *L'Italiana* rarely achieves upper-echelon political power. Italy and the United States are the only two Western industrial countries that have no women as cabinet ministers. In the frequent shuffles at the top of the Italian Parliament, women have never approached positions near that of prime minister. Nor have women ever been considered serious candidates for the mayorship of major cities.

Their strength has been in business and the arts. Giuseppina Araldi, head of the family steel-tubing company; Marisa Cantoni Bellisario, head of the complex Olivetti Operational Planning Department; Marisa Rubiolo, the venerated head of public relations at Fiat Motors—all are examples of the formidable *Italiana* as business executive. In the media, women are also often in control. Witness Inge Schoental, book publisher; Adeline Tattoli, magazine publisher; and the important popular film directors, Lina Wertmüller (*The Seduction of Mimi, Swept Away* . . .'') and Liliana Cavani (*The Night Porter*).

But aside from the dynamic actresses like Anna Magnani, Sophia Loren, Gina Lollobrigida, Monica Vitti or Oriana Fallaci (one of the world's most flamboyant journalists), the Italian woman rarely succeeds in the international community. Even the works of poet-playwright Natalia Ginzburg and novelist-feminist Dacia Maraini are rarely read outside of Italy.

Of the women I have interviewed—both in important posts and on the street—the major hurdle is simply that they don't care to join the international contest. ''What difference does an American edition make to me?'' one writer exclaimed. ''I want to examine Italy and make a living. If my book did well in the U.S., that would be fine, but that's a big 'if'—if the translation is good, if the publisher is good, if the reviewers have eaten well before they settle down to read my book. Too much of my life could be trapped into chasing those 'if's .' ''

Her comment is typical of the strengths of the Italian woman. She doesn't lose sight of the importance of living life instead of running through it. Not all her attributes translate easily to other cultures of course. Two of her strong points—female-male alienation and aversion to physical activity—may be considered negative aspects by many outsiders . . . although Italians do enjoy a special electricity between the sexes and a low incidence of violence. The important thing is that *L' Italiana* has produced a society where tolerance works, even if not perfectly; where daily encounters with other people have a vivacity that makes them enjoyable in themselves with no thought to their practicality or efficiency, and yet where the business person can still function well in today's economic-industrial world. What more could one ask from a society where people place more importance on sunshine and spaghetti than they do on the trains running on time?

Part Three

The Frenchwoman—

"The Other" Nation

1

The Power of *La Différence*

The French woman. Velvet and steel. Maria Schneider and Catherine Deneuve. Madame de Pompadour and Madame Curie. The woman who has cultivated the mystique of "the Other." *Vive la différence!*

France has a woman as Secretary of State for Women's Affairs. A woman is Minister of Health. A woman is Mayor of Paris. Women serve as trial lawyers in France's most flamboyant cases . . . and as the protagonists in trials that have the most far-reaching effects on customs and mores. French husbands seem willing to accept their wives' love affairs as well as the possibility that their wives may make more money.

One would assume that with such options, *La Femme* would be proud to be a woman. As Eric Rohmer, director of the delicate but incisive film *My Night at Maud's,* commented archly, "We don't need Women's Liberation in France because the women are doing what they like to do. . . . We appreciate women, we think they are wonderful. I think American men are misogynists."[1]

Is the Frenchwoman as happy and secure as she appears to be? In talking with them, it becomes apparent that Rohmer's smugness is unwarranted. The Mouvement de Libération de la Femme (MLF) is the most organized, articulate and angry women's group on the Continent. Every week or so the newspapers light up with another confrontation between MLF and the established order—whether the flash point is unequal job practices, the Marie Claire abortion trial, rising prices in the supermarket or a judge refusing to swear in a woman postal inspector because she was wearing a pants suit.

The first internationally well-known book of the current feminist movement, in fact, was Simone de Beauvoir's massive *The Second Sex,* published in 1949. In it, she defines women as "the Other"—literally a separate class, systematically trained to have different wants and needs from those of the male. But De Beauvoir does not lead one to believe that Frenchwomen relish their role, or that they have achieved the *je-suis-bien-dans-mon-peau* (I-am-content-inside-myself) harmony we ascribe to them. De Beauvoir, after all, was the one who said,"To be a woman, if not a defect, is at least a peculiarity."[2] Just as she was one whose father patronizingly boasted, "She thinks like a man."

The position of woman as the Other vis-à-vis men arose out of the French preoccupation with ordering and categorizing life, with making lists and checking off characteristics. If ever a people has trained itself to utilize either/or thinking and computer logic, it's the French. Their technique is to name, then to systematize.

Words are so significant that inability to express oneself is listed by leading psychiatrist Dr. André Haim as the first cause of suicide.[3] The psychotherapist, Emile Coué, believed that words "created" reality, and taught that one could heal the body by repeating the "Every day in every way . . ." formula. The importance of words is reflected in the common maxim, "He who says nothing must have an empty head," as well as in an extreme sensitivity to mockery.

This *esprit de système* (spirit of systematization) also manifests itself strongly in daily life where schoolchildren present their daily class reports in the classic form of logicisms. Thesis: all good points. Antithesis: all bad points. Synthesis: reiteration and reconciliation. It means long, intricate, precise recipes, and tidy housework schedules. It means the structuralism of Jean Piaget and Claude Lévi-Strauss applied to such nebulous subjects as child thought-patterns and primitive dream archetypes.

Systematizing is important because of the way it forms the French personality. A child selects a basic character type—groupist or individualist—early and adds new attributes methodically, year after year, like an artist applying clay layers to a wire armature. In no other country are the dividing lines between these two basic types more clearly defined. The only restriction is that—whether an individualist or a groupist—the Frenchwoman must be Female First; i.e., she must be different from the male. She must be the Other.

La différence is considered so innate, so basic, that it goes deeper than groupist/individualistic designations, defying description. When Malraux's hero thinks of his mistress in *Man's Fate,* he is hardly thinking of the cheery English chum, or the Italian mamma, or the American competitor. "Once more," he murmurs to himself, "that body was beginning to take on the intensely mysterious quality which a sudden metamorphosis produces—was becoming dumb, blind, lunatic. And it was a woman. Not a variation of the male. Something else. . . ."[4]

The Italian feels that the woman is essential and the male accessory; the Anglo-Saxons perceive woman as a second-class man; the French believe she is a different species. As incomprehensible as a visitor from another solar system or a cuneiform inscription, she is full of importance and magic. Writer Jules Michelet conceives her as the *Sorcière,* an ancient being more in touch with the wisdom of nature than man—perhaps the Devil incarnate. The Frenchman talking about woman is likely to conclude, *"La femme c'est plus qu'une femme"* ("Woman is more than she seems"). She is a force to be won over or conquered. She is a source of power and inspiration. She is the revered General Joan of Arc. She is the awe-inspiring, manipulating wife or mistress of the man in power. She is Marianne, the symbol of *La Belle France* herself, demanding blind loyalty and sacrifice.

Inside their "Other" Nation, Frenchwomen have enjoyed freedom in the areas of both mental and physical activity. Madame Curie was born in Poland, but she was a product of French education and the French scientific community. Of her daughters, surely French, one received a Nobel prize in physics and the other achieved a noted career in letters. For centuries the literary salons of Frenchwomen have dictated style and content to French writers, and they continue to influence politics, literature and life-styles even today.

Women have always been highly regarded as writers from the time of Madame de Staël to Beauvoir and Colette. French military history includes not only Joan of Arc and the march of the women on Versailles, but also the legends of such figures as Marie Thérèse Figuer, a washerwoman who fought with Napoleon. She supposedly became the Duchess of Danzig, though retaining her rough ways. When Napoleon threatened her with expulsion from court, she brought out one of his old unpaid laundry bills. He let her stay.

How did *La Française* come about? With her historic ties to the Catholic Church and to the Latin language and cultural heritage, why has she evolved so differently from the Italian woman? Why has she carved out her role not as *la mamma* but as *l'autre*?

If we examine the Italian inclinations toward matriarchy during the Etruscan period, we see that France at the same time consisted primarily of Celtic tribes, constantly on the move and at war with one another—the perfect society for patriarchal, soldier-king mores. While the Etruscans were worrying about the tranquillity of their homes and about developing group value systems of interdependence and trade, their Northern neighbors were deserting one meager homesite for another, devoting their energies to capturing the next food source or the next herd of breeding females.

With Roman hegemony, patriarchy was codified into law in both France and Italy. Women were considered not a part of the group, but a *possession* of the group. Highest status went to the soldier, with generals becoming heads of state.

The tradition of the self-sufficient, all-important family protecting itself from the outside world by inner cohesion—the necessity that mothered *mammismo* (Momism) in Italy—began to put down roots in France particularly in the peasant class, oppressed and plagued during the Middle Ages. That influence is still obvious in rural French family life today.

Among the French aristocrats, however, the etiquette of chivalry was developing in a different direction. Although the exact origins of the European Courts of Love are not fully known, they appear to have first become a widespread phenomenon in Southern France. When Eleanor of Aquitaine escaped Henry II, she returned to Provence where she built her glittering court. She had Capellanus codify the rules of chivalry in the document *De Honeste Amandi* (*Concerning the Art of Loving Honestly*), which included a detailed enumeration of the virtues required of a knight who aspired to be a lover.

Eleanor, who had accompanied her first husband, the King of France, on a two-year Crusade to the Holy Land, used the call of chivalry to lure the knights back home. Her court was soon copied abroad—first in Germany, then in Italy and Spain; it had practical economic advantages because the Crusades were beginning to drain coffers everywhere.

Although specific chivalric debates—for instance, should a lady, once married, withhold her favors from a previous lover—seem quaint now, the idealization of Love and the archetype of the Lady continue to reverberate through European and American cultures.

Two tenets of chivalry developed particular strength in France. The first was the notion that love and marriage are inimical. (This was also accepted in Italy, but not in Germany.) The second, unique to France, was the concept that a woman should use *l'amour courtois* to further her own personal power interests. Eleanor was a firm propounder of both these beliefs, and set the mold for the intelligent, upper-class Frenchwoman who seeks fame and power for herself, not for her family.

The archetype of the powerful woman was also known among the French peasantry, and from their ranks rose one of the greatest Warrior Women of European history—Joan of Arc. Society as a whole scoffed at her visions and defiled her for cutting her hair and living among the soldiers, but the undercurrent of approval was strong enough to weld an army, and eventually bring about the crucial defeat of the English at Orléans in 1429.

Joan and her martyrdom became the rallying cry for the whole of France. Family fidelity in the peasant classes and courtly love among the aristocrats both came to be channeled into love for *La Belle France*. The citizen soldier, who—like Joan—fought for love of country, rather than because of fear or avarice, wielded decisive power by the end of the 1700s. People came to feel that they could shape destiny only if they placed France first and family second. This movement totally bypassed Italy, where the Family First ideal remained intact, resisting the comings and goings of another century of foreign rule.

Napoleon raised the mystique of Frenchness to new heights. He put the official seal on the practice of categorizing and systematizing all things. He introduced the metric system and uniform currency, both based on orderly divisions of ten. He also established the family laws of 1804, which placed women firmly at the bottom of the heap. Married women were no better than minors. They were in bondage to their husbands. Marriages were arranged by fathers for their own economic and social advantages. A woman was expected to tend the home fires just as the hearth cat was expected to catch mice. The short-statured French general, who valued his army above all else and felt defensive with his spirited Creole wife, Josephine, could hardly have been expected to decree otherwise.

Napoleon's Code was not accepted submissively by the women of his court. Not only did he have to contend with Empress Josephine and the Duchess of Danzig, but he also had to suppress the passionate humanist,

Olympe de Gouges, who, in 1796, wrote the "Declaration of the Rights of Women," based on the American Declaration of Independence and Mary Wollstonecraft's similar work of 1792. *Les Femmes Savantes (The Knowledgeable Women)*, so bitterly satirized by Molière a hundred years earlier, were still not willing to knuckle under.

Nevertheless, the Napoleonic Code, coupled with the mystique of the Lady, served to restrict women's energies to backstage intrigue for over a hundred years. Not even during the suffragette movement at the turn of the century, did France take up the challenge. During the 1920s, France was the only major European country where women did not have the right to vote at least in municipal elections.

When Léon Blum's Socialists won election in the thirties, it was hoped that these inequities would be righted. Blum had three women in his cabinet—as Undersecretary of National Education, Undersecretary of Child Welfare and Undersecretary of Scientific Research.

Frenchwomen were not to be franchised, however, until 1945, when they took part in the national vote on the postwar Constitution. Nor were De Gaulle or Pompidou to do a great deal to further women's causes. De Gaulle, enamored with the idea of "a hundred million Frenchmen" shoring up the glory of France, believed a woman's duty was to bear more and more children. He was not about to raise women to top-level Cabinet posts or to revise so much as a comma of the Napoleonic Family Code which had been transferred, practically intact, into the new Constitution despite an explicit guarantee of equal rights in its Preamble.

Since Valéry Giscard d'Estaing has been President, a rapid change has been taking place. He created the Ministry of Women's Affairs, and appointed the outspoken journalist and editor of *L'Express*, Françoise Giroud, to head it. Mme. Simone Veil was made Minister of Health, and promptly set in motion machinery for the legalization of abortion in France.

Frenchwomen are taking up the mantle of power everywhere. Nicole de Hauteclocque is president of the Paris City Council, in effect the Mayor of Paris. Nearly forty of the members of Congress are women. And since 1966, even the Folies Bergère has been owned and operated by women.

2

Motherhood—The Least-Known Role

The French mother is worlds apart from her Italian counterpart. The family does not always come first in France, and the position of *Maman,* although secure and appreciated, is not a position of true power. Her partnership in the creation is not expressed. She says, "He made me pregnant," or "He gave me a child," more often than, "I'm having a baby."

Furthermore, the French child is disliked even more than the English. In the sense that the American child is "born blessed," full of innocence and hope, the French child is "born cursed"—the first crime being ignorance. Only through trials and struggles will the child be able to reach status. Only through self-discipline and hard work will she or he be accepted into the enviable caste of grown-ups.

French parents are honored for their efforts at building character and creating a polished person who can function within the group. They mold a citizen who is *bien élevé* (well brought up). But if a child turns out badly, the blame is placed on the child. The explanation is that the child must have resisted training and yielded instead to its baser nature. In a reverse of the American situation, where parents are always blamed for children's neurotic behavior, French children get all of the guilt and none of the credit for the way they turn out as adults.

France and England each have a history of disinterest and disregard for motherhood. But the Englishwoman submitted to breeding duties before turning the raising of the child over to Nanny, whereas the Frenchwoman simply refused to bear many children. Malthus' family-planning principles caught on better in France than they did in his native England.

Today, despite the dream of a hundred million Frenchmen, despite high government child allowances that heavily subsidize the mother who stays at home and can exceed a worker's salary when there are more than five children, despite the medals publicly presented to mothers of large families every year, the average French wife stubbornly refuses to have more than 2.3 children. Brigitte Bardot sniffs, "There is no question that I should bring a child into the world. People who make children are crazy."[5] Film Director Nelly Kaplan says, "I've never had children; I've had abortions. When I'm working, there's no time for private life."[6] The child heroine of Marguerite Duras' film, *Nathalie Granger* angrily refuses the future her mother wishes for her, and dumps the baby carriage upside down.

An interesting aspect of French birthrate figures is that they have changed less since the arrival of the Pill than those of Northern countries. While the French have fluctuated only three points since 1938, the American rate soared up seven points during the fifties, then dropped below Depression levels in the seventies. Finland, Sweden, Germany, England and Russia have all experienced the same kind of vacillation.[7]

The perfect French family, consisting of a girl and a boy, is thought to epitomize good breeding, self-control and orderliness. When you walk down a Paris street with four little children in tow, men do not stop you to remark, "What a beautiful family!" as they do in Rome. They're more likely to murmur, *"Quel catastrophe!"*

A 1971 SOFRES poll showed that people feel a small family means a better standard of living and more leisure time. It is in harmony with the French inheritance laws, which require the patrimony to be split among all the children. Practically speaking, a large family translates into divided farmlands or bitter boardroom wrangling over which sibling gets which profits. The classic battle between offspring after the funeral is no laughing matter in France.

The tradition of the small French family is not due solely to the low status of the mother and child. The Frenchman also feels that a small family reflects well on his self-control. Before birth-control devices and information became legally available in 1971 under National Assemblyman Lucien Neuwirth's bill, the burden of family planning rested primarily on the man.

An *Elle* magazine survey of fifteen hundred women, between the ages of fifteen and fifty, found that although 90 percent of Frenchwomen believe in using birth control, only 30 percent believe in artificial means. The large majority of women polled by *Elle* reported that their husbands practiced coitus interruptus—"fireworks on the lawn" or "jumping off the train before you get to the station," as journalist Sanche de Gramont reports his cousin calls it.[8] Added measures for ridding oneself of sperm which might penetrate the vagina are provided by the ubiquitous bidet. Apparently in France anal copulation is not used as an alternate method as often as it is in Italy.

Considering the tradition of male birth control, one would think that vasectomy would catch on instantly, but the French are even less informed on the subject than the Italians. Although for practical purposes male and female sterilization is illegal in both countries, Italian magazines *do* discuss the possibility and explain how it has been practiced in England and the United States. In France, media discussions of the Pill and intrauterine devices never mention the possibility. Even among Sorbonne students, I found the unshakable conviction that vasectomy was equivalent to castration.

When the Frenchwoman has an unwanted pregnancy, the blame falls squarely on the man. Danielle Nègre, a dancer, is probably the first woman in the world to take her husband to court for fees lost when she became pregnant against her wishes. A forty-five-year-old woman I know locked her husband out of the bedroom when she became pregnant, despite his reasoning that by then it was too late. "This is to teach you how to think," she shot back.

The man himself often feels enormous remorse and guilt over an unplanned pregnancy. Witness the crisis precipitated in Sartre's *Age of Reason* hero, who, after an unsuccessful coitus interruptus, describes himself as "a small boy who forgot himself and wet the bed."[9]

After such an accident, it is up to the man to provide the best abortionist possible. Until abortion on demand during the first ten weeks of pregnancy was legalized by the National Assembly in November 1974, Frenchwomen either went to London or to a local quack. Health authorities believed over a million illegal abortions were performed each year in comparison to eight hundred thousand live births. Figures for the first year of legal abortions are not yet available, but estimates suggest that they will be higher than the 1974 United States total of nearly nine hundred thousand, even though the United States has four times the population.

Although Simone Veil, the Minister of Health, deserves a great deal of credit for shepherding the abortion bill through the French Congress, the decision to legalize abortion in France actually goes back to the Marie Claire abortion trial in 1972, which became a *cause célèbre* with a dazzling array of defense witnesses, ranging from Nobel laureates to politicians to Paul Milliez, dean of the medical faculty at Broussais Hospital. After the case was won, the Mouvement de Libération de la Femme pressed for new legislation, and was rewarded, in 1973, by the government-sponsored bill to lift restrictions in cases where the mental health of the mother is threatened, in cases of rape and incest and in cases where the baby is likely to be seriously malformed.

At present, fees for an abortion during the first ten weeks of pregnancy are set by the government, and the Health Ministry has already begun prosecuting doctors who refuse to perform the operation.

The Frenchwoman is more than twice as likely to keep her illegal child as the American woman. Forty-five percent of the unwed mothers in American cities keep their babies.[10] In France, where fifty thousand illegitimate children are born annually, the overall rate for both city and country is 90 percent.[11]

The French girl limits her choice to either abortion or raising the child. The ones who decide to go ahead with the pregnancy don't consider consigning the child to the state orphanage system, which is nearly as antiquated and poorly run as Italy's. They go ahead with the pregnancy because they want the baby, either as a manifestation of their relationship with their lover or because they want to be a mother.

Although the illegitimacy rate is one-third less than it is in the United States—6 per hundred births in France compared to 9.7 per hundred in the U.S.—French society appears to accept the unwed mother more completely, both in practical and emotional terms.

In a country where childbearing is encouraged by subsidy, the unwed mother draws the same monthly family allowance as her married sister. She receives additional allowances if she works and places the child in a nursery. Finally, she has a fixed income of $260 to $320 per month, depending on how many children she has.

Nurseries, *les écoles maternelles,* will take children as young as three months from 7:00 A.M. to 7:00 P.M. daily. In the summer, the children can attend *colonies maternelles,* camps in the mountains and at the seashore. These child-care facilities are inadequate for the demand, but the unwed mother is automatically placed at the top of the list of applicants. If she is unable to pay the nursery, the state reimburses the institution for her, and, of the 25 francs ($5) per diem fee for the summer camp, as much as 17 francs can be paid by the government.

French inheritance laws once denied the illegitimate child any legal rights and claim to patrimony. In 1973, these restrictions were dropped, and it is now possible for an illegitimate child to be recognized by the father, even if he is married to another woman, though in that case he has to have his wife's consent.

Social tolerance is also slowly increasing. The art and theater community in France has always been more casual about marriage protocol than its American counterpart, and today an illegitimate child is considered *de rigueur* in some circles. Catherine Deneuve has Marcello Mastroianni's child. Dominique Sanda has film director Christian Marquand's. Pierre Clementi, star of Buñuel's *Belle du Jour,* and Maria Schneider, star of Bertolucci's *Last Tango in Paris,* were both *fils naturels*—the offspring of unmarried parents. Clementi says he never knew his father, and Schneider, the daughter of a well-known music-hall singer, says she didn't meet her father until she was sixteen.

The general public is likewise more tolerant. There was open-minded reaction to the press stories of a woman's decision to have her baby without marrying the father, but with a joint raising schedule; i.e., she takes care of the baby some of the time at her home, and the father takes over the rest of the time at his.[12] Readers offered suggestions and applause. They weren't shocked. They didn't feel society was threatened.

Even the French Catholic Church appears to confront the unwed mother with honesty and a degree of acceptance. The magazine *La Vie Catolique (The Catholic Life),* for example, has presented the story of the mother faced with the situation where *"Ma Fille Sera une Mère Célibataire"* ("My Daughter Will Be an Unwed Mother").[13] The woman is married to a businessman and has two daughters, one fourteen, one seventeen. The seventeen-year-old starts work as a secretary. When the mother discovers her daughter is pregnant, she is scandalized—her daughter must be mocking her. Then she realizes how upset her daughter is, and relents, saying, *"Non, tu n'es pas seule, ta maman est là."* ("No, you are not alone, your mommy is here.")

She asks if her daughter can't marry the father, but the girl answers firmly, *"Maman,* I don't love him and he doesn't love me either. How can you live together without love? It would be a horrible thing for the child to grow up with parents who didn't understand each other.''

The mother talks the situation over with her best friend, who exclaims that this will be a scandal for the family. "Maybe they could try a civil marriage for a year or two. Or she could have the baby someplace else and give it up for adoption. Or . . . but, of course you wouldn't think of that. . . .''

The mother returns home, wondering how she is going to tell her husband. Her daughter has already done it, and, "He understood, much faster than I did, the essentials—respect for life, responsibility for the child. I went to René, with his marvelous ability to give our girl the best aid possible, the image of a united and loving family. And it was on the shoulder of my husband that the long-awaited tears came."

Frenchwomen view pregnancy rather pessimistically. There is little of the fuss that accompanies Italian pregnancy, little of the feeling that the woman is producing society's most important creation. Grandmothers do not hover protectively. The woman herself does not think of her pregnancy as marking the transition from innocence to knowledge, from irresponsibility to status and a sense of purpose.

The Frenchwoman chooses the American approach of keeping her body as close to its ordinary shape as possible. She dresses in trendy clothes (so she won't look "like an unmade bed" as one fashion writer said). She follows exercise regimens. She eats only a little more than normal. She fights against the innate qualities of *la grossesse*—French for pregnancy, but literally "the bigness."

After pregnancy any similarity with the American mother ceases. Frenchwomen's magazines on the whole devote one-third of their space to practical articles for mothers,[14] and the tone of these pieces is that modern motherhood is hard work, requiring vigilance and intelligence. The French *Parents* magazine, for example, details the following from *"L'École des Mamans Parfaites''* ("The School for Perfect Mothers") at the maternity clinic of Baudelocque:[15]

"It is very important to weigh the baby each morning the first week, then twice a week until the end of the first month. Afterward, once a month is enough. The baby must gain 15 to 40 grams per day. The pharmacies have the proper baby scales to check whether the baby is normal, too fat or too thin. The baby nursed on the breast should be weighed before and after each suckling.

"The choice of milk—powder, concentrate or fresh—is always established in the hospital. After that, don't change the brand, as this risks disturbing the appetite, the digestion and the growth of the baby. In order not to run out, the mother can ask her husband to bring a provision of milk with him on return to the house.''

Compare this to Dr. Spock's quick 'n' easy directions for the self-sufficient baby. He does not limit the baby by scale weight or hospital feed lists. Scales are mentioned only as an afterthought: "Most mothers don't have scales. . . .''

As for proscribed food quantities, "The formula slip is concerned with the details; it forgets to tell you that the food is for a human being who has strong feelings about how much he wants and when he's hungry again . . . the baby is the one who knows how many calories his body needs and what his digestion can handle. . . . Take his word for it, and get in touch with the doctor.''[16]

The differences between the two attitudes are striking. The French make a stringent list of dos and don'ts, and that's the end of it. The brand of milk will be established in the hospital. Afterward, stick with it. Don't listen to the baby, weigh her. Don't check with the doctor, check with the list. The list goes on to detail baby's room temperature—"15 to 18 degrees (centigrade) at night, 18 to 20 degrees during the day"; the baby's bath water temperature—"37 degrees, verify with bath thermometer"; and an outing schedule—"the first outing at 18 days for 15 minutes if the weather is good, next day for 20 minutes . . .''

French mothers tack these lists on the nursery bulletin board. Their desk drawers contain carefully clipped enumerations of how much the average child should weigh aged six months, aged nine months, aged one year, aged one and one-quarter years, aged one and one-half years. . . . These carefully worked out formulas for baby care—as for life—are more impoitant than capricious baby demands or doctor suggestions.

It's interesting and important to note that the experts who give advice to the new mothers are *sages-femmes* (midwives) and *puericultrices* (roughly, child specialist nurses). This means that the mother feels she is working with a companion or a sister, who simply has specialized training. The mother is more ready to discuss her fears with such an instructress than she would be with a man.

The drawback is that caring for the newborn becomes an isolated female field, where men are neither wanted nor needed. This is one of the few times when the Frenchwoman takes part in the mystique of motherhood. The French father is not invited to parent-preparation classes, or encouraged to be present when the baby is born. French magazines are beginning to run stories about the rare father, such as rugby player Pierre Tosse, who enjoys taking care of his infants. Such examples are still atypical. The majority of men feel that babies are *une affaire de femme.*[17]

Much of the baby-care ritual is new to France. Authorities comment, "Not so many years ago, women had their babies at home. The baby was put immediately in the charge of its grandmother or another woman of the family, who already had experience with babies. The new mother learned from her over a period of weeks, with the older woman constantly at her shoulder, offering counsel and encouragement. There was no brutal rupture between the ten days at the clinic, where everything was done for her, and the home, where she had to cope with everything alone."[18]

Bath and body thermometers, scales, the preference for bottle-feeding over breast-feeding—all of these are new to France. The emphasis on discipline and time schedule, however, is no innovation. The French have always tended to treat their children the way Louis XIV treated the garden at Versailles—nature must be disciplined to be enjoyed.

The French mother still handles her baby more than the Anglo-Saxon does. She holds a crawler in her lap while talking to friends, not the least worried that baby is missing out on the experiences of exploration. She plays with her baby during the day, not only at bath or feeding time. She carts her child around on quick trips to the bakery, or while she is doing the gardening. Although she is not so likely as the Italian mother to take a nude bath with baby, she is not afraid of the sensuality of touching the child.

As the child begins to walk, the father enters the scene as a playmate. Although he takes on the role of disciplinarian with older children, playing with the small child represents a period of release and freedom for him. Surprisingly, in contrast to the Italian father's practice of playing adult verbal games with his children, French fathers play physical games. Generally, they seem to enter into the child's world, rather than trying to teach the child about adulthood. French camping grounds are full of fathers taking their children for walks, teaching them to swim and pushing their swings.

Mothers utilize these periods to tidy up or visit with neighbors. They play with the child, but it is rare for both mother and father to enjoy the child at the same time. It appears that alone each feels free with baby, but the presence of another adult forces them to be more decorous.

From the beginning, children are made to feel separate from adults. The language is carefully structured to emphasize this; the child is called *"tu"* by grown-ups, but she or he must address them with the formal *"vous."* In some families, this tradition is dropped within the home where everyone addresses the others as *"tu,"* while outside adults are always called *"vous."* (This family-versus-outsiders language structure is common in Germany and universal in Italy, where family is addressed as *"tu"* by everyone, but outsiders are always *"Lei."*)

The primary separation points between adults and children are based on verbal skill and the ability to reason. In his book, *Village in the Vaucluse,* Laurence Wylie, the noted Harvard linguist and social observer, gives a detailed explanation of how children are carefully taught to be *raisonnable* (reasonable). The French invariably give reasons with their commands. "Don't cross the big road at the end of the block," is illuminated with, "The cars go too fast to stop on that street." Blind obedience to authority, still often taught in Germany, is disparaged in France. In adulthood, this results in situations where drivers, stopped by the police because they've run through a red light, can argue their way out of a ticket by saying, "It's after midnight, officer, and I could see that no one was coming."

Punishment is directly related to how *raisonnable* children are. If they break rules that have been carefully explained, they are taunted about having turned into babies: "What happened to you? You're acting like a two-month-old." If taunts don't work, freedoms are taken away: the child can't go out to play, and so on.

When children assume added responsibilities or win good grades, they are applauded with rewards ranging from praise to special food treats, from new freedoms to actual presents. An important factor in these rewards is that they must be earned. They do not come as a "natural" part of birthdays and Christmas.

The "natural" happiness of childhood seems unimportant. Crying babies are checked for open diaper pins and so on, then left to cry. Nobody tries to distract them. Accustomed to Italian behavior, I spoke to a wailing child in a Paris park, only to earn a glare from the mother. When I asked a friend why she left her baby alone when he was howling, she said, "Oh, he only does that because he's little." My own flustered guilt when my baby cried amused her. Why did I feel guilty when I had done nothing wrong? The child should cope with its own problems.

Leaving children alone in their rooms to play quietly—or, more likely, to work on lessons, a paint book or stamp or rock collections—is practiced to the point of desertion. This is particularly true during family leisure time. Parents prefer to take their vacations alone. Driving through the country in August, the month when French industry shuts down and 85 percent of the population takes its vacation, three out of four cars on the road contain no children. This in spite of the fact that the occupants are mainly couples in their thirties. The children have been sent to summer camps, where the parents feel they are learning how to manage on their own. A commonly stated reason for school being held on Saturday is that mothers and fathers need the day to themselves. Parents and children are not expected to spend a great deal of time together. The primary union is between the two parents.

Although French children are allowed to stay up late for family dinners, as they do in Italy, they are rarely their mother's confidants. Recently a mother wrote to a women's magazine, asking what she should tell her eleven-year-old who wanted to know how much her father earned. Children are not considered a part of the adult world.

It is not surprising that it was the well-known pedagogue Dr. Jean Piaget of French-speaking Switzerland who formulated the theory of the child mind that operates in a totally different way than the adult mind. The non-verbal child, who thinks in clusters of emotions and impressions, is an outsider, an apprentice to adulthood.

There is, however, a carefully articulated school of thought on the value of "natural man" individualism in France. As an integral element in this concept, children have often been portrayed as ideals in French literature. They may be impish, clever and lazy, but—like the drunken puppet, Guignol—they are quick to help if they find someone in need. Often such archetypes are contrasted with hollow "Gaston-and-Alphonse" symbols of *politesse,* courteously lifting their hats to accident victims, but never offering to help.

Antoine de Saint-Exupéry's *Le Petit Prince (The Little Prince),*[19] a story of an excruciatingly wise Tom Thumb from Asteroid B 612, is a primary example of this kind of character. The narrator is a boy, who, having read about boa constrictors swallowing their prey, draws a small snake with a large lump inside. Adults think it is a hat. So he carefully draws an elephant inside the lump. Adults tell him to quit thinking about such things. "Adults never understand anything alone, and children get tired of explaining everything each time."

This kind of nonlinear imagination is sometimes appreciated by parents, but on the whole society conspires against spontaneity. Coloring books are titled *J'observe la nature et je colorie (I Observe Nature and I Color).* Like Italian coloring books, they are furnished with sample pages, so that the child knows the sky must be blue and the clown's nose must be red. Clothes put on in the morning are expected to stay clean until evening. Despite promotion of easy-to-wash durable fabrics during the past few years, ten-year-olds still lack the dinnertime-disaster look of Anglo-Saxon children. In city parks, children are discouraged from making friends with strange children, and are told frightening tales about the dangers of passing dogs. As Pompidou once intoned on the eve of a national election, "The path of the unknown always leads to unhappiness—always."

At home, children as young as three are expected to help look after the baby and assist in chores. Both girls and boys are sent on errands outside the home after age eight, but are expected to return immediately. Helping Mommy when she is sick is a favorite children's-book topic, with children commonly buying *Maman* a bouquet of flowers out of their pocket money while doing her shopping. The task is not difficult, for the French child usually has shops within a block of his or her home. At the table, the *"Mange et tais-toi"* ("Eat and keep silent") rules are still enforced in traditional homes.

French mothers are not usually the family disciplinarian. For one thing, they are reluctant to employ physical punishment and abhor such things as the martinet—a small cat-o'-nine-tails made explicitly for spanking and still available in hardware stores for use by a limited number of fathers. In general corporal punishment of any kind is derided as a crude means of controlling children. It is not, after all, *raisonnable.* When the offense is serious, however, the father administers whatever measures he deems necessary. "I can't do anything with the children when my husband is away," is a common wifely complaint. Father is boss. His word is as unquestioned as the government's right to imprison any suspect on the grounds of "preventive detention."

Until recently, the father's authority was firmly backed by the law. A mother had no right to decide which school her child would attend—even if, as in many cases, she and the child had been deserted by the father. Today, a family-court system handles parental litigations, as well as divorce cases, nonpayment of child support, and so on.

Although statistics on family-court decisions are difficult to analyze, a French lawyer involved in such cases told me she believes as long as the couple are legally married the father wins most litigations about authority over the child. However, children are ordinarily awarded to the mother after a divorce, and she then has the right to make decisions concerning them and to deprive the father of his visiting rights if he refuses to pay child support.

At age twelve, French children enter secondary school. At home, this marks the time when the boy is pushed from the nest while the girl is encouraged to emulate her mother. By then the mother has discharged her primary duties toward her children. She has made them understand who she thinks they are. She has told her daughter and son whether or not she thinks they will succeed in a profession and why. She has told them whether or not they will succeed in love and why. The boy is thought to be ready to enter the men's world, where other adults—primarily the father, older brothers and teachers—take over his training. The girl has reached the point where the mother must explain to her in practical terms *how* she is to make her way as a woman. Often the mother—particularly if unmarried or widowed—takes on the role of friend, accepting the girl as an equal.

French parents, like the Americans, devour articles and books on sex education. Having broken with the tradition of the grandmother passing on her information to the mother, and thence to the children, the French are now interested in modern theories and methods.

A survey conducted early in 1972 by the weekly news magazine, *L'Express,* indicates that most fifteen- to twenty-year-olds feel comfortable with their parents' views on sexual matters. Sixty-seven percent reported that their parents liked their choice of boyfriend or girlfriend. Of the girls who favored making the Pill available to under eighteens, 54 percent said they would ask their parents before taking the contraceptive.

If the girl accepts her mother's offer of friendship at this point, she usually adopts a life-style very similar to her mother's. It's common to see teen-agers having with their mothers the kind of long conversations that usually only take place between women of the same age in the United States. Often, they are discussing their jobs, and the girl is learning the same profession as her mother, be it midwifery or public relations. Literature is also full of exceptional mother-child relationships like that between Colette and her adored mother, Sido.

If the girl does not accept her mother's friendship, *Maman* can console herself with another traditional stereotype, that of the ingrate child: Children—willful, uncivilized little beasts that they are—simply don't know any better.

3

Learning to Be "The Other"

            The educational system in France plays a significant role in the formation of the Frenchwoman. School, after all, is the place where one learns to be articulate, to recognize the importance of order and logic, with its roots in the famous Cartesian statement, "I think, therefore I am." Schooling in these vital fields is considered a privilege. Only by dedicating herself totally to learning can a girl—or a boy for that matter—win the keys to successful adulthood.

    Universal equal education in France has always had to struggle against intellectual elitism. Public education did not arrive with the Revolution. Free primary schools were not open until 1881. Even today, workers' and peasants' sons make up only a tiny fraction of the students attending the postgraduate-level *grandes écoles*.

    Educational opportunity is bestowed through a rigid system of national exams, which automatically advances the most studious and verbally precocious to the top30 schools and from there to the nation's executive suites and civil-service department headquarters.

Despite an enormous amount of time spent in studying, students tell me that practically everyone they know has had to *redoubler*, i.e., repeat a year of schooling somewhere along the line. Passing into the next grade is determined solely by end-of-the-year exams. Although the pass/fail method still exists in some form all over Europe, France's system is recognized as the most rigid.

Students dread two exams above the others. First is the *sixième,* an oral and written test taken by eleven-year-olds at the end of sixth grade, which determines whether or not they qualify for college-preparatory courses. The *sixième* annually sends back one out of every four students for *redoublement*.[20]

If failure of the *sixième* causes a major family crisis, failure of the *baccalauréat* high-school-graduation exam is equivalent to disaster. The students take the pressure seriously and there is an annual rash of adolescent suicides following the publishing of exam results in the spring.

Only students with top *baccalauréat* grades are admitted to good universities. Universities are state-supported and the students receive a living allowance grant to attend, as they do elsewhere in Europe. After university, the best students can take further exams to qualify for entrance to graduate schools, which also operate on a scholarship-grant basis. The very best of these pass the exams that allow them into the *grandes écoles*. Three of these schools quite literally run the country: the École Polytechnique, which supplies the technocrats who head France's businesses and some of the civil service; the École Normale Supérieure, which supplies France's university professors; the École Nationale d'Administration, set up specifically by De Gaulle in 1945 to supply the country with civil-service administrators. Graduates from these schools have career guarantees. The state bureaucracy and the nation's corporations take everyone and automatically promote them to top positions in due course.

Although women's universities did not appear in France until 1855, almost fifty years after Mount Holyoke was opened in the United States, today's daughter of the Establishment has almost the same opportunity as her brother. Forty-one percent of the college student body is female, a larger percentage than that of any other Western country except the United States and Finland. Frenchwomen constitute 13 percent of the students in basic and applied sciences, nearly twice the percentage studying in comparable fields in the United States. In 1972, the Polytechnique was the last *grande école* to open its doors to women. Anne Chopinet topped all the applicants as *le major* on the combined written and oral entrance exam.

Children are placed in a structured society at a very early age. There are five thousand full-day nurseries in France that take children from three months to three years. Some will even accept babies eight weeks old. The daily fee ranges from 0.50 francs (12½ cents) to 26 francs ($6.50).[21] The nurseries are often overcrowded; there is a long waiting list and the facilities are not the best. Still, mothers prefer to have the child in school as soon as possible. They feel the education, social contact and discipline are invaluable.

I spent several summer afternoons talking with a teacher at a public nursery just outside Paris. The building where she teaches is dark and poorly ventilated. Classes are jammed with as many as forty pupils and there is little equipment for them. They do have plenty of paper and pens and they spend their time learning simple arithmetic, the alphabet and some words. They are expected to sit at their desks much of the day, either working or listening to stories. The teacher said that even the two-year-olds in her class showed interest in learning. The children attend a full twelve-hour day, from 7:00 A.M. to 7:00 P.M, with one hour set aside for playing games and singing songs. There is also a rest period in both the morning and afternoon.

The most serious breach of discipline the teacher could remember involved a boy who bit off another's thumb. She laughed—but was embarrassed—about this, and said the offender was simple-minded. It is rare, she assured me, that the children get out of hand. "Most days they don't even get their smocks dirty."

Unlike the Italian ones, their smocks open in the front so that the children can button them by themselves. They are important symbols of school life: not only do the smocks define the difference between the outside world and school, but they also make the children uniform in appearance, creating a unisex look, because, as in Italy, the boys wear short pants underneath. Everything emphasizes that the child has joined a group where everyone must stick to the same rules. This regimen is not lifted until after the eleven-year-old's exams.

Regular six-hour public nurseries for young children have existed in France since the boarding-school tradition began at the turn of the century, but the number of children attending has grown appreciably since World War II. The percentage of two- to four-year-old children attending public and private schools has risen from 15 percent in 1948 to 48 percent in 1964 and 66 percent in 1971. The percentage of two-year-olds enrolled doubled between 1963 and 1971 from 9.7 percent to 18 percent.[22] Regular classes begin at age four, and by age five 95 percent of the children are in school. Mothers insist that if facilities were available, this number would climb even higher.

The reason for the popularity of schooling is twofold. The first is the principle that children need as much learning as they can get; that verbal, structured, group knowledge is the best tool for coping with life. French mothers are not reluctant to add the second reason—that they themselves need time away from the children. Usually they want that time in order to take a job.

As soon as the child enters school, education takes up the major part of the day, which soon consists of going to school, returning home, working on lessons. Usually the child works straight through until suppertime, and then goes to bed.

The child studies reading, writing and arithmetic. Stress on sciences is a recent development. There is little art, music or drama instruction. The classic French view is that school is for training the mind, while culture and character are the responsibility of the parents. Oddly, considering French pride in cultural achievements, few children take private lessons. Only one in ten, for example, has music lessons.[23]

One to three hours of physical education (P.E.) per week are taught, in addition to a daily hour and a half of recess time (a half hour in the morning, a half at lunchtime, a half in the afternoon). P.E. training consists of exercises and individual accomplishments. Individuals, however, cannot choose what they want to do, but must do what the teacher decides. Children compete against themselves—that is, their running time is contrasted with their own performance the previous week, not with what their companions do. Equipment is limited and little effort is made to encourage children to excel in sports. Neither sex is extensively trained for group efforts. The result can be seen in international soccer matches and at the Olympics where individual French athletes do superbly, but overall team performance is weak.

The schools themselves are structured around optimum study priorities. Teachers use peer pressure relentlessly to maintain the emphasis on academic achievement. Hardworking, verbally oriented children are rewarded with front seats in the classroom, honors and teacher affection. Teacher's pets have status among their peers, but class clowns—although they may have cronies outside school—are deserted in class, and often blamed for everything by schoolmates.

Children with learning problems suffer the most. If they have dyslexia or other handicaps, or if they have emotional blocks, there is only one public school in the whole of France that will pay particular attention to them— the C.e.s. expérimental Jean-Lurcat, started in 1969 at Saint-Denis, Paris, under the control of the Institut national de recherches et de documentation pédagogiques.

Children who get low grades are derided in front of the class, and can expect to be jeered at by schoolmates during the lunch break. Friends call them names and ostracize them from games. Parents and teachers also ignore them, and, by their very lack of interest, encourage such children to accept their lack of ability.

If children are late, they do not interrupt class to explain the reason to the teacher. They must go to the *surveillant général*, who listens to the excuse and then writes a note to the teacher permitting the child to be admitted to class.

If children receive three such notes, disrupt the class or fall behind in their studies, their parents are notified. Children are supposed to be disciplined at home. If they still don't straighten out, their parents are called to the school. There the child's misdemeanors are discussed in a *conseil de discipline* composed of parents, teachers and school authorities. The adults close ranks to condemn the child's behavior. It's a far cry from the "defensive parents" situation that occurs in America and Italy. The case is laid out so that—logically, *reasonably*—there is only one culprit: the child. The French child, as a result, is always on the defensive in relation to the world, always trying to earn group approval.

This school training serves to make the French child feel singularly alone. No one will help in moments of failure; no one is there to make excuses. The French child soon realizes that life is hard, that harsh punishment is to be expected for mistakes.

The child must stand up under the strain. The purpose of all this is not to intimidate children into blind obedience, but to teach them the precise limits beyond which it is unwise to go and to encourage them to develop their individuality to the fullest within these limits. If children cultivate their strong points, they can expect praise and comfortable relations with others. If they are lazy or rebellious, they can expect society to turn away from them.

The result is a Mondrian-like, geometric person. Every characteristic is clearly articulated and outlined. Whereas the American system attempts to make the age and social limits of childhood invisible, developing the "I can do anything" feeling, the French technique is to make children so aware of themselves and their limitations that they can fully cultivate their good points and feel, "Anything I do, I do perfectly."

The advantage of the French system is that it gives children an early sense of self-definition. French children are told from the moment they become verbal, exactly what the family hopes for them. If a girl is pretty but has big ears, at age five she knows how to arrange her braids so that they cover offending appendages. If she is a hard worker but not very quick, by the second year in school she has accepted the fact that she must stay at the kitchen table doing homework longer than other children.

Both girls and boys are taught that their adult life will include both a family and a job, that a well-balanced personality will include a desire for affection as well as a desire for knowledge. It is not surprising, therefore, that the Frenchwoman is certain of who she is, what pleases her and how she can go about controlling her destiny.

Fifty percent of secondary schools are sex-segregated. In contrast to the rapidly integrating Catholic schools in Italy, the great majority of Church schools in France are still divided. Urban schools are more likely to be co-ed than country schools.

Sex segregation is even more fundamental for the French girl than it is for their English sister, since the French child's world revolves around school and studies. The secondary school has an entirely different aura as well, for there are no masculine-looking English girls' school uniforms or English group sports to emphasize her membership in a group. Here, in fact, she no longer wears the primary-school smock, and her task is to build her own individual personality in a world where her "Otherness" vis-à-vis the boys is the first rule of self-definition.

Like their English counterparts, French proponents of sex segregation insist that children need to pass these difficult years with no distraction from their studies. They explain that if a twelve-year-old girl doesn't have boys around to tease her as she experiences the changes in her body, she can cope better at her own speed. She doesn't have to join the battles of sex until she is old enough to know herself well, and already has the vital high-school-graduation exams behind her. Only when she has surveyed her options, decided who she is and in what direction she wants to develop, should she start learning about the opposite sex and determining what kind of relationship she wants.

There is also a positive practical reason for maintaining the segregation. Frenchwomen are emotionally well equipped to enter the career world. Evelyne Sullerot, the noted French sociologist, has commented that 80 percent of the university women in France plan to continue working after marriage. This is a far cry from the American college woman, who often fears success and may subconsciously believe that ambition in a woman equals neurosis. The Frenchwomen's career orientation is fostered by a number of things, and the lack of interplay between the sexes at an age when the girl is feeling her first powerful physical urges to form a family cannot be discounted, particularly when one observes that this aggressiveness occurs among all classes of women—just as sex-segregated schooling does.

Opponents decry the neglect of interpersonal relations. Girls complain that they come out of school terrified of boys. Women insist that they never overcome their sense of "Otherness" instilled by the separation. Feminists denounce the differences in education—separate is not equal in France either.

Sex segregation, along with the other strictures of early self-definition, constitutes the major drawback of the French system. A girl is channeled into a personality before she has had the experience that equips her to make her own choice. In adulthood, she has the right to choose, but the pattern her parents and her teachers have dictated is already ingrained. Thus, the female college graduate has only an either/or choice—to accept the definition given her, or to become its opposite.

There is no Jonathan Livingston Seagull mystique to save her self-esteem. She does not believe that she will become Dreamgirl or Supersmart. *C'est comme ça* (It is like it is).

The ravages of self-hatred are as visible in France as evidence of *amour-propre* (self-love). It's not only the teen-ager who commits suicide when he or she fails the *baccalauréat*. The adult Frenchwoman is 50 percent more likely to take her own life than her American counterpart. She is more than twice as likely to die from cirrhosis of the liver caused by France's soaring alcoholism rate.

She does not turn against the group in times of stress. She is not as likely as the Italian woman to take the destiny of her family in her hands and leap in front of a train clutching her children. Her murder rate is only one-third as high as that of the United States. She destroys herself instead of society.

The other side of her total acceptance of self-responsibility is that the Frenchwoman often has the fortitude to battle her way to brilliant success—this despite the belief that people cannot change their natural lot, that the only *raisonnable* attitude is to define and accept oneself, that education offers the only key to fortune. Colette was an undereducated woman from the provinces, when she married Henri Gauthier-Villars. He cooped her up in her room four hours a day to force her to write her first novel, *Claudine à l'école* (*Claudine at School*). He signed it, had it published and put her to work on another book. After a few years of this, she divorced him. Still virtually unknown as a writer, she went into burlesque and for many years led a life that would have been the envy of a Hemingway or a

Kerouac. Slowly she became known for her columns in *Le Matin* and for her books, which she never stopped writing. By her fifties she was famous and launched upon her third marriage—to Maurice Goudeket, twenty-three, who had decided when he was twelve that she was the only woman for him.

Edith Piaf was another child of the streets who became a success with the intellectual elite. Violette Leduc still another. These are spokeswomen for the "noble savage" archetype. They have been ambassadors of the inarticulate class, full of sensuality and awe-inspiring emotion.

4

"The Other" Rearticulated

              The Frenchwoman's best-known role of "the Other" is cultivated not only by the educational system in which the schism between the sexes is institutionalized, but also by the dissimilar ways in which parents treat boys and girls.

From the beginning, the sexual difference between the French girl and her brother is carefully delineated. The girl is cuddled and given dabs of perfume behind her tiny pierced ears because, *"Tu es une fille"* ("You are a girl"). She is told she is more fragile than her brother, though she is allowed to run, swim and play ball with him.

The French *fille* is also not expected to work as hard or be as serious as the boys. When she grows older, she will feel freer to choose a life that pleases her over a life that is practical. Ultimately this will mean that as a mother she does not need to play the role of family conscience. The nagging "inner voice" that society instills in individuals to foster self-discipline is not exclusively female in France as it is in Italy and, to an extent, in

England. In France, the man must be the most self-controlled, disciplined and practical.

As in Italy, the year-old French toddlers of both sexes are encouraged to urinate on the street rather than wet their pants. This early freedom, however, contrasts sharply with later discrimination. Simone de Beauvoir describes the French three-year-old boy who is singled out for initiation to the standing position by his father. She goes on to illustrate the denigration of the girl. "To urinate, she is required to crouch, uncover herself, and therefore hide: a shameful and inconvenient procedure."[24]

De Beauvoir notes another difference between the ways in which girls and boys are treated. French mothers accentuate their sons' sexuality. Gargantua's and Louis XIII's teasing nurses are a matter of literature, but modern mothers also give pet names to the boy's penis, and encourage him to think of it as an "alter ego, usually more sly, more intelligent, and more clever than the individual."[25] This may be a direct outcome of the French mother's practice of retracting the uncircumcized foreskin on the penis during washing to facilitate cleanliness. In contrast, De Beauvoir says that the girl child is not allowed to touch her vaginal area, and her self-examinations are considered improper.

As in Italy, children's fighting is more often verbal than physical. Mothers tell their children,[26] "Argue, yes, but don't hit." Today, however, a theory gaining acceptance is that it is "natural" to let children "find their own balance" through fighting it out alone without adult intervention. This can and does develop into fistfights, but name-calling and clever mockery are still considered the most potent weapon. A French girl feels at ease taunting the boys, and is subtly encouraged to play tricks on her friends.

One sees national differences in physical training in European summer-camp grounds. The Italian children are least interested in swimming or wrestling games, and the girls show real fear of the water, dogs and dirt. As things get rougher, the French children of both sexes are the next to drop out. American, English, German and Swedish boys will fight it out to the bitter end. American and English girls usually drop out if the going gets very rough, and only the German and Swedish girls will actually wrestle boys to the ground. It is, of course, impossible to rank children in verbal conflicts, since the language barrier puts everyone at a disadvantage.

A girl learns about herself through contact with adults, a pattern reflected in the French attitude toward pets. A provincial man will have a mongrel dog at his side—a dog that behaves perfectly, accompanies him at heel everywhere, never barks while the master speaks, never chases a passing cat and never, never spoils anyone's living-room rug. A few Parisian society women have poodles or exotic pets to complete their image. But children—malleable, and as yet undisciplined themselves—are not allowed to have animals. French girls are taught social responsibility by gradually assuming duties for their baby sisters, not by taking care of a pet. I know a French suburban family with seven children that was upset when the youngest came home with an animal. After much consultation and argument, she was finally allowed to keep it. It was a turtle, hardly the kind of animal to cause any consternation in a Northern European household.

The dislike of animals is intertwined with a feeling that they are base and evil. *"Vous êtes un âne!"* ("You are a donkey!") a teacher will say to a child she doesn't like who flubs a difficult verb declension. *Politesse* and articulateness are the ultimate qualities of superiority—the characteristics that demonstrate that a person is not an animal. Sensualist adults, like Colette and Bardot, may champion the warm, loving, "natural" qualities of animals, but the majority of parents reject any nonverbal influence on their children.

The female archetypes of today's children's literature are not as strong-willed and individualistic as those of the 1930s and 1940s. Girls' books of the pre-World War II era in France, as in the rest of Euro-American society, portrayed self-sufficient heroines setting out to make their own way in the world. A favorite series starred Becassine, an eccentric ladies' maid, who sought her fortune in New York.

Today, girls are offered the Martine series. *Martine at the Park, Martine at the Zoo, Martine at School, Martine at Home.* Martine embellishes her garden and plays *la petite maman.* She has no fanciful adventures. Those are reserved for the boys' series—*Tintin in the Congo, Tintin in the Temple of the Sun, Tintin, Objective: Moon.*

Most of the adventure stories for younger children, like those in England, have brother-and-sister protagonists. Unlike the English stories, however, when Daniel and Valérie get into difficulty, the boy is not able to save the day alone. An adult comes along to help. Small children are not shown to be self-sufficient when danger threatens. The greatest preponderance of books for the six-to-twelve age group, in fact, are encyclopedias or *comment fait-on* (how-to) instruction books, where the child learns directly from some adult figure.

"Little Prince" rebel archetypes, so popular in adult French literature, are few and far between in children's books. Marguerite Duras did a book, "forbidden for adults," starring a character named Ernesto, who refuses to go to school because it's too difficult, and then one day—after his parents have despaired of him—he magically learns how to fly. But such books do not appear to be widely popular.

Older boys have adventure stories, like the Alix series, where a teen-age hero wages victorious battles alone against Roman gladiators, Vikings and fantastic machines. For girls who want adventure, there are the usual enchanted-princess fairy tales. A modern addition is the one ponytailed girl in the "Four Aces" humorous adventure series. The Four Aces have a protagonist for everyone to identify with—the Chubby Gourmet, the Bookworm, the Real Boy, and the Real Girl. When danger threatens, Chubby is forever preoccupied with eating, Bookworm is lost in his book, Real Girl is looking in the mirror and combing her hair. Only Real Boy seems to have a bit of real sense.

In analyzing what French children read, one other series should be noted: "Corinne et Jeannot," comic-book characters roughly equivalent to the "Nancy and Sluggo" strip in the United States. There is nothing innocent about Corinne and Jeannot's games, and there is no question as to who is the *vilaine* (bad child). It's Corinne. She will ask Jeannot if he doesn't want to climb a rope. Then, after he's started up, she'll set fire to the end of the rope just to see him scramble up faster. When the two come across a baby crying on a doorstep, Corinne tells Jeannot he must take the baby to its home which, she says, is across town. As soon as he leaves, she goes up the step, rings the bell and tells the mother who answers, "That boy just kidnapped your baby." Jeannot is thrown in jail.

The truly amazing thing is that the end frames of the episode show Jeannot in jail writing a letter that says, "Corinne is a monster, so I need another companion. But she must be *jolie* [pretty] like Corinne, intelligent like Corinne, adorable like Corinne. . . ."

Privacy is one of the most prized rights of the French individual. The family usually tries to have separate rooms for each child, even when they are of the same sex. In old-fashioned boarding schools, girls' dormitories had long rows of beds, but each was partitioned off from the others by white percale drapes—an arrangement that emphasized the fact that you could do anything . . . as long as you were quiet.

Noisiness is the major threat to privacy, and children are constantly told to shut doors quietly, to lower their voices and so on. Privacy is also an adult status symbol, and both fathers and mothers often have rooms—or at least sections of rooms—that are wholly theirs, serving as a study or sewing room.

There is no Grand Central Station atmosphere in a French home. Friends of the same age are not considered necessary and often the child is allowed to play with other children (of widely varying ages) only under adult supervision at school or summer camp. Mothers do not encourage their daughters to invite friends home. Teen-agers, even in modern families, are surprised at the idea of children younger than ten inviting friends to stay overnight.

The games children play outside school are individual-oriented. The emphasis is on skill and imagination. The French boy will play soccer and other team ball games, but he is not as passionately involved in such sports as Anglo-Saxon boys. Nor does he use brute force. Instead he plays *boules*, a kind of outdoor bowling, or concentrates on swimming or fencing or horseback riding.

French girls play hopscotch, skip rope and learn juggling—a peculiarity of France. Only a few speak passionately of dressing-up games. French girls learn the art of capitalizing on their assets and dressing themselves imaginatively, but most do not learn it from other children. They learn from watching their mother or older sister, or through long afternoons, spent alone in front of the mirror, judging themselves.

Being alone and looking to grown-ups for conversation, the French girl is encouraged to know herself well. She learns to understand her good points and minimize her bad ones. The technique of defining oneself, accepting oneself and making the best of oneself is taught gently, by casual statement. "Well, you're lazy, so you must find a clever way to do things."

A child is also taught that a droll comment, a smile and a lilting voice often get the best vegetables at the greengrocer's and a candy at the tobacco shop. *Sois sage* (be wise) and *sois raisonnable* (be reasonable) are the common parental admonitions—a far cry from the English and Swedish encouragement of "cheeky" little girls.

By the time the French girl has reached her teens, she is quite aware of her sexuality, whether or not she has attended an all-girls' school. At a very early age, she has developed the *savoir-faire* about appearance which has given the Frenchwoman the reputation of being the *"most beautiful woman in the world,"* [27] among European and American observers. She succeeds in looking beautiful, because she looks upon herself as unique. She is her own creation.

This is particularly true of girls who don't conform to conventional ideas of beauty. The French invented the term *jolie laide* for the woman who makes success out of ugliness. And Frenchmen often profess a preference for this type of woman. They are intrigued by these female Cyrano de Bergeracs, who totally shape themselves.

The well-known *jolies laides* women themselves—Jeanne Moreau, Simone Signoret, the electric Zou-Zou—are all casually proud of their ability to mold an original look. Their lives often include a Pygmalion. Zou-Zou commented, "When I was 18, I hated myself. I wanted to be blonde with blue eyes and a little nose. But then I was lucky to meet a man—Jean-Paul Goude, who is now a magazine art director in America—and he said he loved my face. He said it was the greatest face in the world. That gave me confidence, and now I don't want to change it."

Entrepreneur Jean Bernardin his turned his ability to "exploit the faults in a face and make a woman feel as beautiful as she is" into the Crazy Horse nightclub fortune.

Both men and women build their images carefully. They are adept at using artifice to create a "natural" appearance, but they rarely let nature take care of things. The French look is not the fresh-water-and-soap face of England. Women over sixty-five, generally felt, in other countries, to be exempt from beauty regimentation, are fastidiously made up every day in France. Hair is not swept into the bubble concoctions of Italy, but has a windblown look that comes from a monthly cut as well as intricate brushing and combing rituals.

The hourglass figure is watched vigilantly, and every young woman has a personal exercise-diet regimen to keep herself in trim. Health is a major preoccupation, and one can find more health-food products in French supermarkets than anywhere else south of Scandinavia. Even bralessness hasn't made it in France, despite Maria Schneider and a determined push by *Elle* magazine. Teen-agers continue to protrude just as defiantly as their mothers. They don't like the free and floppy feeling. They don't enjoy a body that's undisciplined and disorganized.

It is this pride in self-creation, this *amour-propre*, that is the secret of French beauty. A French woman concentrates on finding her physical type and cultivating it, making it—like her personality—as pure and definite and unique as a flower.

Once the components of body and personality are assembled, the mold is rarely broken. Just as Deneuve would never play the role of the Earth Mother, Brigitte Bardot would never play the upper-class snob. For that kind of flexibility, we have to look to a Glenda Jackson or a Liv Ullmann.

Sex as an art form is one of the most envied accouterments of adulthood, and society guards such knowledge jealously. The philosophy has been to keep these secrets from the young until a benign adult teacher bestows the gift of sensuality on the innocent. The adolescent is to be helpless until the adult condescends to notice him or her.

Writer Christine Collange's childhood included a schoolmistress who told girls to lower their eyes whenever temptation appeared. Temptation took the form of any young man.[28] French mothers insist that their daughters may not go to London to study because of the "deterioration of morals." A French father won his damage suit against Air France for the "scandalous" showing of the film *Benjamin* on board the plane on which he was traveling with his eleven-year-old daughter. *Benjamin* is a boy-meets-*femme-fatale* story, and the seduction scenes take place in voluminous costumes.

Sex education in French schools was illegal until 1973, when the iron hold of the conservatives was broken by a series of court cases, culminating with that of Nicole Mercier, who introduced Dr. Jean Carpentier's *Apprendons à faire l'amour* (*Let's Learn to Make Love*) in her high-school philosophy class. Dr. Carpentier's major tenet is: "In all sex practices, what counts is desire and the pleasure derived from it. There is only one danger and that is the frustration of one's desires. Abnormality doesn't exist."

Although the students had voted to discuss the booklet, one, Christine Jaujard, was outraged. Her father, an army colonel, took the teacher to court on a morals charge that carried a two-year jail sentence and a $3600 fine. Mercier won the case, and a few weeks later the Minister of Education announced plans for sex education in high schools.

The first French sex encyclopedia for children also appeared 1973, when Hachette brought out the five-volume *Encyclopédia de la Vie Sexuelle*. It is an age-graded presentation starting with volume I for seven to nine-year-olds.[29]

When one compares these developments to practices in "conservative" Italy, one can see how reluctant the French have been to impart knowledge to their youngsters. Italian sex encyclopedias were available nearly a decade earlier.

Advertising is another bête noire of parents who wish to shield their children from sexual stimulation. Here again the French censors are more conservative than those in Italy, where newsstands and film posters displayed nudes photographed from every angle except genitalia close-up. In 1957, a Paris publisher was condemned for showing a girl *en bois*, that is, with one leg up. Ten years later, the first nude man (frontal but shadowed) was used as an advertisement in magazines, but an ad for underpants was forbidden for street posters. Not so long ago, the Metro subway system was still refusing an ad for *The Naked Ape* which showed a rear-view picture of two apes and a man, woman and child—all nude.[30]

As a result of these restrictions, sexual experimentation is the major symbol of the French adolescent breakaway rites. Students who claimed that sex-segregated schools had deprived them of partaking in *la vie vraie*, scrawled "Pleasure Without Obstacles" on the walls of the universities during the May 1968 revolution. France's Dear Abby columnist, Marcelle Segal, has a special name for today's teen-ager. She calls her *La Vierge Honteuse* (The Shamed Virgin) who "carries her virtue like a blemish." Girls write her with questions that range from "I have to admit that I'm 13, and I've never been kissed . . . do you recommend any books on how to do it?" to "I'm 21 and desperate. I have the impression that I'm not normal, for I've never been able to give myself to a man."[31]

The first nationwide report on sexual mores, the Simon Report,[32] appeared in late 1972. It found that 54 percent of young people who marry today have already had relations with each other before the ceremony. This compares directly with a similar 1972 study of American girls under nineteen, where, again, 54 percent were no longer virgins.[33]

The picture, however, is not as permissive as worried French parents fear. The Simon Report stresses that the majority of girls who had intercourse did so with boys they had known for more than a year, and that the young couple discussed the idea at length. French teen-agers were not advocating promiscuity, but rather the long-term "trial marriage" relationship, a practice supported by a full 80 percent of the under twenties. In fact, a *L'Express* magazine survey of fifteen- to twenty-year-olds conducted the same year showed that 70 percent believed it was wrong to have sexual relations if one was not in love.

These same French young people proved to be more conservative about marital fidelity than their parents. Following the logic that if you've worked out difficulties through trial marriage, you should be able to enter a legal relationship in full possession of your senses, only a tiny 1 percent of the young marrieds believed that occasional infidelity on the part of either partner was "normal."

The only part of the picture that might prove socially difficult was that 43 percent of the young unmarried couples engaged in sexual relations were not using any birth-control methods. This appeared to be a higher percentage of ill-prepared couples than in the past.

The miscalculation is apparently due to misunderstanding. Whereas the French boy once took full responsibility, today's male expects the girl to be on the Pill, but often she is not. This is not because she is searching for the romantic "magic moment" of her English counterpart. She simply has no information, and birth-control Pills and devices are not legally available to anyone under eighteen.

The French male's initiation to sex, like the Italian's, has traditionally been in the hands of an older woman—whether a professional or a woman he knows as a friend or member of his family. Film director Louis Malle has even made a film, *Souffle au coeur* (*Sighs of the Heart*), portraying the "ultimate taboo," mother-son incest. The mystique of the older woman is reflected in the newspaper comic strips, where young, prince-like heroes are forever finding their way into the castle-like abodes of fascinating, mysterious, wealthy, intelligent, queen-like women. The picture is filled in sensually by Colette in *Le Blé en herbe* (*The Ripening Seed*), when sixteen-year-old Philippe becomes acquainted with Madame Dalleray, a beautiful lady-in-white, who lives with her many-colored parrot in a lush, dark, velvet-and-silk lair.

A unique aspect of French mating rites is the *ménage à trois* (literally: household of three) two boys and a girl, or two girls and a boy. In the summer, they can be seen in the countryside, setting up their single tent. In the winter, they stride along the boulevards arm in arm—not only in sophisticated Paris, but in the province of Alsace as well.

It's a relationship based on the French sense of rationale. They state emphatically that there is no logical reason why three can't build a relationship as well if not better than two. Simone de Beauvoir describes sharing Sartre with women friends on several occasions and finding her relationship with him growing better because of the addition.[34] The complications that these relationships occasionally take on are accepted by the French as a small price to pay for the added pleasure that all three find in one another's company. As De Beauvoir points out, three make self-exploration more intriguing and accurate because each reflects unique facets of the other two.

5

La Femme

In French, the word for "woman" is the same as the word for "wife." The meaning of *la femme* is so bound up in the idea that marriage is woman's natural state, that Frenchwomen often define themselves by how close they approach that norm . . . despite the large number of successful career women . . . despite the articulate and apparently self-confident Lesbian factor . . . despite the women who reject tribal marriage rites.

One of the main reasons *la femme* enjoys status as a wife is because the man has status as a husband. As in Italy, a family is one of the trappings of success, a symbol that the man is *sérieux* (serious). The French bachelor, as long as he is young, represents virility and he is expected to sow his wild oats. But, if he stays single as he grows older, it is viewed as a sign of failure. When presidential candidate Valéry Giscard d'Estaing wanted to charm voters with his stability, he took his wife with him on the hustings. The popular actor, Jean-Louis Trintignant, is often interviewed while working for his film-director wife, Nadine. Men are portrayed as needing "the Other" and enjoying the stimulation of her company.

Since France is a society where children are taught to cope with their problems by themselves and pride in self is instilled from birth, one would assume that it would be difficult for the individual French person to form a union with someone else, much less to move deliberately into such a stable and lasting relationship as marriage.

It would be—except for two things. First, *l'amour* is glorified as the ultimate experience for both men and women. Second, marriage is thought to be the "natural" way of life—even for individualists. The secret lies in maintaining one's separate individuality inside marriage. It is rumored that Eric Rohmer has never told his wife that he is a film director. Colette never appeared before her husband without first putting on her makeup. The key to these relationships is that the partners never allow the day-to-day intimacy of living together to co-opt the sanctity of their personal lives. Privacy in close quarters is religiously maintained.

Not all Frenchwomen are willing to sacrifice their independence before the marriage altar, however, and Lesbian or bisexual alternatives are more visible in France than in any other Western European country. Lesbianism has long been accepted in French intellectual circles. The subject has been treated in books and films since the twenties—sometimes as something titillating and scandalous, but often with seriousness and genuine sensuality. It was not chance that led Gertrude Stein and Alice B. Toklas to live most of their lives in *la Provence*. Colette openly discussed her bisexuality, while today Maria Schneider flaunts her relationship with Lucie Garcia.

As Violette Leduc explains in her sensitive yet self-possessed autobiography, *La Bâtarde*, love of Like for Like is a natural outgrowth of *amour-propre*. It is credit to the strength of French *logique* that this principle appears to be as acceptable for women as it is for men.

Opting out of the female/male scene is not the only possibility for a Frenchwoman who regards matrimony as stifling. She can choose from a whole range of other roles. Brigitte Bardot, for example, says, "I leave before being left. I decide. I think it would be terribly boring if you always had to stay with the same man." Past forty, Brigitte is the Joe Namath of France. Men give interviews on such subjects as "For 18 months I was BB's *petit mari*."[35]

Simone de Beauvoir's long "association" with Jean-Paul Sartre is representative of an entire generation of principled women who refused the marriage ceremony. "During the twenties and thirties, we were all determined not to give in to social strictures," said a woman from the south of

France who has lived with the same man for thirty-six years without what she calls, "A piece of paper from the grandfather's office." She continued, "Why bring outsiders into it? What you feel with your man is nobody else's business."

It is not only the desire to control one's own destiny which encourages the Cult of The Affair in France. *La Séduction* is an art, deeply rooted in the tradition of *l'amour*. It's a national game in which both players look on each other as desirable objects.

Marie-Claire, the largest and most successful quality woman's monthly, devotes issues to "Seduction in the Summer" and "Love in the Winter" and "Why Some Women Are Passionate." These articles are pragmatic. One dealing with a woman's use of seduction to further her career discusses the disadvantages as well as the advantages involved. After all a woman may suffer loss of status as a result; her boss may be jealous of her career and her devotion to it; he'll be furious if he discovers her motive is avarice; her women co-workers will be jealous and hinder her progress; and her boss will be inclined to tell her next boss. Advantages are also explained without coyness. The emotional excitement of an affair can spice up a boring job, bring better pay, more luxurious social activities, job security.

The possibility of marriage resulting from an affair is described as unlikely, although real-life stories do exist. Madame Cino del Duca, for example, was a typist who married into the business and went on to become the millionairess boss of a publishing empire stretching from the *Paris Jour* daily newspaper to true-love romance magazines. Practically speaking, however, class differences separate the secretary from her superior, and the instances of men divorcing first wives to marry mistresses are rare. The French women's magazine reader wants to look at an affair clearly, and make her decision coolly, without the illusion of church bells and organ music in some distant future.

Both men and women commonly enter into relationships for financial reasons and they are disconcertingly forthright about this. A man asked a magazine columnist if she thought it was ethical to make a deal with his mistress: he'd give her a baby if she'd give him a new car. The columnist said she thought it was better than trying to get the car underhandedly. Classified marriage ads will often read: "Pretty young woman, 28, desires marriage. Broke."

There are other practical reasons for seduction: to get oneself out of a fit of despondency . . . to find a drinking companion . . . or a dancing companion . . . or a helping hand at work. All of these motives are expressed openly. Again, the French prefer to define a relationship clearly from the beginning.

As might be expected in this either/or society, affairs and other dyad relationships fall into two classes—*l'amour fou* and *l'amour sage*. The first is mad love—the passionate loss of all reason, the blind drive into self-destruction with "the Other." The second is a stable, practical love that grows through the years—closer to our definition of "affection."

Both possibilities are open to women. The Parisian girl who spends her time packing and unpacking her suitcase, flitting from one apartment to another, leaving a string of lovers in her wake, is as familiar an archetype in France as the swinging young bachelor.

A girl who left Lyon to join the Paris scene earnestly described this life to me, and said, "It's part of the joy of being a woman—a man doesn't have the freedom to do this, you know. Unless his family really has money, and he can pay his way, he has to be serious, even if he wants to spend all his life as a bohemian painter. We women can go anyplace—somebody will always give us something to eat and a bed to sleep in."

It is considered natural for some people to maintain a *sage* relationship with one person, yet plunge into *l'amour fou* for a short time with someone else. A well-known example of this is Yves Montand's marriage of twenty-three years to Simone Signoret, which was interrupted by a passion for Marilyn Monroe. He speaks of both relationships gently. "One is quite capable, I believe, of loving two persons at once. I was really in love with Marilyn . . . but Simone is another thing, and she is wise enough to understand that. . . . As you grow older, you don't agitate for *l'amour* with *le grand A*, but for something tender, the rapport becomes singular."[36]

Purists will argue that such "side trips" are not true examples of *l'amour fou*, because the individuals concerned were not destroyed by their emotions. "They were only visiting a foreign country. They had no intention of emigrating," said one Frenchwoman, herself an admitted *amour sage* type.

Perhaps it is this belief that a person will never change type which enables the French to look upon the affairs of political leaders with aplomb. Flings are considered irrelevant to one's normal serious demeanor.

Flings, however, are less excusable for "serious" women than for men. The Gabrielle Russier affair demonstrated a venomous social hatred for the "serious" woman who breaks with her stereotype. Russier was a literature professor in Marseilles. She and one of her students, Christian Rossi, seventeen, fell in love. His parents insisted that the relationship stop, but Gabrielle and Christian continued to see each other. His parents sent him to boarding school. Gabrielle had a breakdown. Christian ran away, and his parents charged Gabrielle with *détournement de mineur* (literally, "diverting" a minor) and declared that she was the cause of his defiance. They had her placed under arrest until Christian gave himself up, then sent him to a private clinic for psychiatric treatment.

Gabrielle spent eight weeks of preventive detention in a Marseilles jail before her trial. She was given a lenient sentence. The public prosecutor immediately appealed for a stiffer penalty, which would have left her with a criminal record and barred her from teaching. At age thirty-two, with the second trial coming up, she taped the windows in her apartment and gassed herself to death.

Debate over the Russier incident has preoccupied France since Gabrielle's suicide in '69. Would there have been such a clamor if *he* had been older and the professor? Why did Gabrielle and Christian act so unreasonably when they saw how determined his parents were? Why did the parents act so unreasonably when they saw how determined Gabrielle and Christian were? Perhaps the answer is simple. The definition of *l'amour fou* is closely tied with the idea of self-destruction. French society seemed compelled to demand the fulfillment of this definition, just as the lovers seemed compelled to prove their passion by self-immolation.

Ninety percent of the French prefer to read about *l'amour fou* rather than to practice it. As portrayed by Bulle Olgier in Jacques Rivette's *L'Amour Fou* film, such passion is destructive even when one succeeds in marrying the love object.

As lovers, the French have been described as both mechanical and magnificent. Writer De Gramont comments: "Treatises have been written to explain that the singularity of being French consists in the paradox of a totally uninhibited but totally disciplined attitude toward sex. There is no false shame or false modesty; considerable masculine pride surrounds the diligent pursuit of agreeable sensations. French lovemaking is less passionate than technically proficient, its vocabulary reminiscent of two housewives discussing a complicated recipe—do this, then do that, now here, that's right, turn a bit, not too fast, simmer but do not let come to a boil."[37]

A unique feature of French lovemaking is the preoccupation with accompanying conversation. It's not surprising that such a verbal nation would enjoy sharing intellects as much as sharing bodies—and at the same time. The jokes, the innuendos, the comments on everything from daily trivialities to geopolitics—all signify as much to both parties as the sex act itself.

French lovers do not play the same roles in bed as the Anglo-Saxons. The woman is often the initiator. Technique ranges from a subtle look signaling that she would like to be accompanied home after a party to a murmured, "You must be very passionate." She also feels less need to hide both her previous experience, and her desire to try something new. The Simon Report indicated that over half the younger generation had made love standing up, and nearly three-fourths had had oral sex.

The belief that all women must lose themselves totally in the sex act is almost universal. De Beauvoir disparages immature girls who have lost their virginity but have never experienced "genuine erotic reality" and explains: ". . . They look on physical love as a game and, if they happen not to be in a mood for such diversion, a lover's demands seem coarse and importunate; they retain feelings of disgust, phobias, adolescent modesty. If they never get beyond this stage—as according to American men, many American women never do—they will spend their lives in a state of semi-frigidity. True sexual maturity is to be found only in the woman who fully accepts carnality."

She goes on to describe explicitly the passion of the mature woman: ". . . Feminine sexual excitement can reach an intensity unknown to man. Male sex excitement is keen but localized, and—except perhaps at the moment of orgasm—it leaves the man quite in possession of himself; woman, on the contrary, really loses her mind; for many this effect marks the most definite and voluptuous moment of the love affair, but it also has a magical and fearsome quality. A man may sometimes feel afraid of the woman in his embrace, so beside herself she seems, a prey to her aberration. . . ."[38]

The belief in woman's innate passion is reflected time and again in literature, but it turns up in daily life as well. When sex-education classes were introduced into French schools not long ago, the first lessons described the aggressive female cat in search of a tom. The principle also places the burden of birth control on the man. Since it is the woman, not the man, who is driven by sexuality, it is the man who must be practical and—often quite literally—restrain himself in order to prevent pregnancy.

Romance and *l'amour courtois* are frequently quoted as major reasons why Frenchwomen enjoy being women. References to the magic of love are everywhere. Makeup ads offer "the look of a woman in love." Vacations away from the children are "times for love." Electricity "helps you to live. It gives you the time to take your time. The time to love." And Madame Soleil, probably the most consulted astrologer in the world, with a widely read daily newspaper column and a program on the radio, puts it simply: "Love is the quality of life."[39]

One would assume, therefore, that courtship and marriage would be highly emotional experiences. Yet, again, the French have rationalized the procedure until it often seems mechanical.

Broken engagements can still be treated as broken contracts, and the injured party can take the other to court if either feels that her or his career or good name has been damaged. Marriage contracts, even more common in France than they are in Italy, are usually quite explicit about the financial duties of each party.

Marriage rites include several preliminary trips to notary publics and the priest. There are two ceremonies: first at the mayor's office and then in the church. The man may have a bachelor's dinner beforehand (at one time this was the scene of a "burial of bachelor life" ceremony complete with coffin). There is no bridal-shower tradition. Instead, the bride's family gives her a trousseau and as fabulous a wedding gown as they can afford.

The wedding feast is the highlight of the occasion, for eating together is a major sacrament to the French. Food is so important that one sees the photographer clear guests away to take a sentimental picture of the virgin, food-bedecked table.

At one time a honeymoon was possible only for the wealthy, but today nearly all young couples expect to get away for at least a few days even if only to an inexpensive campground. The possibility of visiting a relative living elsewhere is another means of overcoming economic restrictions, as it is for many Italian newlyweds. Such a honeymoon emphasizes the change the marriage makes in the couple's social status, rather than their new sexual license.

In marriage, most Frenchwomen step into second-class citizenship. The majority of marriages are dominated by a dictatorial father figure. The woman, as mother, has little of the power and admiration accorded the Italian mamma. As wife, she is expected to revolve around her husband. Frenchwomen refuse to join "boring" women's clubs and seem to "come alive" when a man enters a conversation.

A Frenchwoman's status in society is decided by her husband's success and by how well he treats her. She measures her worth by the number of little favors she gets during the day—from her husband and all the other men she meets.

"What do you do when you have a flat tire?" asks an advertisement appealing to the girl on the go (who is shown skydiving and waterskiing). Answers: First "Redo your makeup." Second, "Wait, and *voilà!*" The final photograph shows the coquette leaning against sports car, and a man, half hidden inside trunk, pulling out the tire.

De Beauvoir called this kind of manipulation, "A whole tradition, [which] enjoins upon wives the art of 'managing' a man; one must discover and humor his weaknesses and must cleverly apply in due measure flattery and scorn, docility and resistance, vigilance and leniency . . . this is indeed a melancholy science—to dissimulate, to use trickery, to hate and fear in silence, to play on the vanity . . . of a man, to deceive him."[40]

The wife who dedicates her life to the "melancholy science" must be forever attentive and submissive. She helps her husband put on his coat and then carefully dusts his shoulders before he leaves the house. She cooks "for others, [and] picks the worst food for herself without even thinking about it."[41]

In Georges Simenon's latest volume of his autobiography, the world-famous mystery writer sings songs of praise to this very French style of homelife and the joys of living with a meticulously organized woman. He requires complete fidelity from his wife, but refers to what he calls "light" sex with nightclub dancers and others he meets casually, as a way that "dreams and vague urges are purged, which . . . poison most marriages. . . . I have to push myself to do it." As for his wife, D. (as he calls Denise), he admits that she is subject to fits of depression, but he adores her. She is his "companion, businesswoman, buddy, mistress, mother."[42]

Adultery is an eternal preoccupation. It is the favorite theme of the boulevard comedies that dominate Parisian theatre, of popular French literature and of the costume dramas on prime-time television. Newspapers regularly report the *crime passionnel*, and a special French twist is the woman who throws oil of vitriol in her unfaithful lover's face.

Such crimes pass under the eyes of judges who are as lenient to "understandable passion" in France as they are in Sicily. In 1972, a Parisian Garde Républicain was tried for the murder of his wife. She had wanted to continue working after their first child was born. When he disapproved, she asked for a divorce. He refused. She joined a drama club and began staying out late and buying clothes "like the girls in *Elle.*" A true traditionalist, he still brought her the little bouquet of lilies of the valley on May first. She refused it. He grabbed a kitchen knife and stabbed her twenty-eight times. Taking into consideration the dead wife's near-criminal involvement in *féminisme*, the judge sentenced the garde to five years—parole available after two.

Foreign visitors are often surprised at this decidedly patriarchal cast of most French marriages. Those outside the country are more familiar with the French version of Open Marriage so often described in literature.

In these relationships, neither partner dominates, and both usually work. The well-organized wife streamlines the household, the husband helps. Many decide not to have children, preferring the privacy such a relationship affords. They eat their meals in tiny candlelit restaurants—sometimes *à deux*, sometimes with friends or business colleagues. They take business trips alone, and sometimes spend summer holidays separately.

They look on extramarital relationships as natural but incidental to the mainstream of their lives. Even an extracurricular pregnancy is apparently taken in stride. An art editor told me that she had become temporarily involved one summer, when she was unable to fill her Pill prescription in Turkey. When she knew for certain that she was pregnant, she discussed abortion with her husband. "Between adults, certain things must be discussed without hypocrisy." They decided to have the child, since he was sterile. He does not consider the child his, but he loves the little girl (and has given her his name) because she belongs to his wife.

The wife in these open marriages is often the more radically antimarriage of the two. Singer Juliette Gréco keeps spice in her marriage to film actor Michel Piccoli by declaring, "You are the one with the idea of a 'couple.' Me no! I can pack my bags and leave any day."

Such *laissez-passer* relationships are in a minority in France. They are found almost exclusively among professionals, although there is a strong tradition of ribald wife/husband individualism among peasant marriages.

The important thing is that French society accepts these marriages. And they exist often enough to accommodate most of those who want to take advantage of them. People who define themselves as soon as they begin to talk rarely let themselves get caught in the deadly embrace of the Garde Republicain and his career wife. Divorce—even though it has existed off and on in France since Napoleon, and today includes an ambiguous "grave psychological injury" clause—occurs only in one out of ten marriages. This figure has not fluctuated significantly in the past thirty years. Despite feminism, and the increasing number of wives who work, the French fatalism still holds: "There are few good marriages . . . but even fewer good divorces."[43]

6

The Professional Housekeeper

Along with her mystical role as *la femme*, the French wife has another status role to play—that of housekeeper. Even her title, *la ménagère* (the manageress), reflects the professional value of her work. She is the keeper of the nest; the meticulous, well-organized, creative mistress of a craft that the entire society appreciates.

Setting up the new household as the marriage begins is complicated. A major problem is *obtaining* housing. France has the least postwar housing construction of any major country except England. As late as the sixties, some two-thirds of all housing in France dated from before World War I. Rent control and soaring land values continue to encourage landlords to keep a house empty. They want to be ready if a truly affluent buyer shows up.

If renting is difficult, the young couple finds their buying power is practically nonexistent. Property has more emotional value than money. Money, landowners explain, is forever being devalued. One must offer a very large amount of cash to buy a house, even if it's been empty for years.

173

Wealth is still unevenly distributed. Economist Jean-Jacques Servan-Schreiber has estimated the ratio of the very wealthy French to the poorest sectors as 35 to 1,[44] whereas, in America, the upper fifth sector is only seven times more wealthy than the lowest fifth. Very few young couples can afford to buy a home when they are starting out. Nor is the Italian tradition of the parents providing the bride with a home at all common.

Mortgages are hard to obtain, customarily cover only two-thirds of the assessed value of the house, carry a 10 percent interest rate and must be repaid within fifteen years. This is an interest rate approximately 30 percent higher than that of any other country we are discussing, and the French term of payment averages twelve years shorter.[45]

A great many couples, therefore, find they must spend the first year or two with in-laws. This situation is accepted bitterly by both parties. Unlike their Italian counterparts, the young pair does not feel it is natural and the senior couple does not feel it is an investment in old-age insurance.

Housing shortages are often quoted as the reason for small families. One twenty-six-year-old woman from a suburb in northern Paris described it this way: "I live with my husband, an electrician, in a little apartment of two rooms. We have two children, and with the family allowance and his check, we have sixteen hundred francs a month [approximately $400]. The children have the bedroom, and I spend the whole day in the other room.

"At night, we push the table up against the wall and unfold the divan. When I found out I was pregnant the third time, we decided that I should have an abortion. We'd tried to get a bigger apartment five years ago, before the first baby. We'd like a place with bath—here you have to wash yourself in the kitchen, and the toilet is on the ground floor. But we've never gotten anywhere with finding something else."

As she indicates, modern conveniences are hardly universal in French homes. In fact, apart from middle- and upper-class housing in urban areas, accommodations are often more primitive than in Italy. According to a mid-sixties European Economic Council Report on Family Budgets, 55 percent of Italian wage earners' households had television sets, compared to 37 percent of the French; 57 percent of the Italians had refrigerators, compared to 55 percent of the French; 29 percent had telephones, compared to 6 percent. France has a larger percentage only in washing machines—43 percent in France compared to 20 percent in Italy. According to the 1962 census, one out of four French homes was without running water, and 60 percent were without private bathroom.

The French household is designed in harmony with the isolated, self-contained, self-sufficient French family. Not for the French are the picture windows and doorless rooms of the American home. There is a professed appreciation for English "comfiness," but the furniture the French buy is stiff and bony.

Houses are set primly in the center of flower and vegetable gardens. These gardens are not places for children to play, but places for them to learn how to care for the plants—how to water, weed and train each seedling to keep to its proper place in the garden order.

There are usually two doors to the house; one opens at a right angle to the other. The "front door" often does not face the street, but is placed around to the side. Secluded and sedate, it is used only for guests. The garden is surrounded by a fence. Often there is a sign on the gate: *Chien Méchant* (Vicious Dog). These dogs are usually small, but they can be nasty with unwanted outsiders.

The "back door" faces the front gate and opens into the kitchen. Whereas the Italian woman would be mortified, the Frenchwoman thinks nothing of a passerby seeing her at work inside. It shows how industrious she is. The arrangement has the further advantages of allowing her to speak to peddlers and knife sharpeners who pass, and to keep track of the children.

If there is only one door, it faces the front gate and opens into a hall which serves both as an entrance and a master nexus with a door on one side leading to the dining room and one on the other leading to the kitchen, and ending in a stairway up to the bedrooms. The kitchen is still positioned with a window that commands the approaches to the house.

All inside doors are kept shut. Walking from one room to the next without knocking is frowned upon.

The city apartment is even more fortified. The street door is guarded by a *concierge* (door person), who has the reputation of being somewhat less friendly than an attack mastiff. The apartment door is barricaded with double and triple locks.

Once admitted into a French home, a person usually must wait in the *foyer* for a few minutes until the entire household is alerted to her or his presence and prepared for the invasion. Then, the alien is ushered into the dining room or a dining room-living room combination. Although the French do not invite outsiders for dinner as often as the Americans and the British, when a guest comes by for a chat, she or he is brought to the table and offered coffee, tea or wine.

The family itself spends most of its time in the dining room; often a separate living room doesn't exist. This is the opposite of the American home where people grab quick meals in the kitchen and often don't even have a dining room. The French family television set is also ordinarily in the dining room, despite common family rules against watching during meals.

The dining room is the center of the household, the place where the family comes together to talk and enjoy one another.

Housework is a demanding daily ritual. The dining room is cleaned inch by inch, silverware is polished, flower arrangements are freshened, until everything is just so. The kitchen and bedrooms are often Spartan, but spotless.

The notion of a husband doing housework is not viewed unfavorably by the Frenchman. SOFRES pollsters have found that 42 percent say they help their wives regularly, and 47 percent lend a hand sometimes.[46] The wives I know say their husbands take out the garbage and fix anything that breaks. Do-it-yourself (*bricolage*) household projects are popular. Men may even take complete responsibility for food, from planning the meal and shopping to the preparation and cooking. Yves Montand says he has never helped his wife with the housework, since they can afford to have it done, but he sees his father help his mother and thinks it's a perfectly *raisonnable* routine.[47]

The garden is a major preoccupation of the French housewife. Forty-seven percent of the wage earners' households have gardens, and even more women tend flower and herb window boxes. According to the EEC Report on Family Budgets of 1963–64, the French are more likely to have a garden than any other Western Europeans except the British. In Britain, however, the garden is the man's responsibility.

Le jardin (the garden) is an ongoing creation. Visiting the market, the Frenchwoman will stop to select seedlings for shady corners, and discuss at length staggering the planting so that her border rows are ablaze with color from April to October and so that her beans and tomatoes do not all ripen in one overwhelming week.

The Frenchwoman is likely to sew clothes and home decorations. Although other European women now rely on mass-produced goods or seamstresses, the Frenchwoman is determined to fashion her own look. She may buy the basic model ready-made, but she adds ruffles, ribbons or scarves to create a unique outfit.

One part of her life—shopping—is becoming streamlined. Presently, women must keep track of innumerable details. The street market, for instance, is open only in the morning; the butcher shop is closed on Monday but open Sunday morning; the household goods shop is closed on Wednesdays but open until nine thirty Tuesday nights; the milk store is closed Saturday afternoons but open Sunday; the light bulb and electrical supplies shop is open only evenings from six to ten.

This inconvenient but traditional system is being superseded by the hypermarket—an airplane-hanger-like building that houses a no-nonsense shopping center, with regular hours. The hypermarket offers an admirable selection of goods, many on bulk purchase discount—Italian Parmesan, German venison, Danish pastries, La Poule Roussette eggs, Dutch-made home appliances, English clothes. The shopper has a wide selection of TV dinner concoctions—more often canned than frozen—but very few mixes. Obviously the French feel that if the woman will go to the bother of mixing, she wants to use her own recipe.

France is the land of the legendary *mères Lyonnaises* (the women cooks of Lyon); French children are given five-course meals in school cafeterias; the food stores in small towns are more elegant than the clothing stores; *bon appétit* is a common salutation. The French appreciate creative energy spent on the art of eating well. And the wife, who oversees the performance and guards her secret recipes like the Drambuie fortune, has important status.

It is interesting to observe how she supervises her domicile. A 1973 survey by Acumen, a leading marketing firm, suggests that she is hardly a slave to her cooking responsibilities.[48] She controls her five-course family dinner in this way: The first course is a *pâté* bought fresh from the neighborhood *charcuterie*. The second course is steak (French beef is the best on the Continent) and French fries. The third is a tossed fresh salad, which may have been cut for her by the greengrocer. The fourth is fresh cheese. The fifth is a bakery tart or fruit.

This meal does not take a good deal of preparation time *if* a woman runs a well-organized kitchen and organizes her shopping so that delicate vegetables and fruits are always used the first of the week, *pâté* is kept properly in airtight containers and her husband brings home fresh bread and dessert on schedule. If a woman runs this kind of well-organized kitchen, she can also serve her family the *cassoulet* and the *pots au feu* and marinated *boeuf en daub* that require preparation a day in advance. This is the cooking French wives have described to me as normal, now that meat prices are soaring. To those accustomed to impulse cooking it seems hard to conceive.

The French-cooking tradition becomes most apparent when guests are invited. One expert found that wives spent an *average* of three days in preparation.[49] Not for special occasions are the *charcuterie* thrush pies or the *pâtisserie mille-feuille* presented in bakeries on crystal platters surrounded by a garland of flowers. When the Frenchwoman entertains, she wants to display her own abilities, not someone else's. Guests respond with personal compliments: "Oh, this is so delicious! You're a mistress of *la cuisine*!" No, "Where did you buy this?" No, "What brand is it?" No, "Oh, it only took a minute to prepare," self-effacing response either.

Entertaining, like other homemaking tasks, is considered a skill in France. The books and magazine articles offering professional know-how on the subject emphasize organization, which translates once again into strict scheduling. They are also detailed with instructions. "If you entertain once a week, it is best to do so on Friday night," they intone. "Best twice-a-week evenings are Monday and Friday. One must be certain that other members of one's social group have not already taken Monday and Friday evenings. If a wife does not like to entertain, a sensible husband should not ask her to do so more often than once every three months. The guests should be friends, not business associates, and the conversation should be cultural not shop talk."

Although the Frenchwoman could not open a bank account without her husband's permission until the sixties, she has often been responsible for the family budget. Family men say they hand their pay envelopes over to their wives and add admiringly, "She does it all. She has a ledger of everything from the mortgage payments to the children's allowance."

The wife's approach to the family bookkeeping is practical. She pays particular attention to long-term planning and saving. Women's magazines may carry a feature titled "A Year of Organization," with tips on discounts available for children at state schools and summer camps, on the best times for buying cut-rate skiing equipment or obtaining discount flowers on a weekly subscription basis, and on investigating "Special Sale" advertising.

The underlying attitude of this kind of feature article, with four-color photographs and cover headlining, is that budgeting . . . and gardening . . . and cooking . . . and housework . . . and child care . . . are all demanding, serious, complicated tasks. The information is not intended to make the woman's life simple. It's to keep her informed so that she can handle her job more professionally.

The sales pitch for convenience appliances is often, "You work hard. You deserve beautiful surroundings and up-to-date equipment." It's the "name on the door deserves a Bigelow on the floor," approach. Even packaged foods don't emphasize how they simplify cooking. Instead, they appeal to a woman's *connaissance* (knowledge and perception): "Your husband doesn't know quite what he's missing, but you do. You know he needs a corner of his childhood. The taste of sugar and butter and the best ingredients that take him back to the days when he was a boy."

This catering to the housewife's professional knowledge stresses the fact that the French *ménagère* has the best of two worlds. She has the status and *joie de travailleur* (work enjoyment) of the Old World home-creator, and the conveniences of the New World appliance industry.

One group has been left out of the above picture—the women who inhabit the suburbs. The housing projects in France march across the hills outside large cities—ten stories high, blank-walled concrete, with small unadorned windows overlooking blank unadorned green areas, where children are often forbidden to play. Stairwells bear signs: "It is forbidden to allow children to play on the landing. . . . It is forbidden to leave things standing in the stairwell. . . . It is forbidden to make loud noises. . . . It is forbidden. . . ."

These developments were begun with Sarcelles, built outside Paris over twenty years ago, and are outgrowths of the dreams of the controversial architect, Le Corbusier. At first they were hailed as the answer to France's chronic housing problem. The arrangement was all right for husbands, who were happy to come home to peace and quiet. But within a few years, wives were complaining that they were suffocating. The apartments were built as "bedroom dormitories." Good for sleeping, but not for living. Often there was no shopping available, no cafés where one could meet friends, no place where the women could work, no organization that could take care of the children and sometimes not even any public transport to the cities. Since many of the women couldn't drive, and their husbands took the only car off to work, they became—quite literally—prisoners.

Paradis, a development forty kilometers north of Paris, was begun in 1965 and is typical. Madame Brigitte Gros, mayor of the area and the nearby town of Meulan, describes the problems in detail: the developer, who refused to put in a café, saying, "You would create two factions—those who go to the café versus those who watch from behind their curtains and gossip"; the government, which refused permission for inhabitants to use the school as an evening meeting place; the lack of firms to offer the women employment because there was no telephone service. There was also no daytime television.

Gros explains that the women spent their time "washing the windows every other day and counting the cars that passed." When a connecting bus service to the city finally started running, the women appeared to be so mired in lassitude that they rarely took advantage of it.

Worried by statistics showing that suburban wives often turn to prostitution, drinking and suicide, Mme Gros consulted a psychologist. She was told it was too late, unless she could mount massive job-training courses and psychotherapy facilities. "These women have become professional neurotics; they are no longer good for anything," Gros concludes. "They feel incapable of assuming any responsibility; they won't take on the slightest obligation."[50]

Typical suburban couples feel that the traditional values placed on the wife's role are important. The problem has been that the wife must limit her creative abilities to an efficiency apartment. The energy that could easily handle a full household is caged inside three small rooms. Unless suburban women can completely change gears and join the ranks of jobholders, their future will be a blot on the overall picture of the French *ménagère*.

7

The Natural Career Woman

In 1970, *Elle* polled fifteen hundred readers on women's attitudes. Among the questions was, "What woman do you most admire?"

The answers were a far cry from similar lists compiled every year by querying *Good Housekeeping* readers. The favorites were not wives of famous men, and they did not include any movie stars.

Marie Curie was first choice. Jacqueline Auriol, France's best-known aviatrix, was second and Colette was third. Auriol and Colette were both divorcées. All three—women who forged their destiny by themselves—are better known than any of their husbands.

Not only is the career woman admired in France, she is considered "natural." When one meets a new couple, in an anonymous place like a tiny provincial restaurant, the wife, as well as the husband, often gives her profession when introducing herself. And the question is then returned, "What do you do?"

181

In the *Elle* survey, the outlook was further reflected by 72 percent who said they would accept a woman president, 30 percent who believed there should be a woman's political party, and 50 percent who favored some form of national service for women. The most significant group was the smallest . . . and the most determined. Seventeen percent said they would prefer "individual fame" over "family happiness," an attitude that is unvoiced by women anywhere outside of France.

One can understand how the Frenchwoman develops this desire to create her own place in society rather than resting on a husband's laurels. Despite the honor given women as manipulators of the great figures in history, women who act directly, write their own books and make their own scientific studies are the ones who are most acclaimed. The French concept of self-pride, of *amour-propre*, is bound to cause a certain number of women to renounce putting the family first. The interesting thing is that such women feel sure enough of their position to voice their decision. There is no, "Oh, I *do* want to have a family someday," no, "Yes, I wish I had had children, but . . ." Instead Bardot comments that since men are beasts, why should she be interested? And Nelly Kaplan remarks that she chose abortion instead of babies.

The "natural" career woman finds support in French society. The Preamble to the French Constitution adopted in 1946 contained an equal-rights clause for women: "*La loi garantit à la femme, dans tous les domaines, des droits egaux à ceux de l'homme.*" ("The law guarantees to women, in all fields, rights equal to those of men.") This concept, equivalent to the beleaguered U.S. Equal Rights Amendment, has been enshrined in French law for thirty years.

In France, there are nursery schools for the children of working mothers; there are unions willing to call strikes for women's causes; there are city politicians aware of women's commuting problems and concerned about providing employment inside the suburbs.

More than that, the men are astonishingly at ease with the idea of female competition in the business world. A November 1972 SOFRES poll of a thousand men between the ages of twenty and sixty-five illustrated this clearly. Only 14 percent of the men said they would be upset if their wives made more money than they did; only 9 percent would be jealous if their wives had better prospects in their jobs; and only 13 percent would be unhappy if their wives held more important positions. The report went on to say that 68 percent would accept a woman for a boss.

The viewpoint is not simply an abstract ideal. We see it in operation in every stratum of French society. Wife-husband career teams are common—

not only behind intellectual Beauvoir/Sartre typewriters or in the Claude/ François Lalanne art studios or in the Curie scientific laboratories, but also in the civil service, small offices and family-run stores.

This does not mean that everything is perfect. Average wages for women are 6.7 percent lower than men's. In banking, insurance, commerce and the textile industry, a woman can make 40 percent less.[51] There are not enough nursery schools to meet the demand, and parents have a particularly difficult time on Wednesday, when there is no school. As Mayor Brigitte Gros pointed out, statutes on the lawbooks do not necessarily bring about a government psychologically willing to meet workingwomen's needs.

Even the SOFRES respondents who appeared to be totally at ease with their successful wives were still not reconciled to the whole concept. When asked what they thought was "the best solution for today's woman," a full 16 percent believed she should not work at all; 38 percent felt she should work only until she married or had children; 37 percent believed she should interrupt her career to care for the children until they were of school age; and only 6 percent stated that she should work all her life.

The fact remains, however, that the career woman in France enjoys an acceptance and status that professional women of other countries envy. The latest available statistics show that 34.9 percent of Frenchwomen work—a percentage only slightly greater than England's 34.4 percent, and less than Sweden's 37 percent and the Soviet Union's 48 percent. The important point is *where* the Frenchwoman works. In the civil service, for example, 27 percent of the top administrators and more than half (57 percent) of the middle management are women. France has a higher percentage of women lawyers and engineers than any other Western country. She comprises nearly as large a percentage of her nation's medical profession as the Englishwoman, and fully twice as large a percentage of film directors as women in any other country in the world. In city planning, Brigitte Gros is probably France's best-known current polemicist. In political comment, Françoise Giroud, who was editor in chief of the weekly news magazine, *L'Express*, made the best-seller list with *Si Je Mens . . . (I Give You My Word)*, just before her Ministry of Women's Affairs was created. Ariane Mnouchkine, as the director of the Théâtre du Soliel, is a leader in the Parisian avant-garde.

Frenchwomen were the *causes célèbres* in three of the most far-reaching mores and customs trials of recent French legal history—the Gabrielle Russier morals case, the Marie-Claire abortion case, the Nicole Mercier sex-education case. Their lawyers were also women. So was the lawyer of Christian Jubin, the notorious multimurderer, who escaped during pretrial questioning, when a female accomplice, Evelyne Segard, arranged to bring guns and a getaway car to the courthouse. It was also Segard who ultimately did all the driving and commanding in the escapade.

Sociologist Evelyne Sullerot has argued that perhaps a major reason why the Frenchwoman can choose a career in order to express herself is that she has not been channeled into the volunteer-charity-work outlet of Anglo-Saxons. Community work, like women's clubs, has little status in France, and Sullerot states that the Lady Bountiful figure is unpopular with the younger generation because charity is considered outdated and insincere. Sullerot contrasts this particularly with the United States, where an ambitious and energetic woman is encouraged to put her talents into becoming a "volunteer executive."[52]

This ignores the question of why the Frenchwoman has not put all her energies into the family, as the Italian woman has. The reasons lie in the points we have examined: motherhood simply does not have that much status in France, Frenchwomen take much more pride in their history of fighting for *La Belle France*, shaping the nation's literary tastes and carving out their own careers.

Being a wife is, in fact, the only role that overshadows that of the career woman in France. The wife role has many status symbols. In managing the household, commanding the kitchen and perfecting the sensual arts that most French consider the key components of happiness, the wife is considered a professional in her own right. Even more important is her magical role as the companion of man *(l'être essentielle)*, who motivates or manipulates man to his highest achievements.

The admirable thing about the system is that the woman who chooses a career is still considered a woman. She is not labeled a "sexless bitch," as the ambitious woman in the United States sometimes is. Sullerot found that there was very little "pleasing by self-effacement" on the part of the Frenchwoman. The French university woman did not feel she had to "play dumb" with her fiancé. And the French Beauvoirs and Girouds don't have to forego marriage or lasting relationships with men.

The Frenchwoman, however, faces many barriers. She is not allowed to step into the top command positions. The Establishment—whether it is in the universities, the civil service, politics or business—does not allow her into posts of true influence. That is why there is only one woman ambassador, Mlle Marcelle Campana, in Panama, why there have been no French Queen Victorias, why there have been no women in the Académie française. Though the current political scene offers much more promise than that of the sixties, it does not appear that a modern Eleanor of Aquitaine will preside over France in the near future.

In all of her roles the Frenchwoman has the accouterments of the professional. As a mother and homemaker, she is considered the mistress of an intricate and serious craft. As a career woman, she is considered intelligent and capable of achievement in widely varied fields. As a mistress-wife, she is admired as the power behind the throne. Women and men *both* appreciate the stable advantages of married life and expect to make accommodations to maintain the relationship.

The Frenchwoman enjoys two freedoms that have eluded other Western women: she is not limited in life to playing by men's rules and she does not have to act as society's conscience. These freedoms are interrelated. The child who doesn't have to be as "serious" as her brother falls more naturally into the malicious trickery of comic-strip Corinne. The teen-ager who is not hanging her life on her *baccalauréat*, can devote her energies to *la vie vraie*. The mother who is not required to be family disciplinarian is not isolated in the role of the Holy Madonna, forever sacrificing herself on the altar of the family group.

Her problems are twofold. The first she shares with the Frenchman. As noted before, once a girl has chosen her self-image, determined her course, and set her formula, she is not allowed to change. Once she chooses groupism—or turns from it to individualism—she is forced by society to stick to her choice. "The journey into the unknown always leads to unhappiness. Always."

To the outsider, the Frenchwoman has another restriction which is more pervading—she must be Female First. The problem is inherent in the concept of "the Other" Nation. It is the oppression that De Beauvoir resents most deeply, and yet, it is a Malraux heroine who expresses it most succinctly when she scornfully tells her lover, "You know a great deal, my dear. But you will probably die without appreciating the fact that a woman is *also* a human being."[53]

Part Four

The German Woman—

The New
Brunhild

1

Manipulation and Conciliatory Patriarchs

In the early 1970s, while women in other countries were digesting the heavily annotated and lengthy *Sexual Politics* and *The Female Eunuch*, public attention in Germany was caught by a two-hundred-page essay entitled *Der dressierte Mann (The Manipulated Man)*. Written by a thirty-six-year-old sociologist, Esther Vilar, the book castigates both sexes. Men are "enslaved" and "in love with Non-Freedom." Women are "subjugators" of the opposite sex, while "allowing their own talents to atrophy."

The Manipulated Man was an outstanding best-selling success in Germany and was promptly translated and published abroad. Three years later, Vilar continued her theme in a second book, *Das Polygame Geschlecht (The Polygamous Sex)*, where she defends male philandering, explaining that "rational love" means that a woman should allow her husband sexual freedom because he is forever subjugated to her anyway.

Although Vilar toys with the idea that men enslave themselves to women

189

because of the more insistent male sexual needs, her basic premise in both books is that men coddle, protect and work for the weaker sex because they *need* women to be their masters. "Freedom is the last thing he [man] wants. . . . Only as a slave does he feel safe."[1]

Vilar does not trace her argument historically, but it is important for us to note that "pleasure in Non-Freedom," as she calls it, is a common theme in German philosophy. Although other peoples may be secret slaves to the family, and/or the corporation, and/or the dictates of the individual, none of them consciously exalts its bondage to the extent of the Germans. None sings so many praises to duty. And none so clearly points up the gleam of truth in Vilar's argument.

The love of Non-Freedom—more positively called the love of duty and magnanimous self-sacrifice—is vital to understanding the German woman, but not only for the reasons outlined in Vilar's indictment. In the first place, love of Non-Freedom has been—if anything—instilled more firmly in German women than in German men. In the second place, there is salient evidence that the German woman is throwing off this trait, and breaking away from her past more quickly than any other woman in the Western Hemisphere.

For centuries, the German woman has been defined by the word *Frau*. Like *femme* in French, *Frau* means both "woman" and "wife." Further, in German as well as in the other Teutonic languages of most of Scandinavia, *Frau* (or *Fru* in Scandinavia) is also the equivalent of "Mrs." and signifies the honor bestowed upon a woman for becoming a wife.

It is interesting to note another idiosyncracy pertaining to female-male relationships in Teutonic languages. The word *Mann*, common to all of them, means "husband" and "man," as well as the universal pronoun "one." Linguistically, the male is as locked into the marital role as the woman.

Many of the conflicts faced by German women today stem from the fact that she and her *Mann* have cast her simultaneously into two incompatible roles—that of the Warrior Woman, equal to the man and carrying the same responsibilities and tasks; and that of the Lady, a separate entity with totally divergent responsibilities and tasks.

No part of the German woman's life indicates the enormous changes she is experiencing as completely as her new attitudes toward sexual freedom. This is reflected in the world's lowest birthrate as well as in the rapidly rising number of women who believe that premarital coitus is not only beneficial and permissible, but also necessary to the success of a future marriage.

Changes are not limited to sexuality alone, however. Self-confident young Marlene Dietrichs stride through the executive suites atop Germany's towering glass-and-steel office buildings. Women's rights classes are being taught in state-supported night schools around the country. Family laws were radically liberalized in 1973. Divorce by consent is now possible after a year's separation. Teen-agers over fourteen can have legal sexual relations if they have their parents' permission. And a wife has the legal right to work without her husband's consent and to forgo taking his name in marriage if she so desires.

An ingrained resistance to this new woman still exists, of course. An unspoken but powerfully influential belief persists that women lack that extra, all-important quality of *Wille* (will), that dedication and inspiration which makes great musicians and true leaders. There is still a widespread belief that women must submit to the duties of "natural motherhood," a philosophy very clearly expressed in the recent German Constitutional Court ruling against abortion on demand.[2] The importance of motherhood is further underlined by the continuing practice of half-day schooling, which forces women to spend an inordinate amount of their time on childrearing.

But, on the whole, the German woman's transition seems to be progressing amazingly well. It has the conscientious (if half-suspicious) benediction of the male Establishment. It has the wholehearted support of important leaders like Willy Brandt. Its success reminds one of what happened when Chancellor Otto von Bismarck was faced with a widespread challenge from the rising industrial-worker class a century ago. Bismarck was a classic authoritarian patriarch, but he was no fool. He proceeded to set in motion the world's first social-welfare program, gave the workers a limited vote and told everyone how well they were serving the country—before sending them back to the factories. Today Germany is generally thought to have a model worker-management relationship, where at the bargaining table both sides appreciate the other's problems and needs.

If this kind of reasonable give-and-take can be maintained between the sexes, the German dinner-table interplay should continue to be relatively tranquil for quite some time.

Before continuing, we must try to define the German woman. The country itself presents a particularly complex problem. "Germany? But where is it? I cannot find such a country," Schiller once said,[3] and the national boundaries today are even more nebulous. What about East Germany? When one stops to consider historic and linguistic ties, one runs into Austria, the Germanic cantons of Switzerland and even parts of Czechoslovakia. Germany is not like England, Italy and France, where languages set up barriers that coincide more or less with boundaries shown in the atlas.

The German language is vitally important. It means that the writings of

Goethe, Luther, Nietzsche, Kafka, Freud and Jung are all equally accessible in the original, despite the fact that the last three are from Czechoslovakia, Austria and Switzerland, respectively. Language unity has also fostered a common pattern of thinking. The Germanic custom of building vocabulary by lumping root words together supports the *Weltanschauung* philosophy of life that each individual has a "natural" place in a system of "universal order." When children *(Kinder)* know that their room is the *Kinderstübe* (nursery), that they go to school in a *Kindergarten* (preschool), that their sitter is a *Kindermädchen* and that their games are *Kinderspiel*, it is not surprising that they quickly develop the idea that they are minute cogs in a massive Life Plan.

Language affinity is therefore one of the major reasons I have chosen to include in this section information on East Germany, Austria and the Germanic sections of Switzerland. There are two others.

The first is the important influence of the *Weltanschauung* philosophy of life on women throughout the Germanic culture. The concept of a "natural order" leads to the assumption that it is "natural" for the Big to dominate the Little . . . therefore "natural" for father to dominate the family, and "natural" for the husband to dominate the wife.

This "natural" argument is implicit in the opposition to women's equality the world over, but in the Western Hemisphere it takes its most overt form in Germanic cultures where it has been reiterated ad infinitum. Therefore it is here that its disadvantages—and advantages—are most easily highlighted.

The second reason for including information about all the Germanic countries is their common glorification of duty and self-sacrificing obedience. As already noted, this concept is crucial to the role of women in Germany, and the ways it has been interpreted by the Austrian Freud and the Swiss Jung are certainly as important as those of Adler and Reich—not to mention the importance of observations by Austrian teachers, East German housewives and Swiss secretaries.

A complete profile of East Germany, Austria and Germanic Switzerland cannot be included in the limited space of this section, of course. Parallels and discrepancies will simply be used to articulate Germanic traits, but the focus of this section will be West Germany.

2

From Freya to Dietrich

The earliest references to the German woman occurred in oral myths which were recorded later during the era of Christian scribes.

The pantheon of the most ancient Teutonic gods is governed by Wotan, the god of wisdom, who has lost one eye in his search for knowledge. In the mythical tales themselves, however, his sovereignty becomes overshadowed by the brash and explosive acts of his lieutenant, Thor, god of war.

The female goddesses play a decidedly secondary role, the only important ones being Frigga, the goddess of marriage, and Freya, the goddess of youth and love. Wife and Mistress archetypes, both these goddesses are portrayed as possessions of male deities.

When the conquering Romans attempted to superimpose the Latin hierarchy of gods onto the Germanic culture, they drew rough parallels between Frigga and Juno and between Freya and Venus. As a result, the German *Freitag*, which translates into the English "Friday," was the day of the week dedicated to women, just as, in the Latin languages, the same sixth day of the week is dedicated to women and named after Venus.

The Romans found no equivalents for Minerva, goddess of wisdom and the arts, or Diana, goddess of the hunt. The female deities who played such important parts in their everyday life had no Teutonic counterparts. In many Teutonic myths, even Freya and Frigga overlap and blend into one shadowy character drifting along the fringes of the narrative.

The important Gudrun epic presented the first clearly depicted German heroine. The source of this prehistoric myth in major German legends is unknown. Gudrun is a princess betrothed to Herwig of Seeland. Kidnapped by the King of Norway, she steadfastly refuses to marry him, and for thirteen years is kept as a laundry woman. Seeking vengeance, her lover and brother then attack her captor and make him a captive himself. Gudrun then marries Herwig.

Gudrun's two most important virtues—steadfastness and sexual fidelity —were already known to be strong traits of the German woman. As the Roman Tacitus commented sourly, "German women live in a chastity that is impregnable. No one in Germany finds vice amusing."[4]

In later legends, Gudrun evolved into a fierce Warrior Woman, but the most important archetype of that genre as we know her today is the martial queen, Brunhild. The major legend of Brunhild concerns her vow that no man shall win her unless he can conquer her in feats of strength. Since this is impossible, the man who wins her does so through trickery (a friend provides a cloak of invisibility). Although at marriage Brunhild is deprived of the magical source of her strength and her arrogance, the deception is avenged by her allies.

Brunhild turns up consistently throughout both Teutonic and Norse literature. In Wagner's massive tetralogy *Der Ring des Nibelungen* she combines her physical fierceness with implacable jealousy and vengeance, and in her wrath brings about the final scene of *Götterdämmerung*, where all the gods are destroyed by fire.

Lorelei, the beautiful, passive spirit of temptation, is apparently a latecomer to Germanic mythology. Residing on a cliff at a treacherous bend in the Rhine River, she uses her golden hair and her sweet songs to lure sailors to their doom on the shoals below. Of all the important German female archetypes, she is the one who best personifies the malignant Manipulator described by Vilar.

The Age of Chivalry in the twelfth century witnessed the first fundamental revolution in the role of women. At first German poetry speaks only of a woman's longing for the love of a man, since it was considered "unmanly" for a knight to spend his days pining for the love of a woman.

In 1184, the festivities at Mainz celebrating the conferring of knighthood on the man who later became King Heinrich VI marked the first formal appearance of the chivalric codes developed at the court of Eleanor of Aquitaine. This signified the acceptance of the concept of *Frauendienst* (the service of women), which was then duly written into the songs of the *Minnesänger* (the German troubadors or minstrels). One of the best-known of these, Reinman von Hagenau, called "the Nightingale," described love as unfulfilled, by definition, his most famous dictum being, "Love without suffering cannot be." Although Eleanor of Aquitaine's French poets and knights praised man's adoration of woman and love from a distance, in Germany the worship of chastity became an all-pervading obsession.[5]

Roswitha, a contemporary of the early *Minnesänger*, is known as one of the three most important European women writers of the Middle Ages and is Germany's first dramatist. A nun cloistered in a Benedictine convent, Roswitha developed her plays around the lives of the saints and virgins. Again, the Germanic stress on duty and chastity stands in direct contrast to the themes being developed by the contemporary French. Héloïse and Marie de France, the other two important women writers of the era, dealt with more earthly passions in their letters and their *lais* (songs of courtly love).

The emphasis on chastity for men was dropped as the songs of the *Minnesänger* began to speak of a man's right to "pluck the rose" after successful efforts on the jousting fields. With the rise of German Romanticism, a double standard—one for the ordinary woman, one for the Lady—became a convention. Goethe, whose life and work typify the age, went from one inspirational passion to another—Charlotte Buff, Charlotte von Stein, Bettina von Anim, Marrianne von Willemer. All the women were young and intellectual and most of them were wives of good friends. Although Charlotte von Stein refused to be "more than a sister" to him, Goethe's relationships with the others were not so platonic and his philandering caused constant conflict with Christiane, his wife.

Again and again he reiterated the Romantic thesis that women are man's source of creativity and that passionate love is the highest endeavor of humanity. Yet his ideal Lady, Margaret Gretchen, the heroine of his masterpiece, *Faust*, is a paragon of virtue. As the tragedy progresses, she is so overcome with shame and guilt at having been seduced by the protagonist, that she destroys her illegitimate baby, and is, in turn, sentenced to death for murder.

Later her spirit returns to Faust to aid him in his intermittent struggle to free himself from the Devil. She pervades the story as the personification of the forgiving, loving, faithful Lady. The final couplet, written by Goethe only shortly before his death, after he had spent nearly forty years on the work, celebrates her as the embodiment of goodness, *"Das Ewig Weiblich/Zieht uns hinan"* ("Eternal Woman, lead us upwards.")

After Goethe and Schiller, the German Romantic movement was led by a younger group of writers that revolved around one of Goethe's muses, Bettina von Anim. She, too, was an ardent believer in all the tenets of the epoch. One of the reasons she was attracted to the fifty-seven-year-old Goethe was her mother's involvement with the writer a dozen years before her birth. Besides being an accomplished writer, von Anim was also a sculptress and a musician. Together with her husband and her brother, she published one of the most important literary magazines of the time.

The Romantic Movement in Germany was marked by several important women, although none achieved the fame that Mary Shelley enjoyed in England, after she wrote *Frankenstein*. In music, Cosima d'Agoult was one of the most powerful personalities. The daughter of Comtesse d'Agoult and her lover, Franz Liszt, Cosima grew up in the center of the music community. In 1857, she married Hans Guido von Bülow, a man who had been so impressed by one of her father's performances that he dropped his studies in law to take up music. He became an outstanding pianist and is known as the first of the modern virtuoso conductors.

Cosima left him in 1869 and a year later married the *enfant terrible* of the time, Richard Wagner. Possessing an iron will and dedicating herself entirely to her husband's career, she set to work organizing the Bayreuth festival. From the time of Wagner's death until her own at the age of ninety-three, she was the prime force behind the festival.

Even during the height of the Romantic Era, when German women in certain circles enjoyed intellectual status and sexual freedom, there were several important fields closed to them. Most significantly there were no women composers or philosophers of note.

Although women have not achieved recognition in these fields throughout the Western Hemisphere, the void is particularly distressing in Germany because of its special reverence for composers and philosophers. Western musical heritage is dominated by such luminaries as Beethoven, Bach, Brahms, Mozart and Wagner. In Western philosophy and theology, Luther, Marx, Kant, Hegel, Nietzsche and Schopenhauer all decisively influence contemporary thought.

Unfortunately these ranks not only lack women, they include several of the most vociferous and dedicated misogynists of Western culture.

Before the Age of Chivalry swept Germany in the twelfth century, women had been considered man's helpmeet, his "natural companion." The ancient Romans noted that the German wife would take up arms alongside her husband and that both of them preferred to die rather than to be taken captive. In folk tales, the German woman was sometimes cast as an evil witch, but most often her confrontations with men were open and direct.

In the legendary context of Brunhild, the Warrior Woman, then, it is difficult to understand why a woman never became leader of the country. The answer lies partially in the German assimilation of the concept of the Lady, with its assumption that women as "the Other" lack the *Wille* to concern themselves in men's power games, and instead have a separate realm of their own to tend.

Another important factor, however, concerned the peculiar stresses and demands made on the German leader. Although the monarchies of Germany were based on heredity, each succeeding ruler had to be elected by the regional dukes, and automatic hereditary succession was often threatened.[6] Once a leader was elected, however, his power was thought to be more totalitarian than that of the English or French monarch, and it was believed that the German candidate for the throne therefore had to be a particularly commanding and popular male.

Only once did a woman come close to ruling the Germans. In 1713, the powerful Hapsburg Emperor Charles VI forced all of his supporters to sign the Pragmatic Sanction in which they agreed to recognize his daughter, Maria Theresa, as his heir.

The German-Prussian sector of the Austro-Hungarian Empire broke its word as soon as Maria Theresa ascended the throne, and, with a bloody seven-year war, was able to partition off what is now Poland and much of Germany. Her Hungarian subjects were also deeply suspicious of a female ruler, and a unique arrangement was worked out whereby she reigned in that country with the title of king. Throughout the rest of her vast dominion, which included what is now Czechoslovakia, Austria, Yugoslavia, Rumania and Bulgaria, her authority as a queen was accepted, and her reign of forty years was marked by agricultural reform, great advances in architecture and music and an exceptionally moral royal court.

The last field where the German woman has historically lacked status is one of the most surprising; she has received little social support in her role as the mother.

Although fertility was considered a virtue among the ancient goddesses, there was no personification of Motherly Love. No goddesses or epic her-

198 *The Female Factor*

oines were joyfully benevolent or heroically protective toward their children. Nor were there any who commanded their young, demanded their unceasing filial loyalty or tore them to bits in fits of jealous fury. Later, when Catholicism pervaded the area, there was no preoccupation with the Virgin Mary on the Italian scale. Among the children's fairy tales, the child's friend and benefactor was almost invariably male.

The present century has seen a change in that image. Bertolt Brecht portrayed the unforgettable heroine, *Mother Courage*, eternally dragging her children and her wagon through the war-ravaged land. Günter Grass depicted the mysterious and eternal figure of the grandmother of the potato fields. Erich Maria Remarque linked the Mother irrevocably to the ideals of Home and Peace.

But the German mother who appears in these works is neither good nor evil. She is beyond questions of morality. She suckles her young blindly, without *Wille* or effort, and filial obedience and devotion flow back to her in the same fashion—naturally. Hers is still a job for the dutiful, not the passionate.

The single most important change in women's roles during this century has taken place in the area of political status. German women won universal suffrage in 1919, one year before the Americans, nearly ten years before the English, and more than twenty-five years before the French and Italians. During the twenties, the German woman was considered the most liberated in the West. She also played an important part in her national legislature.

It was during this era that Rosa Luxemburg emerged. Small, crippled, Polish-born—as unlikely a Brunhild as Hitler was an *Übermensch* (superman)—she posed a frightening threat to the mainstream of German politics. A passionate orator and pamphleteer, she was a Marxist who had taken part in the 1905 uprising in Russia. Acquiring a German passport through marriage, she set to work organizing the German Communist Spartacus Party, and, with Karl Liebknecht, edited the party newspaper.

She was jailed for her political activities during World War I, and soon after her release, was picked up again by soldiers for her part in a Spartacist uprising in Berlin. All of Europe was edgy about the repercussions of the Russian Revolution and on the way to prison, Luxemburg was murdered by her captors.

Ulrike Meinhof represented this same archetype—the Warrior Woman who attacks the Establishment and shakes it to the very roots.

The majority of today's women who have achieved power, however, have done so legally and with the acceptance of male society. Women hold office as the German equivalent to the U.S. Speaker of the House, as one of the seven judges who constitute the German counterpart to the United States Supreme Court, as the Minister of Health and the Family. Beate Uhse is one of postwar Germany's million-dollar-a-year business success stories; Hildegard Knef hits the best-seller list everywhere, and Marlene Dietrich continues her peerless career as an international entertainer.

Early in the seventies, the German clothing industry reported that in the past twenty years women had gained half an inch in the bust, lost an inch and a half in the hips, and grown three and a half inches taller. Obviously, the German woman's shift in status is being mirrored by a change in her physical image as well.

There are still no major women composers or philosophers in Germany, nor has any woman candidate been taken seriously for the post of Chancellor. But all the roles that once lay outside her sphere of "natural order" now seem accessible to today's tall, slim Brunhild, and the duties of spouse and mother no longer appear mandatory.

3

The Joys of the Work Ethic—
The *Hausfrau*

The marketing director of a well-known American firm that manufactures self-polishing car wax once mentioned that his company faced a good deal of trouble when it first went into Germany. "There was nothing like us on the market, and we thought we'd be selling hand over fist. We had a strong introductory publicity campaign on television and in the papers. And nothing happened. We sat on our full stocks for a month or more in amazement, and then called in a German marketing man, who told us quite plainly that German customers are not interested in saving themselves work. They like to work. The only thing that sells them is the idea that a new product combined with lots of elbow grease will get a superior shine.

"So we ditched the 'nothing to it' ads, and had our models roll up their sleeves and look like they were really working at that old polishing. And then we had close-ups of the shine that resulted. Within days, stocks began to move.

"We've been able to stress polishing ease these last couple of years, particularly because it's considered 'practical,' but when we first came, 'effortlessness' was always equated with 'quality-lessness.' "

Today's German housewife buys self-polishing wax for her furniture and her floors as well as for her car. She apparently responds to the concept of the helpful "white tornado" in her kitchen as avidly as the rest of her Euro-American sisters.

But visiting a German household, one realizes that "ease" still has a bad name in Germany. It is equated with "laziness" and "second-rate" performance. The concept that anything worth doing is worth doing well still reigns. It's obvious the first morning at 7:00 A.M., when one's hostess begins tossing mattresses over windowsills to air them out, dusting her walls and ceilings with her bright pink nylon wall brush and drilling her children on their homework. She uses self-polishing wax, true, but once a month she has a barrage of other liquids to deep-clean her floors (under the rugs, as well) before replacing the hard wax finish.

Examples of the worship of the tidy household are endless. One American found himself ousted from a German home because he had put his cigarette out in the dessert plate instead of the ashtray. An English resident comments that whenever German women friends are visiting, they seem compelled to do a little housework from time to time, just to release nervous energy.[7] Some German families will demand that everyone take off his or her shoes and wear house slippers provided at the door to avoid scuffing floors. And children are expected to coexist with gleaming battalions of crystalware and tiny china animals adorning tables and sideboards.

The importance of the Work Ethic is legendary in all sectors of German society. Max Weber, the German sociologist, was the first to criticize the concept in his 1904 thesis, "The Protestant Ethic and the Spirit of Capitalism."[8] Before the rest of the world had fully realized that the Work Ethic existed, Weber was tracing it back to Martin Luther and the Protestant Reformation, and denouncing its effect.

His complaints have proved ineffectual. In the 1970s, as in every decade since World War II, Germany continues to have the most consistently growing GNP and the lowest rate of man-hours lost through strikes of any other country.[9] A survey of Swiss between the ages of fifteen and twenty-five reveals that a full 40 percent love to work, another 26 percent are "satisfied" with working and only 20 percent admit that they might like to quit if there were some other way to support themselves.[10] West German Federal President Walter Scheel's best-selling song *"Hoch auf dem gelben Wagen"* ("High Up on the Yellow Wagon") states the message clearly: "Diligence goes forward."

On its most basic level, the Work Ethic as it is expressed in Germany,

Scandinavia and the United States is quite simple. "Work" is first defined as any effort that contributes to society as a whole (as opposed to a "hobby" that contributes to the individual alone). People receive status for making the group contribution. More than money, they are rewarded with private smiles and public accolades. There is a constant reiteration of the belief that everyone who matters works and that, while working, people experience the fullest kind of living.

Those submerged in the Work Ethic *do* mutter from time to time that it isn't universally true. All societies have their rebels. But on the whole people raised in a society dedicated to the Work Ethic feel most satisfied with themselves and most content with their lives when they are doing their work well.

This is in direct contrast with the Italian culture, where no one is imbued with belief in the joys of working for society, and also with that of England, where the Work Ethic is ingrained only in the middle class.

German joy in working is impressive. Gymnastic classes in neighborhood sports centers have an aura of religious fervor. Sex manuals recommend positions and activities requiring awesome agility and feats of strength. Everyone talks about his or her own job, and is interested in the mechanics of other people's occupations. Job titles are often used with a person's name—not only on introduction, but in direct address.

In this environment, the German housewife quite naturally views her profession with Calvinistic seriousness. The workday usually begins with only a coffee and a roll. Father and children have early and different departure times, making big family breakfasts the exception rather than the rule. Once everyone is out of the house, the special task of the housewife's day comes next, for example: Monday, washing; Tuesday, ironing; Wednesday, washing windows; Thursday, washing woodwork; Friday, polishing the silver and/or the furniture; Saturday, extra preparations for the Sunday dinner.

Then the housewife sits down to her midmorning snack. In the past women went through several *Würste* (frankfurters), bread and a salad at 10:30 A.M., and then ate a full meal at one o'clock. Such massive consumption has gone out of style with the younger women, who now indulge only in a midmorning cup of coffee, or perhaps a slice of cheese, if they haven't eaten breakfast.[11]

After this moment of relaxation, it's time to review the shopping list to make sure that all unusual details like cleaning, banking, repairs and knife-sharpening are under control. Carefully ticking off one's duties is as important a tradition in the German household as it is in the French.

The list is then put away. Like the Swede and the American, the German woman prefers to do all her shopping once a week. She has the mammoth hypermarkets to accommodate this kind of shopping and, more important, she is more likely than most of her European sisters to have a car at her disposal.

Shopping is ordinarily done in the afternoon, after the housewife has shed her housedress and her house shoes. She does not exactly dress up for the occasion, but she does put on hose and a dress. If she is over thirty and it is winter, she will most certainly wear a hat—usually a practical type of fedora.

Lunch is hot, and quite often includes soup and another course. Although only a few businessmen in the south of Germany manage to make it home, this is an important meal to be shared with the children. They have returned from school not just to eat, but for the rest of the day.

The German half-day school means that, for the great majority of women, afternoons are arranged around the children, their homework and after-school classes. All Germanic countries have a widespread *Volkshochschule* (extension school) program operating in every neighborhood, where mother and children spend one or two afternoons a week learning everything from flower arranging to Freudian psychology. Although the state school offers some art and music, most of this teaching is left to a *Volkshochschule* that charges only a small fee.

After class, the woman returns home to finish preparing supper, the major meal of the day—despite a five o'clock snack break. German cooking is more arduous than the French. Meat cooks for hours until it drops from the bone. It is then chopped and mixed with other ingredients. Soups simmer for days on end. Dumplings must be made far in advance and chilled before cooking. Strudel dough is one of the most time-consuming in the world to make. One woman told me her strawberry frappé was quite easy—just berries and sugar. "Naturally you have to whip it at least three hours, if you do it by hand," she added casually. "I used to give it to the children to finish, until we got our mixer. Now the machine takes care of it in forty-five minutes."

Mixers are not the only things that make today's cooking faster and easier. The German woman takes advantage of frozen Findus fish and Birds Eye corn. She uses dumpling mixes and dried potato pancake flakes.

But her husband is a demanding man who can polish off three fryers at a sitting, and he is particularly partial to homemade desserts. Sumptuous *Sacher Torte*, tart *Apfelstrudel*, heaps of plum dumplings topped with buttered crumbs and cinnamon—that's the way he likes to finish his meal. As a result, the German wife spends more time cooking than any other woman in Western Europe.

After supper, children of both sexes are expected to carry out household duties, and the husband may help with washing the dishes. Except for evenings spent with family and friends, the majority of couples are in bed by ten o'clock.

The legendary diligent *Hausfrau* receives appreciation and recognition in Germany. Husbands, friends—even children—are aware of the demands of the post, and are quick to praise a job well done—particularly a good meal. (They are even quicker to criticize a job left undone.) The Swiss go so far as to issue the Federally Diplomaed Housewife title to women passing an annual examination.

The encroachment of self-polishing wax and frozen *Sacher Torte* is subtly changing all this, however. The German woman has been suspicious of the quick 'n' easy commodities, which shift status from her to the manufacturer who so cleverly packaged them for her, but she has not been able to resist the appeals to her *praktisch* (practical) nature. Feeling outclassed by the speed and efficiency of the mechanized household (one brand of built-in kitchen units is even called *SieMatic* [The Automatic Woman]), she often complains of feeling guilty and anxious because she is able to finish all the work her mother did in less than one-third the time . . . and then has nothing constructive to do with the rest of the day.

This is a problem facing women everywhere in industrialized nations, and the German woman, like others, is more and more likely to fill her need for status and participation in the community by looking for work outside the home. All too often, this only gives her the opportunity to work on the very machines that give her time to get out of the house—an arrangement that robs her of much community status and also cheats her of the satisfaction of making her own personal creative effort. The steadily diminishing status of housework is a particularly salient problem for the work-oriented German woman, and so far she has not been able to deal with it at all well.

Predictably, the Germans work hard at their leisure activities, too. Weekends are filled with car and household repairs, although a few hours are devoted to sports. Vacations are dedicated to improving health and vitality. Germans are fanatic spa and nudist-camp devotees, and the weeks spent in these resorts are taken up with austere schedules designed around rigorous "work yourself back to health" regimes.

As *Newsweek* reported in 1971, West Germany has one of the briefest vacation periods in Europe. By law, blue-collar workers get three and a half weeks off, white-collar workers a month, and some government employees are entitled to six weeks. Only Americans take shorter vacations. The report went on, "most Americans must work nearly seven years for the same employer before they can claim as much as three weeks' vacation, [and] women, who tend to change jobs more frequently and thus accumulate less seniority, average only two weeks."

Evening leisure time in Germany is often spent watching "Gunsmoke" and the *Deutches Rundfunk* (German state television company) documentaries, which are similar to the in-depth investigations of the BBC. Only a few people spend their time reading. The majority of women I talked with told me they did handiwork sewing projects while watching television.

A number refused to watch TV for entertainment at all. "We watch the news and the documentaries, but those American adventure stories really aren't worth much," they comment. Instead, couples go for an evening of hiking or bicycling. Some are enrolled in unisex gym classes. Everyone who doesn't have a sauna wants one.

The emphasis on the body demands daily and strenuous workouts as well as the vacation-time *Blitzkrieg*. Although slimness has become a widespread ideal only in the past dozen years, the Germans have always equated health and strength with status. It is a mark of the German woman that she has not allowed the Lady mystique to infringe on her health. Although in the past women submitted to whalebone waist cinchers and indulged in the sighs and fainting spells of the helpless, the majority has always firmly believed that good eating and good exercise constitute the best route to a happy life.

Apart from wife-husband joint exercise regimens, relaxation is most often a group affair. Germans entertain in the home, but they also like to meet friends at a nearby *Gasthaus* (inn), where everyone consumes *Würste* (sausages) and beer and *Gemütlichkeit* (hospitality). The big beer halls in Southern Germany are particularly famous for this kind of congenial evening.

Several characteristics set these establishments apart from the pubs of England and the cocktail lounges of the United States. First of all, they are family-oriented. The wife accompanies her husband, and they are usually joined by several other couples. On weekends, they sometimes take their children, who are welcomed with big mugs of nonalcoholic cider. Since all tables rapidly become occupied, it is inevitable that new couples will double up as the evening proceeds. Jammed in, side by side on benches, people strike up conversations easily. The loud, rollicking bands of the large halls periodically play pieces that force people into physical contact with their neighbors, like the *"Einz, Zwei, Drei"* ("One, Two, Three") song, where each firmly links elbows with the next, and the entire benchload sways emphatically to the beat of the music.

At the popular camping grounds, Saturday evening get-togethers also feature "New Partner" dances where one is required to pair off with someone one doesn't know, and "Ladies' Choice" dances, which also encourage new acquaintanceships. Most people use these occasions to tease an acquaintance or make jokes for the crowd in general, rather than to exchange partners, but the atmosphere is light and strangers talk avidly among themselves, as everyone discusses the antics of the one show-off who is actually dancing with her new partner in solitary splendor.

The pursuit of *Kultur* is yet another demanding area of German life. When the German woman goes out, she is more likely to go to the opera, a concert or the theater than to a film. The number of tickets sold to filmgoers in Germany has dropped 500 percent since 1954.[12] In the meantime, the state-supported opera companies have developed impressively, and Germany now has sixty opera houses in fifty-eight cities. The government further contributes heavily to the two hundred legitimate theaters in the country.[13]

German appreciation of music is evident everywhere. People in general are avid fans of the opera and symphony, and they also demand a high standard from their church choirs and organists. The city of Vienna sells over twice as many tickets to opera and concerts as it does to theaters.[14] Esteem takes an odd twist at discotheques. German teen-agers attend in great masses, but the crowds are always serious. A few may sway to the music, and a festival with live performers rouses them to clap, but most audiences are silent and serious, in direct contrast to their singing, stamping elders in the beer halls.

The layout of German villages and houses reflects the "home is your castle" mentality of the Anglo-Saxons. Despite the fact that the cold northern climate works in the favor of apartments with their more efficient heating systems, Germans, like the Americans and the English, prefer living in one-family units.

The most desirable home includes a surrounding yard, where people are more inclined to exercise and sunbathe than to garden. The single-family home is visible throughout all German-speaking countries. Mammoth cities, like Frankfurt and Hamburg, with their towering office-building central sections, are as house-oriented as Los Angeles.[15]

The entrance hall of a German home gives easy access to the living room. A few German architects have followed the American pattern of dispensing with the entrance hall altogether, so that a guest enters immediately into the center of the family. Sometimes the kitchen door also leads off the entrance, but this is kept closed. Surprisingly enough, the German woman does not like to be seen working at the stove, apparently because she does not want to display her kitchen except when it is in perfect condition.

The living room is dominated by a large picture window overlooking the front yard. The German family is more open to its surrounding community than the reclusive French. This makes for more neighborliness, but leaves everyone more vulnerable to neighborly criticism.

In Southern Germany, the living room is sometimes still outfitted with the giant tile *Kochofen* (warming oven), where everyone can warm themselves. These heat-retaining units are built with sturdy round shapes, and more than one person has remarked how "motherly" they seem, with their quiet, dependable warmth. The living room is the place to talk with friends, and also the place where the family often eats and watches television, and where the children do their homework.

All the rooms in the house are carefully decorated and cared for. Visitors are often shown around the entire house, just as in England and America.

Parents have the largest bedroom in the house. Children often double up, or even sleep on a couch. Their second-class status in the family is reflected in the strict rules against them leaving their belongings anywhere but in their own rooms. There are no toys tucked under sofas, no drawings hung over the *Kochofen*. The home belongs to the adults. That's the "natural" way of things.

4

The Joys of the Work Ethic—
The Career Woman

The German woman who works outside the home has an impressive history. Not only did her ancient forebears till the fields and take up the sword, but during the feminist ferment of a hundred years ago, the most clearly articulated women's movement was in Germany. While women in other countries were fighting primarily for equal voting rights, the Germans were zeroing in on equal work rights. This was in keeping, of course, with the status of work in German society as a whole.

Karl Marx is the name most often associated with the view that work is the only valid basis for the exchange of money. Sixteen years after the appearance of the first volume of the monumental *Das Kapital*, August Bebel published his *Woman and Socialism*. In the views of one critic: "No such book had ever come before the reading public, and no such book has gone into battle for the working woman on so many fronts since. . . . It took up aspects of the 'woman question' never discussed at that time in polite society—women's sexuality, for example, and prostitution—and it presented a mass of data and arguments in favor of woman's economic and personal independence and in support of her capabilities.''[16]

A year later, in 1884, Friedrich Engels published *The Origin of the Family, Private Property and the State*. In it, he theorized that a matriarchy was the natural state of humankind, and that it had preceded the Western patriarchy, in which the father, in effect, "owned" the family. Castigating the resultant capitalism as unnatural and defective, he stressed the necessity of economic equality for women. His is still one of the seminal works in the libraries of feminists the world over.

The German working women's organization itself was fired by Clara Zetkin, who first threw herself into politics in 1881. She fought on two fronts; on the one hand she condemned the traditional "patriarchal division of work," which exploited all women who were doing unpaid labor in the home. On the other, she refused to join with middle-class suffragettes, since she feared that, having so much to lose because of their economic security, they would accept too many compromises with the Establishment.

In 1919, as the Weimar Republic was being formed after the conclusion of World War I and German women were gaining universal suffrage, Zetkin was elected to the national legislature. She remained in office until 1932, and that year, at the age of seventy-five, she presided over the opening of the Reichstag as its oldest member. But already the Weimar Government was losing the battle against Hitler and the National Socialist German Workers' Party with its absolute dictum about women as second-class citizens. Hitler was to dominate the German Government completely by 1933, and the issue of women's-right-to-work equality was not to be a major concern for nearly forty years.

Hitler's dictates on women, however, were not as totally effective as they would seem. Under his regime, many women who never would have thought of leaving home to work were wrested from their sheltered nests by the needs of the war machine, which had removed their men to the front.

Germany did not quickly reverse this situation after World War II. As in the rest of Europe, not enough soldiers returned home. Every pair of hands was needed to restore order and German women responded with typical diligence and determination.

The result was the *Wirtshaftswunder* (German Economic Miracle), which has been cited so often that international financial experts no longer bother to note that Germany has the highest monetary reserves of any major industrial nation nor that its GNP has doubled between 1965 and 1973.[17] Currently two-thirds of the German families own their home, a 1500 cc automobile and a color television set.[18] They also have eight million women in the German work force—the largest number of any of the Common Market countries.[19]

Beate Uhse, one of the most successful postwar executives of Europe, highlights the Brunhild archetype so prevalent in the contemporary German business world.

Daughter of the first woman to receive a doctorate of medicine under the Kaiser, Uhse is a Prussian and an ex-Luftwaffe pilot, who tested the first batch of Messerschmitts. She has had two husbands and three children. When the Russians moved into Berlin in 1945, she took her three-year-old son, Klaus, and two wounded soldiers (her pilot husband had been killed in battle) and flew to Schleswig-Holstein, where she was forced to land when the plane ran out of fuel. Her home and her parents' agricultural business had been left behind, and the English confiscated the airplane.

She started her new life selling puppets and toys made by a peasant friend, and giving English lessons. (She had studied in London.) Soon she found that many of her friends were worried about birth control, so she wrote a booklet on the Ogino and Knaus rhythm method. Thirty thousand copies at two marks apiece quickly sold out.

Ten more books followed, of which *The Book of a Thousand Positions* sold ten times as many copies as the first. Uhse became involved in distributing her books, and then moved into direct-consumer outlets. From there came the idea of adding other things besides books to her merchandise—aphrodisiacs, creams, erotic records and films. Thus, over twenty-five years ago began the world's first sex shop, called simply "Beate Uhse."

Today, at fifty-three, Uhse arrives at her large and luxurious office at 7:15 every morning to oversee the company with its million-dollar-a-year turnover and its 260 employees. In her free time she gardens, goes scuba diving and fishing, and pilots her private plane. Her second husband, Ernst Walter Rotermund, is asking for a divorce citing infidelity and demanding a settlement of $300,000. Uhse says that at this moment in her life she finds the most important thing "is to follow an activity which fully satisfies me—in other words, I love to work."[20]

With her short-cropped hair, her easy ironic smile, her casual shirtwaist dresses hanging loosely on a limber body, her offhand acceptance of being photographed in the nude (she is a nudist) or in an old sweat shirt and Bermudas, she seems to have made the transition from the traditional "natural order" role of the *Hausfrau* to that of the modern "professional" with the ease of a salmon slipping from the river into the sea.

This is exactly the way she defines herself. It was perfectly "natural" for her, she says, to take on such a demanding and varied life. With the mother she had, the training she had and her love of work, it would have been "unnatural" for her to settle down to a life of simply keeping house.

Beate Uhse is a familiar, vibrant New Brunhild presence throughout West Germany. Every Beate Uhse shop is a form of self-advertisement, and she is constantly featured in magazines and on television talk shows. Observers maintain that she is better known in her homeland than any current German actress.

The material advantages to be won through arduous application of the Work Ethic can also be seen in other German-speaking cultures. Although the East German standard of living is 30 percent below West Germany's, it still boasts the highest per capita income among the Communist states. Average salaries, in fact, have already surpassed Italy's and Ireland's and are close to England's. The country, which is smaller than Cuba, has a larger GNP than Hitler's prewar Reich, in spite of the fact that there was no Marshall Plan to boost the economy. Instead, the East Germans have paid over $15 billion in direct reparations to the Soviet Union.[21] (The West Germans have paid over $14 billion in reparations to members of the Jewish community.)

East German women have also played a decisive role in their country's economic blooming. Eighty-four percent of the adult women work. They make up 46 percent of the labor force—a larger percentage than that of any other country except the Soviet Union.[22]

Although Austria's economy has not moved ahead as strongly in the past twenty years as that of the two Germanies, it is important to note that the country has the highest rate of female employment—41.3 percent—of any Western country except Finland. Of all the Germanic countries, only Switzerland has a low percentage of women in the work force. It appears that without a war to jolt the economy seriously, Switzerland has remained entrenched in nineteenth-century inhibitions about the woman leaving the home.

Switzerland is also the notable exception among the Germanic states for its lack of legislative support for the female work force. While the Swiss are busy awarding Federal Housewife diplomas, Austria and East Germany have set up extensive child-care centers. The West German system is still inadequate, but manages to incorporate 22 percent of the children of working mothers—the highest in the EEC. The Germanic states also have equality clauses in their constitutions and paid pregnancy leaves in their laws.[23]

Since school lasts only until one o'clock, the problem of what to do with children in the afternoon is a major issue in both West Germany and

Austria. It is being solved only partially by after-school state programs. Citizens' groups have stepped into the gap in some cases.

In others, a simple solution is being applied. Grandmother takes care of the children.[24] This sounds common enough, but in Germany, Grandmother is paid for her work. At the moment, her wages are small—approximately $50 a month—but the concept is important because it not only provides flexible, individual care for the children, but also channels funds directly to the older woman and gives her a creative, responsible place in society.

Former West German Chancellor Willy Brandt is a champion of women's equality. Along with pressing for liberalized Family Laws, he personally backed the December 1972 election of Annemarie Renger as President of the Bundestag (the lower house of Parliament)—a position equivalent to Speaker of the House in the United States. She ranks as the third highest officer in Germany, behind Walter Scheel who is Federal President.

German women have made an impressive mark in the legal profession. Wiltraut Rupp von Brünneck belongs to the exclusive club of four women Supreme Court judges in the world. (The other three are in Scandinavia.) Following in her footsteps, more and more young German women are entering law, and Ursula Dreisback, at twenty-five, is one of the youngest judges in the country.

The most powerful woman in Germany today is Maria Weber, who began her working life as a seamstress, and later became involved in her local union. In the early seventies, she was the first woman ever to be elected as one of the three-member ruling committee of the Deutchen Gewerkschaftsbunder (the German Amalgamated Workers Union). With 7 million members, the DGB is not only thirty times the size of any other union organization in Germany, it is the second-largest labor-union confederation in the world. (First comes England's Trades Union Congress with 9.5 million.)

In other fields, Countess Marion Doenhoff was for years editor in chief of the influential *Die Zeit*, Germany's equivalent of the New York *Times*, and won the 1971 German Peace Prize for her books which urged "an understanding between all nations in East and West."

In traditional business, the vast family dynasties, like those of Krupp and Flick, occasionally produced women like Claire Stinnes, who kept an iron-fisted control over her husband's giant real-estate empire from the time of his death in 1924 until her own in 1973 when she was one hundred and one.

Today's women head businesses everywhere. Ursula Brinkmann, who started as an accountant, is now president of the German branch of Massey-Ferguson, with sixteen hundred employees under her. Dr. Elisabeth Noelle-Neumann heads the Institut für Demoskopie, Germany's largest pollster organization. Lily Joens is president of a Düsseldorf instrument factory.

Once one looks past the outstanding examples, however, the picture of German women takes on a decidedly less optimistic cast. Despite a fairly good record of women in high-level government posts, there are only thirty women members in the 518-member West German Bundestag—down from the high of forty-eight members in 1957. In East Germany, there are 159 female Parliament members out of 500 seats, but only twenty-two women on the 181-member Central Committee, and only one, Margot Honecker, is a Cabinet minister. She happens to be the wife of Erich Honecker, the boss of the East German Communist Party.

A dearth of women is evident in *Capital*, Germany's influential equivalent to *Business Week*, which only rarely uses photographs of women, even in the advertisements for typewriters. It shows up clearly in comparative statistics on the professions. Evelyne Sullerot, the French sociologist, found that, in the sixties, percentages of women in various fields broke down as follows: In engineering—West Germany, 1; France, 3.7; Soviet Union, 37. In law—United States, 3; West Germany, 5; Austria, 7; France, 19; Soviet Union, 38. In medicine—United States, 6; Austria, 18; West Germany, 20; France, 22; England, 25; Soviet Union, 76.

Current East German statistics indicate that women there comprise 33 percent of all doctors and lawyers and 11 percent of mayors.[25] This sounds impressive until one remembers that nearly one out of every two in the East German work force is a woman.

Repression begins in the schools. Germany does not have a high level of university-educated people. A recent survey found that there are nearly as many vacancies in American universities—500,000—as there are German students—667,022. Proportionately, Germany has one of the smallest university student bodies on the Continent.

Elitism is coupled with *de facto* misogyny. Evelyne Sullerot's statistics pointed to the fact that only one out of every five Swiss students was a woman, one out of every four German and Austrian students and one out of every three East German students. In the United States, France, Soviet Union and Finland, the ratio is approximately 1:1.

Second-rate status is reflected in wages. Nearly half of all German workingwomen earn less than $175 per month, another 48 percent earn between $175 and $350, and a minute 4 percent exceed that figure. Yet the *average* German working wage is $370. These figures are going up with inflation, but the proportions remain the same. It is obvious why women's rights groups in Germany consider equal pay for equal work a primary goal.

Despite the predictions and promises of Zetkin, Bebel and Engels, the East German situation is no better. *Time* found that three-fourths of the women workers were "still stuck in the bottom half of the nation's wage structure." Sociologist Hilda Scott, in her extensive and thoughtful report *Does Socialism Liberate Women?*, paints a bleak picture of the East German workingwoman, 57 percent of whom have three or more children at home. The majority reported they never got enough sleep and rarely had any free time.[26] Although they and their sisters in other Socialist countries enter professional fields, they are often not paid on an equal level with men; usually they must interrupt their careers during their children's first few years; and they are almost never tapped for the top posts in management or government.

Dissatisfaction with these inequities is being voiced more and more frequently. An East Berlin woman complains bitterly, "Equality means my husband and I have equal rights. Equal rights means that we both work at full-time jobs. Then I clean the house and take care of the children—while he sits in front of the TV set and drinks beer." And West German politician Aenne Brauksiep echoes, "We can't begin intense work for the party when we're young, because we have to stay at home. When a woman finally puts foot in the Bundestag, the paint has already worn thin."[27]

And yet, the German Women's Liberation Movement is neither widely organized nor particularly militant. There seem to be two reasons for this. First has been the ability of the German Establishment to muffle these protests in that wily Bismarckian style of giving way on everything but the essentials. German men are currently bowing politely to the proponents of woman's equality. They voice strong approval for equal pay in their own legislation and in Common Market pronouncements from Brussels. The German Zeitschriftenverlage pollsters have even profusely apologized in full-page, four-color ads in *Quick*, the German equivalent of *Look* magazine, for having committed the *"männlichen Fehler* (male chauvinist mistake) of asking readers to "Write their *man* in Bonn."[28]

The second thing that seems to hold women back in Germany is that ubiquitous feeling that women do not have the *Wille* to be exceptional. *Wille* is a much more important concept in the German language than it is in English, and is constantly cited as the trait that sets leaders apart from others. *Wille* is a passionate, driving, inarticulate force that catapults the ordinary diligent and dutiful person to the top where decisions are made. As long as *Wille* is considered essentially a male characteristic, the psychological barriers against more than a few token German women making it to the top will remain high.

5

Memoirs of a Dutiful Mother

Nowhere in German society is the woman's traditionally dutiful and self-sacrificing nature more evident than in her role as mother. No one would think of denying that the German mother is important to the family and society, but her responsibility is to raise her children not as she sees fit, but as her husband and society instruct her to do.

The German father has an iron grasp on his children. He has completely assumed the role of their teacher and leader. He does not share ultimate responsibilities for his offspring with his wife or with school authorities. His children no longer address him as *Herr Vater* (Mister Father) as was done in Hitler's generation, but *Vater* is still the arbiter of punishment and reward. He is the one who checks homework and signs report cards. He is the one who lays down the rules about bedtime and television privileges. He is the one who adjudicates when siblings quarrel.

The importance of the father in the child's life is constantly emphasized by society. Family snapshots show children flocked around the father, with the mother off to one side. In parks, one sees nearly as many fathers as mothers with toddlers. In summer, swimming pools are dominated by fathers patiently coaching their offspring.

Eltern, the German equivalent of *Parents' Magazine*, devotes a fourth of its pages to articles of "particular importance" to fathers, and the titles of these pieces are marked by a red star on the index page. *Eltern* pages are full of ads aimed at fathers and touting Conti Stahlgürtle tires and Opel Rekord II cars. *Eltern* cartoons depict Father pretending to shake his fist at a tiny baby sitting on a potty, with the caption, *"Geschäftshilfe"* ("Business Help").

Advertisements in all the media contrast directly with those in Italy. *Vater*, with son in backpack, is off to catch a Lufthansa flight. *Vater* and son are fishing in a quiet, nostalgic place, *Vater* wisely wearing Polaroid sunglasses. In Italy, the children flock around Mamma, and even photographic companies advertise with pictures of a woman cuddling her "newborn" camera.

The German ideal of who is to take ultimate responsibility for the child differs starkly from that of Italy as well. After six-year-old Mirko Panattoni was safely returned home by kidnappers in Italy, he was photographed for the newspapers sleeping in his mother's bed, his mother in her slip lying beside him, smiling and protective. When teen-ager Evelyn Jahn went through the same experience in Austria, she was photographed being hugged by her father.[29]

Finally, the German father feels a personal failure if his offspring turn out badly. The dynamics of patriarchy work both ways—if the father is to have full control, he must take full responsibility. As the family leader, he must put the family's interest above his own. The child belongs to him, but he also belongs to it.

Robert Dostal typifies the ideal father whose work and hopes come to a tragic end. Dostal was an Austrian railway man whose son became involved in crime. Finally, after an impetuous escape attempt, the son was killed in a gun battle with the police. Dostal immediately committed suicide.

Acceptance of patriarchal responsibility as the natural corollary of patriarchal power is reflected in society as well. When five men drowned after an abortive NATO paratrooper practice exercise in September 1974, the West German Army officer in charge of safety for the mission hanged himself. When a large German travel agency collapsed in 1972, leaving twenty thousand tourists stranded, the German Government didn't simply tell everyone they should have booked regular flights as the American Government told American tourists who were similarly stranded. The German

Transport Industry immediately stepped in and paid for Lufthansa flights back home for "their" tourists.[30] And when one of Willy Brandt's close friends and confidants turned out to be a spy, the chancellor promptly resigned.

With the ultimate rewards and responsibilities of parenthood resting on the father, the position of the mother is secondary and supportive. Her role is equivalent to that of the top sergeant in the army; she translates her husband's decisions into day-to-day reality. Her characteristics are "natural" dutifulness and diligence. His are decisiveness and passion—the characteristics of *Wille*.

As already mentioned, the Mother prototype of the past was only vaguely sketched. In German folklore and fairy tales, a persistent theme was the plight of the motherless child. The mother's death in childbirth or from the multitude of "childbed fevers" was, after all, a common fact of life, and the Cinderella and Snow White stories were well known throughout most of Europe.

The two powerful older woman archetypes who do turn up in these tales are consistently evil—the Witch and the Wicked Stepmother. Often the two overlap, becoming doubly vindictive and fearsome.

A feature of the Germanic tales is that these women are contrasted directly with good "natural" fathers. In Hansel and Gretel, for example, the wicked stepmother insists that the children must be abandoned in the woods, so that she and the woodcutter can have enough to eat. The *Vater* protests, "No, wife, that I won't do. How could I find it in my heart to leave my children alone in the wood? The wild beasts would come and tear them to pieces." But, the story continues, the woman left him no peace until he consented.[31]

These stories all reflect a belief that the biological mother of a child will treat it well, but that she's not likely to bother herself about the offspring of others. In other words, blood relatives will fulfill their duties, but women are not innately "motherly."

Another important aspect of these stories is that the mother is portrayed as "replaceable." In the few cases where the father dies and the children are left in the care of their mother, however, no stepfather is introduced. In contrast to English teen-agers' belief that Dads may come and go, but, "You can't get another Mum, can you?", Germanic storytellers never accept the possibility of a substitute father. *Vater* is unique and irreplaceable.

During this century, German writers of children's stories have perpetuated the "replaceable"[32] nature of the mother, and the "unique" essence of the father, but they have quite consciously tried to obliterate the "wicked" part of the stepmother image. The new stepmother is genuinely "mother-ly"—wise, kind, patient and loving—and she takes great pains to help children keep a treasured memory of their natural mother.

The mother figures of adult literature, however, do not display "mother-liness" as that quality is understood in other societies. The contemporary German Mother is still cast as the unknown, the unknowable—a passive link between man and the universe. Günter Grass's grandmother waits for-ever in the potato fields, her earthen layers of skirts offering final haven from the natural elements and from punishment. Brecht's Mother Courage absorbs the evil around her without being infected herself, like a mussel feeding at a cloaca. The positive features of this Mother figure involve the inarticulate, the amorphous, the eternal.

German women take on the responsibility of motherhood in the same vein. They accept it as their role in the inscrutable *Weltanschauung.* They must be there, like the chair at the kitchen table, like the *Kochofen* in the corner, because the Life Plan requires their presence.

Although 90 percent of German women are, or plan to be, mothers, the traditional concept that a family must be "rich in children" in order to be happy has almost entirely disappeared. Germany reached a zero-popula-tion-growth level in the early seventies, and today, West Germany has the lowest birthrate in the world—11.3 births per 1000 population.

This trend reflects a radical change, for in the mid-sixties, Germany ranked second only to the United States as the most populous industrialized country. Now, the German mother is postponing the birth of her first child and considering not having a second. She has social support in this deci-sion. As one reporter summed up current medical and psychological advice, "A woman doesn't have to cross-fold herself for children."[33]

Family-planning clinics in all Germanic countries are state-supported, and information is widely available. All forms of birth control are now practiced, but the right to sterilization and abortion on demand has caused great controversy.

Sterilization was legalized in West Germany in 1973, and became avail-able in Austria in 1975. Swiss law varies from canton to canton, and as doctors can be severely prosecuted for it if patients change their minds, they are reluctant to perform the operation. In East Germany, female steril-ization is legal, but male sterilization is not. There appears to be a subcon-scious belief that the man not only has the "right" to be a father, but also the "duty."

Abortion on demand was legal in East Germany and other Communist countries until the early seventies, when these governments became worried that falling birthrates would mean debilitating labor losses in twenty years, and thus tightened birth-control laws everywhere. (In Russia, it is even difficult to get the Pill.) An East German woman whose health is not endangered by pregnancy can only rarely obtain an abortion, even though it is legal during the first twelve weeks of pregnancy.

Abortion on demand is illegal in Switzerland, although there were certain "sympathetic" clinics patronized by women of all nationalities until other countries liberalized their laws in the late sixties. Abortion on demand was legalized in 1974 in both West Germany and Austria, but the German Constitutional Court has already declared the law unconstitutional, and now abortion is available only for "valid" health reasons.

Obviously, neither abortion nor vasectomy are important factors in the Germanic birthrate decline. Germany's highest illegal abortion estimates have always hovered around two hundred thousand anyway—only one-fifth those of Italy or pre-1975 France. The major component of a declining birthrate—in Germany, as elsewhere—is the status of the Mother in society.

Pregnancy is approached from a practical point of view by German women. Women's magazines are full of medical terms, detailed drawings of the uterus and the womb and photographs of the fetus at different stages of development. A woman visits a doctor regularly, takes vitamins and watches her diet. She gains an average of thirty-five pounds, twice that of the American mother, but some studies indicate that this practice results in a healthier baby.[34]

The German woman follows a rigorous prenatal exercise regimen, and continues regular sports—jogging, tennis, swimming, sometimes even horseback riding and diving—until the latest possible moment. Pregnancy is considered "only natural" and therefore is not allowed to infringe very much on daily life.

Family and friends ask questions about the health of the pregnant woman. Does she have problems with backache, swelling legs or constipation? They aren't sympathetic; they simply want to offer advice if she isn't doing something correctly. If she is healthy, they praise her for keeping herself fit, and her status goes up a notch. A wise woman knows how to control her body.

Delivery is a technical, no-nonsense procedure performed in a hospital by a male doctor and his forbidding *Hebamme* (midwife), who allows no complaining or whimpering. Fathers are only rarely allowed to be present. One recent description of a delivery in *Eltern* magazine gave a complete account of how the placenta is checked for tears, the stitches put in and the mother prepared for her postdelivery nap. Not once did the article mention the father of the new arrival.[35] As in France, a mystical aura surrounds the act of birth itself, and the father is rarely considered a part of the rite.

Both baby and mother are subject to several thorough physical checks ranging from the initial *Levensfrische Apgar* test through the daily arrival of *Herr Doktor* and his battalion of nurses with full equipage and charts. They march through the hospital halls like a panzer division, dispersing visitors before them. In the German hospital, more than in any other except the American, doctors, charts and thermometer dominate the mother's life. In Germany there is also the eternal question: *"Haben sie Stul gemacht?"* ("Have you had a bowel movement?")

Doctor's orders are supreme. In Vienna ten years ago, I was the only woman in the maternity ward not bound into a corset and kept in bed for two days after the delivery. The nurses were astonished and disapproving at my relative liberty, but *Herr Doktor* had left instructions, and they dared not disobey. Nor did they investigate his reason for the order, which was that I had not gained the fifty pounds then popular in Vienna and consequently didn't need so much "shoring up." The practices of corseting and lying-in have now largely disappeared in the Germanic countries, but the initiative for the innovation came strictly from the doctors. Nurses and mothers are not supposed to have opinions, much less to seek an analysis, of the situation.

The hospital stay for those on the National Health Plan is a minimum of three days. Those in private clinics often stay as long as two weeks.

Upon returning home, today's German mother immediately launches a regimen to whip her body back into "normal" condition. There are state-supported classes everywhere, offering tone-up programs more demanding than those of other countries. Friends and relatives stop asking questions. The mother has done her "natural duty" and there is no need to talk about it further.

Breast-feeding has general approval. It is considered "natural" and "best for the infant, both emotionally and physically." Rigid hospital feeding schedules used to dry up all but the most determined mother, but today a more flexible approach means that the majority can and do nurse. Occasionally a woman keeps the child nursing until its second birthday, and this is considered particularly praiseworthy.

In some metropolitan centers it is possible to buy pasteurized human milk for a baby if one is unable to breast-feed the infant. For the slightly older child, the Germans and the Swiss were the first to develop the all-in-one powdered formula, which has been available in both countries for nearly twenty years.

State support for parents is explicit, orderly and relatively easy to obtain. The pregnancy leave (which is mandatory) is six weeks before and a minimum of eight weeks after the birth. If there are complications or multiple births, the postpregnancy leave is extended to twelve weeks. Employers must keep a woman's position open for her, but her wages are paid in full by the national health insurance plan, so that employers are not faced with financial penalties for hiring women. Doctor and hospital expenses are also covered by national health insurance.

The monthly family allowance payments run from $20 for the first child up to $45 for the third and subsequent children. These payments go to all families, including unwed mothers, regardless of income, and do not have the demeaning "charity" associations of Anglo-Saxon welfare. Tax relief for families with children no longer exists. Family-allowance checks are sent to the parent having legal responsibility for the child.

Parents who are unable to look after their children because of illness may claim the assistance of domestic help. When chidren fall ill, *either* parent is entitled to a maximum of five days' paid leave per child per year in order to care for them.[36]

A hundred years ago, the German family patriarch was ruler of one of the most austere regimes the world has ever known. The Germans experimented only rarely with boarding schools and the Nanny system of England, but they were even more convinced of the necessity of hardening a child.

Schools were run by Prussian army officers who demanded that students stand at attention, and salute as the teacher entered the room. *Herr Vater* took his cue from the leading pedagogue of the day, Dr. Daniel Gottlieb Scherber, who recommended back harnesses to prevent slumping, chin straps to prevent thumb-sucking and severe discipline to prevent masturbation. He made his sons sit rigidly straight for long periods and expected the boys to obey commands expressed "merely by eye movements."

Scherber's eldest son committed suicide, and his youngest went insane. Freud based his classic study of paranoia on the younger son's case, but even Freud did not attack the image of *Herr Vater*. Young Scherber's paranoid belief in tormenting supernatural powers, Freud theorized, was due to the son's suppressed homosexual feelings toward his father. The father's prescribed ice baths, harnesses and "eye movements" are not mentioned.[37] Scherber senior, it seems, was too sacrosanct to be questioned.

Today, Scherber societies in Germany are growing roses instead of pruning children, and pedagogue bookshelves are full of Spock and Montessori. Perhaps the most popular German writer in the field is a woman, Elisabeth Plattner. She and most other German child-care experts speak exclusively to the mother, who is often called by the diminutive *Mutti* (Mommy). The father is left to his role as family decision-maker without outside advice.

The mother's first concern is to give her child a firm, consistent environment. Beds are solid. The baby taken out for a stroll is placed in a firm buggy and wrapped tightly. When I carried my baby in my arms on the street, I was accosted by German passersby, who told me disapprovingly, *"Das Becken steht deshalb schief."* ("The back is therefore slanted").

Shoulder harnesses are no longer popular, but good posture is still important. Parents give the baby massages. They exercise the baby's arms and legs by hand and introduce it to climbing ladders and tiny trapezes.

Posture training underlies three abiding concepts in the German woman's character. First: the Body Mystique. A clean, smoothly functioning body is a joy and a social asset. Second: Adults know best. Strong muscles and a healthy body must be assured for a baby by benign elders. Third: The Work Ethic. A healthy body does not come easily. The idea that good things are achieved through diligent effort begins early in life.

For the most part rigid feeding schedules have been abandoned in Germany, but the first confrontation between parents and the child still occurs at the infant stage: thumb-sucking. Chin straps are no longer sold as preventives, but Daumexol antisucking liquid is available everywhere. Parents write worried letters to magazine editors, and are told reassuringly that even healthy children put their fingers into their mouths occasionally. Parents need only "outwit" baby by leaving him or her at the breast or providing a pacifier.

Freud, Reich and others of the Viennese circle theorized that the biggest battle between the young child and its parents took place in the area of masturbation. Reich went so far as to designate repressed childhood sexuality as the primary cause of the nation's blind obedience to Hitler. Children who are forbidden to masturbate, he explained, are never able to trust themselves enough to take responsibility for their decisions as adults.[38]

Taboos against masturbation and sexual expression have largely disappeared since World War II, but the thumb-sucking battle is not the only one still being fought between parents and children. The most important front is one that Freud also discussed: toilet training. The avant-garde American idea of "leaving it until the baby trains himself or herself" has made no inroads in Germany, nor has the Montessori practice of training the child through peer observation.

As in other baby regimens, Father is frequently the parent who takes it upon himself to set baby on the pot regularly and expect a performance. The child's bowel movement is often called *Bescherung* (gift or presentation), a word that in itself emphasizes the adult's approval if the child does as expected (and may have fostered more than one school of psychoanalysis).

Father's supervision of the daily details of many of baby's rituals is one reason why duty and authority are more important in Germany than in other countries. The father is not as inclined as the mother to cajole the child into obedience. Being by nature both stronger and less verbal, and by training less conciliatory, he installs a "you do it because authority tells you to do it" approach. As one German journalist put it, "We have always felt compromise to be slightly lacking in character."[39]

When baby is toilet-trained, the whole family is pleased. The child is then capable of entering a new level of society. Nursery schools, for example, will take only children who are trained. A body that is clean both inside and out appeals to the German sense of control and social acceptance. It is the reason for all the large, luxurious German bathrooms with the Niagara Falls flushing mechanisms—by-products of affluence that are as yet considered of only secondary importance in England, France or Italy.

Toilet training is considered equally important for both sexes in Germany, and toddlers are never encouraged to urinate on the street. The only adult men ever seen urinating in full view beside the German Autobahn are agricultural workers or manual laborers.

German preoccupation with defecation is legendary. Gershon Legman, noted collector and student of pornographic jokes from various cultures, points out that a chief characteristic of German humor is that it is built around a scatological theme.[40] Freud emphasized that oppressive toilet training could scar a child for life. Even going back to the fifteenth century, one finds Martin Luther overwhelmingly concerned with his explosive lower colon. Five hundred years later the world-renowned German-reared psychoanalyst Erik Erikson speculated that Luther's struggles with his biological functions may have set the stage for his fulminating genius.[41]

Scatology is nurtured not only in early childhood, but throughout life. Parents demand, even of teen-agers, "*Hast du Stul gemacht?*" every morning after breakfast. It is one of the first questions asked by doctors.

One must note, however, that this psychological preoccupation is an outgrowth of the simple physiological fact that digestion of the heavy German meal is a difficult task requiring conscious effort.

Toilet training in the German context is considered a part of the Body Mystique, which is stressed in every way possible. A girl learns to wash herself daily, and is awarded with her first "grown-up" status when she can take a bath alone. She sees her *Mutti* exercise every morning and is often encouraged to join in. Parents work hard to teach their five-year-olds how to swim and ride a bike and play soccer.

This training is interlocked with an inculcation of the Work Ethic. *Mutti* expects toddlers of both sexes to help her by picking up their toys, setting the table and doing the dusting. With great patience, she oversees an industrious preschool girl who has set herself the job of cleaning the bathroom mirror. *Mutti* always insists that every streak be obliterated; she is teaching duty and responsibility, and is disdainful of the "quick results" Work Ethic of the Americans. "Sesame Street" was turned down by a third of the German broadcasting stations because, the Frankfurter *Rundschaus* daily snapped, "In Germany, learning and laughing have never been considered together, and work and play are considered as opposites."[42]

Parents are called upon to watch over all forms of the child's development. Guidebooks explain how to overcome childish fears and stuttering. Long explanations are devoted to helping the child make friends.

The most important duty that the parent must perform is building the child's character. Anthropologist Rhoda Métraux found in the early fifties that the Germans felt, "A child at birth was neither good nor bad; it was an unformed potential. If misguided or left to its own devices at any point, the child is believed to be incapable of developing its own good potentialities, but, with guidance, the bad ones can be eliminated. This is the basic justification for total parental authority over the child and for self-education of the [parent] educator himself. . . . The intention of this education is not to prepare the individual to make choices, but rather to know what is right, and to have the strength and fortitude to do it."

Métraux further observed that it was not considered a good idea to use threats or rewards, since this was confusing and might turn a child into a "cool calculator, who works only for the sake of rewards." Beyond that, answering "why?" questions only gives the child a means to escape a duty or a punishment, and "may become a source of danger when the child insists on a reason when action—like avoiding an oncoming car—is imperative."[43]

German children are expressly not taught to articulate who they are or why they do things as they are in England and France. The "immutable" quality of a command is implied in the way it is expressed: "Whoever opens the door must close it," not, "The door has to be closed or the cold comes in."

Corporal punishment, so popular before the downfall of the blatantly totalitarian Nazis, is now thoroughly repudiated. The most common device currently used to teach obedience is repetition, and it is ordinarily the mother's task. She must tell the child as many times as necessary, "Knives you may not touch," and take the knife away. Under this guidance, small children can soon be heard murmuring "Knives you may not touch," when they see their mother leave one on the kitchen cutting board. If the mother is consistent and patient, pedagogues insist, children will internalize the lesson to the point where they do not touch knives even when no adult is present.

"With this upbringing," Plattner explains "at a later age, when will and consciousness are more fully developed, a simple and friendly word—for instance, 'Do your homework now'—will be obeyed and taken for granted, and the wish to play more will be overcome. How beautiful the life of the school-age child can be if we have laid the right foundation in the small-child age."[44]

There is a fundamental difference between German and American popularized interpretations of Freud's principles. Americans used Freud (as they now use R. D. Laing) to support the Blessed Baby ideal; i.e., parental efforts to mold the child are always in error because baby is born naturally good, and needs only to be *allowed* to reach its potential.

With their image of the child who must work to *become* good, the Germans thought Freud was simply criticizing *some* of the methods of *some* parents. They resented his comments, but modified many of their child-raising techniques as a result of his theories. They have not, however, deviated from their belief that parents are the rock upon which the child is constructed. The parent is considered the single most important influence in society, and gains status from this responsibility.

The mother's supportive place in this system is considered vital and dignified, but "only natural." Blindly, placidly, patiently, she does her duty. She, after all, has been taught her place in the Life Plan by her own mother.

6

The German Child—A Part of the "Wholeness of Things"

The German child does not ordinarily start school until age six, and then attends only half a day. Although there were innumerable youth clubs and sports activities for primary-grade children, most of them are run by a patient adult who echoes the values that parents instill at home.

There is a conscious desire on the part of educators to offset the omnipresent influence of adults on children and help them develop their *Selbständig* (literally, self-standing) nature. *Eltern* magazine, for example, regularly runs features explaining that parents must trust their five-year-olds on a trip across town to visit grandmother, because only if children try their wings will they internalize the lessons they have been taught.

Little Red Riding Hood, however, does not believe that she can cope with emergencies alone. She is a singularly trusting child, having never come across mendacious shopkeepers or unfriendly policemen. A few boys develop "Hansel" abilities to cope with trouble through using their wits,

226

but on the whole both sexes are taught to rely on authorities to take their part and be helpful. In return, they are respectful and appreciative toward adults.

At one time, the girl was less likely than her brother to be caned for wrongdoing, but today corporal punishment is rare for either sex, although spankings are more popular in Germany than they are in Sweden. Today's German child lives in a controlled environment, where temptation rarely presents itself. Commands are gently but persistently reiterated. Children are asked to be "normal" and "natural"—i.e., to act like everyone else in the group. Deliberate infractions are punished by deprivation of things like bicycles, roller skates, pocket money and television-watching time.

Children are taught that they are being punished for their own good, that if they persist in resisting their parents' authority, they will surely fall afoul of some terrible law of the *Weltanschauung*. The children's cautionary tales in *Der Struwwelpeter* give graphic examples of what happens to children who play with matches or fail to cut their fingernails, for example. The offenders are burned to a crisp or turn into deformed social outcasts.

However, none of *Der Struwwelpeter*'s protagonists are ever warned in advance what their fate will be if they don't do as they are told. Nor do they figure out the probability for themselves. They aren't daring to embark on a dangerous mission; they're simply willfully disobedient, and they get their just desserts. *Der Struwwelpeter* was first published in 1845, and it is still one of the most popular books on the market for young children.

In a direct reverse of the French and Italian value systems, a verbal crime—not a physical one—is the worst a German child can commit. Lying, trickery and deceit are considered much more serious than direct confrontations of the *Wille* because they carry the added sin of premeditation. "I know all children make mistakes," mothers explain, "and these must be corrected, of course. But if a child lies to me, then I know that there is evil in his heart."

The precept is echoed in literature, where writers like Hermann Hesse lace their books with praise for the "modest, unspoiled" child as opposed to the "adroit, clever" ones who are calculating, sly and untrustworthy.[45] The verbally precocious, it is believed, are simply prattling away to cover up their shallowness of spirit.

Hostility toward people believed to be overly verbose and/or liars is intertwined with a suspicion of knowledge. In Germany, the Biblical evil of eating from the Tree of Knowledge is predated by the ancient tale of Wotan's loss of one eye in search of knowledge. The Desire to Know was the supreme sin committed by Goethe's *Faust*. And Immanuel Kant based his system of philosophy on his demonstration that reasoned logic was by its nature circular and inconclusive, and that therefore the way to knowledge lay not in words but in belief and *Wille*.

Distrust turns up even in institutes of learning. Rudolf Steiner, the founder of anthroposophy, is best known in Germany for his pedagogic teachings, and one of his prime tenets is that the child must spend its first fourteen years learning to imitate and to feel. Only after that should training in verbal skills, analysis and evaluation begin. Rudolf Steiner schools are popular today throughout Germany, Switzerland and Austria, and they are also in operation in London, Paris and New York.

In the state school system, distrust of verbal knowledge is not so overt, but during the past thirty years, the schools have turned away from elitism to the values of universal education. And one of the first things to disappear was the old emphasis on pass/fail written and oral exams. "Today we don't make decisions by end-of-year examinations at all," a principal of the Frankfurt school system told me. "The teacher has seen what kind of work a child has done throughout the school year, and he or she is in a better position to know if the child is ready for the next year's work than somebody looking at a piece of paper."

Children are expected to work hard in school, of course, and those who can memorize well are rewarded with the best grades. But personal character and not knowledge is the primary thing being taught.

Valerie Levy, an American who taught in the Austrian public schools during the early seventies, explains it this way: "The main concern of the teaching staff was the grades students were to receive in 'attitude.' We used to have meetings to discuss pupils who were threatened with a 2—failing—in attitude. We had five marks in regular classes—1, the equivalent of an A, through 5, the equivalent of an F—and teachers never talked about those decisions. But with 'attitude,' a student either passed or failed. With more than one 2 in attitude, she could be expelled, and then might very well not be able to get into another school. There was one girl who asked a teacher, 'What for?' and was taken to the principal and threatened with expulsion."

If children run into trouble at school, they have a big advantage over French children when they talk with their parents. German parents will listen to the child's side of the story, and defend the child to the teacher. Fathers have been known to take their child's case all the way to the *Landesregierung* (state head of schools) to get the record changed.

The second-class status of verbal ability has some important advantages for society. Closely tied to Germanic brilliance in the worlds of music, mathematical theory, philosophy and theology is the Germanic support of the awed, inarticulate, dreaming child in search of the unnamed and undefined *Weltanschauung*. Albert Einstein is one of the best examples of this. Unable—"or unwilling"—to speak until he was age three,[46] he probably would have been placed in an institution for the subnormal if he had been French. As it was, he developed theories of physics which have never been fully translated from their mathematical equations into words.

The belief that girls should not join in rough-and-tumble games has few adherents. "I don't pay attention to whimpers because of cuts and bruises from either my son or my daughter," a German father will explain. "I tell both of them to hit back if they are pestered, and I correct both of them in the same way if they ski incorrectly." Girls are encouraged to compete with boys. Some schools have mixed judo and karate classes, and the only single-sex sport is boxing.

Violent competitive team sports, however, are discouraged, and violence in children's television programming is not allowed. Although Germany was one of the last European countries to restrict the sale of guns—its legislation went into effect on January 1, 1973—toy guns in children's departments have been difficult to find since World War II. The German favorites are how-to kits for both sexes. If there is a small bin of toy guns, it is often hidden in the corner or behind the counter.

For girls, this physical training without the threat of true violence results in distinct advantages for those who are athletic. Their dedication to sports is encouraged from the beginning and they are given unqualified support when they succeed. Nobody tells them they must be careful. Nobody asks them how they can catch a husband with all those muscles. The problem lies in the fact that only a few can win in physical fields. The rest are denied the alternative verbal battlefield.

Meanwhile, since verbal agility is considered a negative trait, the lists of German writers to compare with Iris Murdock, Natalia Ginsburg, Colette or Mary McCarthy are empty. Internationally recognized women writers like Nelly Sachs and Hannah Arendt are most commonly influenced by a Jewish verbal upbringing and/or an adult life spent away from Germany.

Without *Wille*, the natural "career" that the girl-child has to look forward to as an adult is fulfilling her duty and responsibility to her family. Here the German girl is given across-the-board support by her culture. As a child, she is the *Schwester* (sister), a name almost synonymous with the willing servant. The professional baby-sitter, after all, is called *Kinderschwester* (child sister); the nurse is *Krankenschwester* (sick sister); the nun is *Klosterschwester* (cloister sister). One of today's most popular books for girls is *Lottie und Lisa*, the story of two sisters who diligently work to reunite their divorced parents. A more traditional series concerns Wildfang, the eldest daughter of a widower, who willfully refuses to be responsible for her younger sisters and brothers. One day, while she is playing on a swing she has been forbidden to use, the swing breaks, and she is paralyzed from the fall. Although she was not told the reason why she shouldn't play on the swing, she feels repentant and learns through her hardship to take responsibility. First, she becomes surrogate mother to her own siblings. When she grows up, in later stories, she marries a widower, and once more becomes a loving "replacement" mother.[47]

The joy of submitting to one's duties is considered a positive attribute in both women *and* men in Germany, but women appear to have slightly better success at practicing it. Freud's case study of Dr. Scherber's paranoid son, for example, detailed his intense desire to *become a woman* in order to serve God completely. And although German writers from Goethe to Kafka have eulogized dutiful subservience, it is a woman, Ilse Aichinger, who most completely explained the dynamics and paradox of its emotional appeal.

Aichinger's "The Bound Man" is the haunting story of a nameless man who awakes in a field to find himself inexplicably tied from head to foot by a thin rope. He rises and finds he can hobble forward, as long as he makes no sudden movements. Before he has a chance to free himself, a circus man persuades him to demonstrate to audiences his miraculous ability to move inside his bonds. He is an immediate success.

After that, although the circus proprietor "often remarked that there was no reason why he should not be untied after the evening performance and tied up again the next day . . . no one took the idea of untying him seriously. For the bound man's fame rested on the fact that he was always bound, that whenever he washed himself, he had to wash his clothes, too, and vice versa, and that his only way of doing so was to jump in the river."

He spends his summer thus, tended by the gentle, wondering proprietor's wife, and is finally attacked by a wolf, which he kills, feeling a "slight elation at having lost the fatal advantage of free limbs which causes men to be worsted. The freedom he enjoyed . . . was having to adapt every movement of his limbs to the ropes that tied him—the freedom of . . . the wild flowers that sway in the evening breeze . . . he was in no way hampered by the rope."[48]

In the midst of all this patient consistency and exaltation of the faithful Job who dutifully withstood all the trials the Devil could devise, there is an extraordinary fact. A German woman made an international name for herself as being the most violent woman of the seventies.

Ulrike Meinhof was indicted for sedition and murder as the leader of a group that the German government considers to be its worst threat in recent history. Was she one of a kind, or the portent of a newly antisocial Brunhild?

Ulrike Meinhof was thirty-six at the time she began her campaign of violence, and hardly seemed the type to throw herself so totally into confrontation with authority. A journalist, she was first known for her work on *Konkret*, a leftist publication edited by her husband, Klaus Rainer Röhl. She was the mother of eight-year-old twins. When she and Röhl were divorced, she gave him custody of the children.

Her decision to embark on violent action is said to have come in 1970, while she was covering the trial of another leftist, Andreas Baader, twenty-seven, who was convicted of turning his fiery rhetoric into several blazing department stores. Meinhof, together with her journalist comrade and lover, Peter Homann, and two other intellectuals, freed Baader from the prison library in a dramatic rescue at gunpoint, which caught the imagination of the entire country and launched the drama of the Baader-Meinhof Gang. Meinhof was known as the "mind" of the group, Baader as the " daredevil."

From the beginning, the female leader was no anomaly. There were more women than men in the band. Use Stachaowiak was one of the few "worker-class" participants. Before taking up bank robbing and arson, she had been a car mechanic.

Women were also among the most widely publicized martyrs. Petra Schelm was shot to death when she pulled a gun at a car spot checkpoint. Monica Hertl, who was implicated in the Hamburg murder of Bolivian Consul Roberto Quintanilla, was killed in a shoot-out with police.

In May 1972, the group blew up the American Army officers' quarters in Frankfurt. Four men died. Radical Chic support among intellectuals faltered. By mid-June, some twenty of the gang that claimed sixty members were in jail. Ulrike Meinhof was captured when police raided an apartment in the middle of the night after an anonymous tip.

For the trial of Meinhof and three other major figures in the gang, the German Government erected a special $5 million courthouse in Stuttgart, complete with an underground causeway to their prison to forestall rescue attempts by those of the gang who are still at liberty, still robbing banks, still assassinating judges.

Since Meinhof's death, it has continued to be the women of the gang who have most captured the public eye with new shootings, new skyjackings, new arrests and new escapes.

In the main, the women in the Baader-Meinhof group are too old and too middle-class "normal" to be easily discounted the way "black" Angela Davis and "young" Bernardette Dohrn and "rich kid" Patricia Hearst have been in the United States. They are also more dedicated to violence, more serious, and . . . more diligent.

The female-rebel archetype fits into the dark side of the German pattern. Germany has the highest murder rate in Western Europe—1.4 fatal assaults per 100,000, compared to Italy's 0.9, France's 0.8 and the United Kingdom's 0.7. (It must be noted that the United States has by far the worst record with a rate over four times higher than Germany's.[49]) The German per capita road toll is also appalling—twice Italy's and three times Great Britain's.[50]

The suicide rate further confirms the overall configuration of strain. West Berlin—a city with an atypical problem of an older population facing a claustrophobic situation—has the highest suicide rate in the world, an incredible 41.3 per 100,000 population. Austria, despite an overwhelmingly Catholic population, has the highest national rate in the West—23.1 per 100,000. Sweden comes next at 22.0; Germany is third with 21.6.

It appears all too clear that those who choose to resist the *Weltanschauung* often feel compelled to do so violently. The most surprising thing about the Ulrike Meinhof Warrior Woman archetype is that it took her so long to express her *Wille*.

7

Sexuality and True Love

The German *Sexwelle* (sex wave) is most often described as a part of the general Western movement toward equality of the sexes and liberation from Puritan values. This analysis is perfectly valid. If one were to draw a chart to indicate which countries put the least restrictions on sexual activity, Scandinavia would be first, with England, Germany, the United States, France, Italy and the Soviet Union following in that order. Germany falls more or less in the middle. But such a chart would not include the provocative variations in German sexual attitudes and how they reflect the overall personality of the German woman.

In the first place, today's international sexual revolution can be directly traced to Germanic thinking. Sigmund Freud started it all in a very simple—and very Germanic—way. He called sexual inhibition "unhealthy." Not "illogical" as the French would have called it. Not "impractical" as the Americans would have called it. Not "ridiculous" as the British were already calling it. But "unhealthy." Against the "natural order" of things.

233

The indictment struck a resonant chord. Unhealthy? Not an attribute of self-control and iron *Wille*? There were thunderous roars of "Blasphemy!" and "Anarchy!" But Freud had found his lever, and Germany was one of the countries where inhibition came crashing down the fastest.

Freud's denunciation of sexual oppression combined with Engel's censure of patriarchal politics to make "free love" one of the major catchphrases of the twenties. Hitler saw the philosophy as a dangerous threat to his image as Father of the Country, and immediately set to work to extinguish it. He rallied against "irresponsibility" and "dirty minds," told the world there was nothing so holy as the German mother, went into rabid diatribes about the dangers of syphilis and homosexuality and chased Freud out of Austria.

Behind these frenzied frontal attacks, however, the Nazi hierarchy practiced innumerable aberrant acts in private. Homosexuality within the Brown Shirt Storm Trooper organization was ubiquitous and violent.[51] In recent years, the rumors of Hitler's own deranged sex life have been given authoritative reality by more than one biographer. In his detailed psychological profile, *The Mind of Adolf Hitler*, which was actually prepared for the United States Government during World War II, Dr. Walter Langer stated: "It is probably true that [Hitler] is impotent. But he is certainly not homosexual in the ordinary sense of the term. His perversion has quite a different nature, which few have guessed. It is an extreme form of masochism in which the individual derives sexual gratification from the act of having a woman urinate or defecate on him."[52]

Reactions against the public Puritanism of the Hitler years were immediately evident in Germany after World War II. As the Continent began to regain its emotional balance and economic viability, Germany came to the fore in the sex revolution. As early as 1950, Vance Packard found that the number of unmarried Germans who had sex was higher than that of any group except the Scandinavians and "rather spectacularly higher than the French." He quoted surveys showing that 70 percent of German women had relations with the opposite sex before marriage, 43 percent of the English and only 30 percent of the French.[53]

Statistics in the seventies indicate that the French are still the least sexually liberated, with 43.4 percent of the teen-agers having sexual relations in comparison to 75 percent of the German girls.[54] Sexual liberation and experimentation have become an integral part of the German postwar culture. Beate Uhse sex shops and Eros Center massage parlors dot city shopping streets. Sex education is included in every school curriculum; nudity and explicit sex play are common in advertising, and *de rigueur* in nearly all German-made films.

Quick and *Stern,* Germany's equivalents of *Life* and *Look,* have spent several years' worth of covers featuring nude models. One *Stern* cover probably takes the prize for forthrightness. It starred a nude female posterior adorned with the words *Kauf Mich* (Buy Me).

Pundits are now predicting that the *Sexwelle* has passed its crest. *Quick* and *Stern* cover models sometimes wear clothes again. Recent box-office returns from sex films have not been as high as those from the Hong Kong karate adventure movies that only briefly include fully clothed, misty-faced maidens.[55] And tour operators report that interest in Hamburg's notorious St. Pauli red-light district is diminishing.

Beate Uhse sales figures keep climbing, however, as do the number of people publicly declaring the satisfaction a liberalized sex life has brought them. As one thoughtful businesswoman analyzed the situation, "We're going past the 'Look, look' stage, where everybody must see how *others* are supposedly doing it, and we're into the Scandinavian mold, where everybody expects to do sex as part of their own natural way of life."

Ideally, the pattern of adult sexuality in Germany begins with a sister-brother relationship. German sibling ties are always carefully nurtured, and, with the emphasis on sexual equality, sisters and brothers have far more opportunity to share each other's lives than their counterparts in England, Italy or France. This initiation is designed to help future adults base their relationships with the opposite sex on a familial kind of love and trust rather than on purely physical involvement.

Whether or not they have brothers, German girls spend most of their time in mixed-sex groups. Schools are integrated. So are sports and games. German girls learn to cope with physical challenge better than their Latin sisters, but without verbal competitions where they can show their own superiority, male dominance becomes the "natural" course.

Esther Vilar has shown how this environment fosters an ignorant "child-bride" manipulator, but Günter Grass has also illustrated how it can lead, quite literally, to penis envy. When tomboy Tulla Pokriefe swims out to the boys' half-sunken boat in *Cat and Mouse,* she pesters the leader to show her his organ. Although he has never done so for his male companions, he finally draws his penis forth, and "under Tulla's questing, much-scratched fingers" it leaps into bloom, "fully a half span longer" than anyone else's, and "a matchbox bigger around. . . . It seemed much more adult and worthy of worship."[56]

As the individual girl reaches her teen years, she is still treated like a child by her family. While girls in other countries are already budgeting their own allowances and spending nights with friends, the German child of either sex is still considered very much in need of their mother's help and their father's protection, guidance and criticism.

Around age thirteen, adults outside the family begin addressing the girl in the formal *Sie* instead of the intimate *du,* and girl-boy games turn from tussling into dancing. In today's initial courtship ritual, as in the past, the underlying precept is that of the aggressive, adventuresome male, impressing the passive, stationary female. A current film advertising "Mo-mo-moped!" motor scooters illustrates the point. Six boys on scooters are attracted to a girl wearing pigtails and a pink sweater. Showing off, the boys demonstrate their daring and ability. Besides performing feats of skill, they tease an elderly woman by grabbing her hat and then jamming it back on her head before she can collect her irate wits.

The leader—always a little more daring and speedy than the others—finds a ball a small child has lost outside its garden gate, and he magnanimously throws it back. He also initiates a project to remove a large, dangerous stone from the middle of the street.

After racing past the girl several times, the leader finally wins her by daring to cross a particularly narrow and treacherous bridge the others are afraid to attempt. Throughout the film, the girl is openly flirtatious, conscious of her appeal. And waiting. Despite today's frankly libertarian attitude toward the body, German advertisers obviously still find that the chivalrous brand of romance sells motor scooters.

It is revealing to contrast this film with a contemporary one done for Ciao motor scooters in Italy. Both films forgo words, so the exaggerated mime effect highlights their ritualistic features. The Italian film is aimed at the same fifteen- to twenty-five-year-old age bracket. Both last between five and seven minutes, and are shown during intermission in general-release movie houses.

But the "hidden persuaders" of the Italian film are very different from the German ones. There is no glorification of power and feats of skill. The emphasis is on freedom. There is no story line, simply a series of short takes showing riders puttering down backwoods lanes, wind blowing, sun shining. Occasionally, riders maneuver easily through traffic-choked streets, obviously more in command of the situation than those caught in larger, more cumbersome vehicles.

The riders are both female and male. At times the camera zooms in on a girl and boy gliding along side by side, but the predominate motif is that of the individual, regardless of sex, enjoying the freedom of going wherever he or she wants to go.

In Germany, love does not fall into one of two types—wise and foolish—as it does in France. Instead, the German believes in only one magnificent obsession—True Love. This *ganz schön Zwänge,* idealized so often in German literature, is an entirely different concept from either *l'amour sage* or *l'amour fou.* It is not even a combination of the two. It has little to do with logic and articulated reasoning, but is more constant and less sexual than the self-consuming pyre of *l'amour fou.* The concept expressed in English of being "true" to one's love derives, in fact, from the German word *treu,* meaning "true." It is interesting to note that at one time the word in both languages was also used as a woman's name—True or Truw.

In Scandinavia, True Love involves the sharing of friendship, interests and values on an equal level. This principle exists in Germany as well, but equally as strong is the ideal of the *Minnesänger's* Lady, with her entirely separate, incomprehensible world.

In Germany, as well as in America, the conflicts between the value systems of the Lady and the Warrior Woman leave countless women and men floundering in confusion. On the surface, everyone agrees with Esther Vilar that a woman should be envied for succeeding in the Lady's world of noncompetitive work and manipulation behind the scenes, but no one ever honors her directly with money or power.

Instead, women are asked to be both types at once. Women in German health camps are expected to be formidable swimmers and soccer players *and also* to listen respectfully while their husbands instruct them three times on the lay of the land: "That is the washroom, right for men, left for women. . . . That is the laundry room, only open until 8:00 P.M. . . . One goes to the lake along that path on the left—the one on the right is to the snack bar. . . ." Tulla Pokriefe is portrayed by Günter Grass as being both a tomboy *and* the only person who can cajole the protagonist to expose himself.

Couples caught in the conundrum of conflicting values often perform strange rites to maintain balance. Goethe's Gretchen/Margaret coped by simply dying and then dealing with Faust from beyond the grave. Kafka's real-life fiancée, Felice Bauer, tried to accept his love by correspondence, but finally despaired and married someone else.

Today's couples, equipped with Freudian analysis, sexual liberation and no-fault divorce, still run into trouble. When journalists Barbara and Manfred Frunert did their taped sociological study of their own troubled union, she complained that he constantly and intentionally demeaned her, calling her stupid, cowardly, dishonest and sly. Neither of them point to the fact that they were *both* asking her to be the gentle, noncompetitive Lady *and* the straightforward, honest, competitive Warrior Woman. In the end, they decided to stay together because of a mystical obsession that neither could articulate.[57]

Outside the confusion caused by the conflicts between the Warrior Woman and the Lady value systems, there is one other pathological pattern between the sexes that occurs in Germany often enough to be of import: masochism.

Germany has no patent on masochism. De Sade's *Juliette* or Réage's *Story of O* certainly attest to the masochistic element in France, and recent cross-cultural sociological surveys indicate that the English, at least at the college level, are by far the most likely to have engaged in "whipping or spanking before intimacy."[58]

The fact remains, however, that overt social acceptance of masochism is most visible in Germany. The two sex/massage chains, Sex mit Herz (Sex with Heart) and Eros Center, are both equipped with workout rooms for the masochistic client. Advertisements in the "services" columns of newspapers are often highlighted with references to "treatment that may be painful but beneficial," and books like Günther Hunold's *Vergiss die Peitsche nicht* (*Don't Forget the Whip*) are big selling successes.

The word "masochism" was derived from the name of the nineteenth-century Austrian writer, Leopold von Sacher-Masoch, who described the syndrome in popular novels, of which the best known is *Venus in Furs*. The masochist worships the Lady, the Gretchen/Margaret figure, whose fragile physique and resilient soul make her the personification of a "blessed" taskmaker.

The fixation is a logical outgrowth of the belief that punishment is beneficial. It is related to Esther Vilar's assertion that men revel in Non-Freedom. In a sociological sense, masochism is not reprehensible, for violence rarely gets out of hand unless combined with extreme sadism. But it is doubtful that it will receive open, conscious approval in other current societies, because the trend in Western culture is for the individual to resist all subjugation.

Until recently, the passive wife–dominating husband pattern appeared firmly entrenched at all levels of German society. Once they passed their sexually liberated late teens, the majority of women seemed to settle into the *Frau* role of meek subordination. Even jealousy was *verboten*. The pattern was personified by *Frau* Gerda Bormann, who bore her commandeering husband ten children in as many years. When she found that Martin had taken up with an actress, she wrote, "It's really a shame your girlfriend still doesn't have children. We could work it out that she had a child one year and I had one the next—that way you'd always have one woman totally dedicated to you."[59]

Intellectual women who do not view their destiny purely in terms of creating their husbands' happiness are still willing to accept—even offer solace to—their husbands' mistresses, as well as let their own careers take a back seat.[60]

This pattern is predominant in German society. The aggressively popular *"Ein Herz und eine Seele"* (*"A Heart and a Soul"*) television series, a takeoff on Archie Bunker, features a rabid Hitlerish husband and a weak, Eva Braun kind of wife. Men often weld their families into regiments, demanding adherence to a rigid daily regimen of exercise, work, meals and relaxation. Politicians' wives speak of the joy of remaining in the shadow of their husbands, and agree with one's comment, "Thank God it's not like it is in America, where the whole family has to stay in the spotlight."[61]

But there is a growing acceptance of something else. *"Ich liebe, wann ich will!"* ("I love whenever I want!") has become the battle cry of the married actress as she is being interviewed on her plans for the future.[62] Women at discotheques are becoming as casually aggressive as their Swedish counterparts. One woman has even set about establishing a Male Companion salon in Hamburg's notorious St. Pauli district. And women customers in Beate Uhse shops or at erotic movies appear at ease, although the right to go alone or with members of the same sex still appears to be reserved for men only.

The emerging sexually aggressive woman is perhaps best typified by Helga Goetze, fifty-one, housewife, married to a banker, mother of seven children. "During my thirty-one years of marriage," she reported on *"Das Podium"* talk show, "I always went to bed gritting my teeth. Love to me seemed something dirty."

Then, in the summer of 1969, she and her husband were vacationing in Sicily, and she had her first affair. "It changed my life," she said, with a shy smile. When she returned to Hamburg, she advertised in the St. Pauli *Nachrichten* for a partner "to enjoy an intelligent encounter once a week." Her husband knew about the ad and had agreed to spend the night away from home.

Soon Goetze was joined in her weekly "encounters" by her three daughters—Swanhild, fourteen; Mechthild, seventeen; and Adelheid, nineteen. Now Goetze has started a league for sexual freedom based on the belief that extramarital relationships make for *harmonisches Familienleben* (harmonious family life). Her husband substantiates the fact that their life together has been more satisfying since the Sicilian vacation, and states firmly that his wife has the right to whatever sex life she wishes.

Helga Goetze personifies the new woman who is throwing off the cross-breed Warrior Woman–Lady archetype so derogatorily described by Esther Vilar. She is a woman who has expressed her *Wille* and then proceeded toward what she wants. Unlike Ulrike Meinhof, she has not been forced to destroy all that was valuable in her past in the process.

She, like politician Annemarie Renger, and union boss Maria Weber, is vitally important in the picture of the German woman. These women indicate that changes are taking place with the average person, who has a firm stake in the old way of doing things, as well as with the young rebel. Their success suggests there is little chance that Germany's birthrate will shoot up again or that women will neglect to take advantage of new family and work laws to achieve greater individual independence and responsibility. The status of individual *Wille* is too high for that.

Part Five

The Scandinavian Woman—

The Dynamics of Equality

1

Pippi Longstocking—Self Sufficiency as a National Archetype

"Pippi Longstocking was nine years old and lived alone with her monkey, Mr. Nelson, and her horse and a suitcase full of gold coins in Villekulla Cottage. She was a very remarkable child, and the most remarkable thing about her was her strength. She was *so* strong that in all the world there was no policeman as strong as she.

" 'But,' asked her friends, 'who tells you when to go to bed at night and that sort of thing?'

" 'I do,' said Pippi. 'The first time I say it, I say it in a friendly sort of way, and if I don't listen, I say it again more sharply, and if I still don't listen, then there's a thrashing to be had, believe me!' "[1]

In terms of international sales records and film, radio and television eulogies, Pippi Longstocking is one of the three most important children's heroines to have appeared in literature in this century. The other two are Lyman Frank Baum's Dorothy in *The Wonderful Wizard of Oz,* and Caro-

243

lyn Keene's Nancy Drew. The three mark a profound change in the way society expects little girls to behave in their daydreams. Gone are the celebrations of marriage and motherliness found in *Little Women*. Even *Alice's Adventures in Wonderland* lacks the determination of these three. Other heroines of our era have been attached either to brothers or boyfriends.

Of these contemporary child heroines, Pippi Longstocking best personifies independence and brashness. And from the very first page those characteristics are offset by a thoroughgoing self-discipline. If she is so strong that no policeman can tell her what to do, Pippi also accepts the responsibility of making herself go to bed. No characterization of the Scandinavian woman could define more clearly her interlocking liberty and responsibility.

The main focus in this section will be the Swedish woman, because throughout Scandinavian history, it is Sweden that has most frequently achieved predominance politically and economically and this continues to be true today. Furthermore, the Swedish woman exhibits a living experiment of many of the ideals that other women wish to put into practice for themselves.

Denmark, Norway and Finland are different in many important ways from Sweden, but the complaint of many Scandinavians—that they are often grouped together simply on geographical grounds—is not entirely valid. All but the Finns have a common linguistic heritage. All were part of the vast Viking culture a thousand years ago, and none was as influenced by either Christianity or the cult of the Lady as the rest of Europe. Today, they share a common approval of social welfare. Most importantly, their women share a common belief that they should take a place in society alongside their men. Furthermore, the various Scandinavian countries are officially supporting that philosophy.

For the purposes of this study, then, differences among Scandinavian countries will be ignored except when they clarify the roles of women in their respective societies. In this way, the impact of the Scandinavian woman can be examined on a broader scale, and her place as the leader of sexual equality for women be better evaluated.

During the early sixties, observers often derided Sin in Scandinavia (invariably a misnomer for free love in Scandinavia). Scandinavian women, it was said with a mixture of scorn and awe, were sexual superwomen who refused to play second fiddle to anyone. By the end of that decade, however, Vance Packard was already gathering significant evidence that America and the countries of Western Europe were experiencing the same sexual revolution.[2]

Little was said about the actual situation in Scandinavia at the time. While other countries were analyzing Scandinavian society and Scandinavian women only in terms of the free love "revolution," the Scandinavians themselves were beginning the next debate. In 1962, before any of the major current women's rights books except *The Second Sex* had appeared elsewhere, a collection of essays appeared in Sweden, entitled *Kvinnors Liv Och Arbete (The Changing Roles of Men and Women)*. In it the Scandinavian lead in revising the woman's place in society was established.

In the foreword, Alva Myrdal, one of Sweden's leading sociologists, comments, "As early as the 1930s, we had succeeded in convincing the Royal Commissions to accept the idea that a career for married women should be viewed as 'normal.' This was the time when the family role of women first came to be regarded as an ancillary, though highly important part, of her life-plan. The official formulation of the demand was not the 'right of married women to work,' but rather the 'right of workingwomen to marriage and motherhood.' "

Myrdal, a member of the government committee that had shaped the most profound changes in family law in modern times, went on to say that many of the programs she had hoped for in the thirties had not materialized. She regretted that collective approaches to housework had not become widespread and that crèches for the children of working mothers were still "almost irrelevant to the need."

But, she insisted, the sixties marked a new dawn in the family revolution, a time when the tax subsidies given to "Men who want to divert female potential to care for their personal wants in marriage" were being attacked, an era when women's liberty and responsibility within society were being supported as never before.[3]

Myrdal herself was a living example of how the socially responsible woman can live her life. Born in 1902, she married Gunnar Myrdal, and when she was thirty, they published *Kris i befolkningsfrogan (The Population Crisis)*, a vastly influential book which led to both heading different ministries.

In training and philosophy, Alva Myrdal is close to Margaret Mead, but there has been a vast difference in the amount of acclaim awarded the two women by their differing societies. Mead is accepted as a dean of American anthropologists, but this does not mean that she has been called to Washington to head Cabinet offices.

In contrast, Myrdal is unhesitatingly identified by everyone I have met as "the most famous woman in Sweden." As well as serving in the Swedish Cabinet in various positions directing home policy, she has been the Swedish Ambassador to India and head of the Swedish delegation to the nuclear disarmament commission in Geneva. She and her husband have received the West German Peace Prize. The Swedish Government's current effort to make both marriage and divorce a contractual agreement on a par with business arrangements stems from her 1973 report on social conditions and the Swedish economy.

Her husband also has a demanding career in social analysis and political policy-making, and is perhaps best known outside Sweden for his book on racial problems, *The American Dilemma.* The couple now lives just outside Stockholm, continuing to write and conduct sociological studies. In the *International Who's Who (IWW)*, Alva lists her hobbies as reading, travel, the theater and cooking; Gunnar lists his as travel and reading. Their son, Jan, is also listed in *IWW* for his reports on China and the European political Left.

If this is the likely result of "a pair of careers," as Myrdal once described her marriage, it's surprising that there has not been a thundering herd of women headed for Sweden.

The overall picture, however, is not uniformly successful. Scandinavian statistical data reveal an ominous upswing in venereal disease. The female suicide rate, although not as high as in Austria and West Germany, is still higher than in any other Western industrialized culture, with Denmark the highest among the Scandinavian countries.

When one checks the charts on alcoholism, drug addiction and divorce, again the picture points starkly to the fact that the Scandinavian woman is paying a heavy emotional price for her place in society.

In 1964, Eva Moberg published *Kvinnor och människor (Women and Human Beings).* In it, she argued that women should no more have the right to "choose" an exclusive career in the home than men, and that women must not shirk their responsibility to society as a whole. Men and women, she insisted, each carry the entire burden of one role—that of human being. Both should be equally responsible in society and in the home.

This is the stance that Sweden is increasingly accepting. The idea has much to offer other cultures, but it has one essential drawback. Far from offering greater liberty, it is simply forcing people to exchange one socially imposed role for another. If this is the pattern Western women are bent on following, we should examine its disadvantages as well as its advantages before accepting it blindly.

2

A Fork in the Road for Brunhild

The self-sufficient, egalitarian women of Scandinavia share with the Germans the ancient Gudrun/Brunhild archetypes. For all the Viking women, fidelity and bravery were the highest virtue.

During the first through the tenth centuries, however, enormous changes took place, making the Scandinavian woman's image of herself and her position in society vastly different. To the south, the Teutonic tribes were first conquered by the Romans and then overwhelmed by Christianity. The Norse, on the other hand, maintained their autonomy. Their laws and their daily lives were little changed by the Roman concept of paterfamilias, and they did not widely adopt Catholicism until the twelfth century. For women, this meant something quite fundamental. The Lady—with her Otherness, her piety and her power through manipulation—never gained the upper hand as the ideal of womanhood.

Instead, Viking women maintained near-equal status and responsibility with their men, both in legal theory and in everyday practice. Jacqueline

247

Simpson, in her investigative *Everyday Life in the Viking Age*, points out that women ". . . could own land and manage their own property, had complete authority in household matters, and often must have run farms single-handed while their husbands were abroad. . . . If the sagas are to be believed, their implacable energy kept many a blood feud alive when the men would gladly have ended it. There are accounts of women wielding personal power, such as Aud the Deep-Minded, widow of a Viking king in Ireland, who led an immigration of her family and dependants to Iceland, and who apportioned land among them like a chieftain."[4]

The wife did not change her name at marriage and never severed her ties with her kinsmen. If a feud arose between them and her husband, she could side either with her relatives or with her husband. Two heroines in the Völsunga Saga are praised for personally taking a gruesome blood vengeance on their husbands for the sake of their dead brothers.

Divorce was granted on the demand of either partner, and carried no stigma for either. The wife returned to her kinsmen's tribe, where she continued to hold a position of responsibility. The sagas record divorces as being granted for "impotence, the wearing of breeches by a wife and of an effeminate shirt by a husband, and a husband's friendliness towards the man who had killed his wife's brother."[5]

Tribes either made peaceful arrangements for intermarriage or captured brides through raids. The eldest man was ordinarily head of the family, but upon his death his widow often took up the mantle of power, and tales of her bloody victories in maintaining her position run throughout Viking history.

Land was inherited according to a code of primogeniture, but the eldest son was required to pay compensation to his siblings for their portion. If all the sons were dead, the widow was next in line, with the sisters coming last. The claims of the nuclear family always came before those of any other relatives.

Younger sons commonly left the tribe to try their fortunes with the Vikings. The name actually means "pirate" in ancient Scandinavian languages, but their behavior was vastly different from that of the queen's fleet in Elizabethan times. The Vikings' women often went with them, and they were looking for land to settle as much as for bounty.

Despite the Viking woman's reputation as a Warrior Woman and her legal status, there were many vital areas where she had little say. When a child was born, for example, it was the father who examined it. If it was deformed or if the family was impoverished, he would have it exposed. Otherwise, he christened the child, often naming it after himself.

The man also had the right to take as many concubines as he could maintain. The wife's position was higher than that of the concubine, but these women also had certain legal rights. Their offspring could be legitimized by the father in a simple ceremony, and even without formal recognition they usually had a small share in the inheritance.

When a renowned leader died, particularly among the Rus tribes from Sweden who settled in Russia, one of the women in his household customarily committed suttee. In Birka, close to modern-day Stockholm, women's skeletons in twisted positions have been found in both men's and women's tombs. The women who had been walled up alive in the men's tombs wore ornaments that indicate they were probably wives.

Out of the milieu of vengeance, tribal responsibility and bravery rose the Warrior Woman queens of the north. The first to be notably honored in history was Blenda, from a county district in southern Sweden. Blenda led an army of women to victory over the Danes, who had invaded the province of Värend. As a reward for valor in war, the women of Värend were granted equal rights with men in matters of inheritance and marriage.[6]

Two centuries later, Earl Birger, the most powerful Swedish nobleman of the day, issued laws prohibiting the taking of any wife by force. He also stipulated that a daughter should have inheritance rights, although she was entitled to only half as much as her brother.

In the 1300s, Birgitta Birgersdotter, one of the earl's descendants, became renowned throughout Christendom for her religious and social pilgrimages. Her revelations, which were published in the vernacular as well as in Latin, are considered by many authorities to be the first Swedish works of interest.

Birgitta knew her religious calling as a child, and very early had a vision which was to influence her throughout life. Nevertheless, at thirteen she was married, and during the next two decades bore eight children, one of whom became St. Catherine of Sweden.

Accounts vary, but in 1344 she and her husband either parted amicably or he died. At any rate, she retired to a convent, where her revelations were recorded, and soon began a pilgrimage to Rome for the Holy Year. She petitioned the Pope to found an Order, and her wish was granted in approximately 1370. Although nearly seventy, and deeply involved with administering to the poor, she immediately began making plans for the pilgrimage to the Holy Land in 1371. This she completed two years later, but her health was ruined and she died soon after. The Bridgettine Order was housed in the famous convent built on the royal estate of Vadstena, in

Sweden, which had been bestowed upon Birgitta by her kinsman, King Magnus.

St. Birgitta (Bridget) is known today as a Lady archetype. The patron saint of Sweden, she was canonized both for her administering to the poor and for her visions. Aside from an iron physical constitution, there is a unique facet of her character which starkly differentiates her from the Latin Lady archetype. She preached sexual equality. The Bridgettine Order, based on commands Birgitta received during a vision of Christ, was open to both sexes, and both the nuns and the monks who belonged to the order were under the authority of the abbess.

Late that same century, the Brunhild archetype blossomed in the form of Queen Margrethe I, the daughter of the King of Denmark and the wife of the King of Norway. When her father died, she had her infant son, Olav, crowned king because it was illegal in Denmark for a woman to be sovereign. While Margrethe's husband remained in Norway, she ruled Denmark as regent.

When her husband died in 1380, she had Olav crowned king in Norway, again with herself as regent. She began pressing for her son's claim to the Swedish crown. Although Olav died soon after, she continued as ruler of Denmark and Norway, waged war against the Swedish king, and succeeded in defeating and capturing him in 1389.

Eight years later, she was able to forge the last bonds of the Kalmar Union, a territory stretching from the polar ice cap to the 55° parallel, including control of the Baltic and Norwegian seas. In name, this empire was headed by her nephew, Eric. In reality, it was ruled by Margrethe, the regent.

Margrethe I was the first European woman to control vast dominions. She was, according to Dr. Irene Scobbie, a former Cambridge professor of Swedish literature and history, "one of the most successful rulers in Scandinavia in the Middle Ages."[7] She was the only person who ever truly united the Scandinavian countries under one leadership, since after her death in 1412, the Kalmar Union was again divided by wars and jealousies.

Her example as a strong and able female leader has never again been equaled in Scandinavia. Christina, daughter of Gustavus Adolphus, assumed the Swedish throne in 1632, when she was only six. She was raised in a man's world and taught to rule as monarch. She set up one of the most impressive literary courts of the era, and was renowned for her intelligence and knowledge. Yet, only ten years after she came of age and assumed full responsibility for the crown, she abdicated in favor of a male cousin, and left Sweden for Catholic Rome.

A hundred years later, Ulrika Eleonora was elected Queen of Sweden after the death of her brother, Charles XII, but, feeling incapable of assuming the responsibility, she, too, abdicated—this time in favor of a husband.

Swedish women everywhere were being recognized in the arts during this era. The best-known was Hedvig Charlotta Nordenflycht, a poetess and a feminist, who had a noted literary salon and was so esteemed for her work that she became the first Swedish poet to receive a state pension.

Fredrika Bremer, Sweden's Mary Wollstonecraft, was born in 1801 (four years after Wollstonecraft's death), and became well known for her novels depicting women, parents and children. Totally dedicated to the issue of women's rights, in 1856 she published her didactic novel *Hёrtha*, starkly outlining the plight of unmarried women. Two years later, a law was passed giving women the right to take legal decisions at age twenty-five.

Women outside the intelligentsia also had careers. From the 1600s through the 1800s, cloth in Sweden was money, as well as the main source of trade. To maintain this backbone of the economy, fifteen thousand textile workers were needed and 70 to 80 percent of them were women. The same percentage is true in the industry today. More important, today nearly half the textile managers and many of the company executives are women.

By the end of the nineteenth century, feminists were making appreciable progress in Sweden. Grade-school attendance of all children became mandatory in 1842. Women sat for matriculation exams in all academic university fields except theology and high law. In 1873, a law was passed reinstating married women's right to dispose of their own property and any money they might earn. Women started independent businesses, became doctors and lawyers and championed the cause of free love.

But, still, the major problem was the unmarried woman. Improved medical care had led to overpopulation in the countryside, and hundreds of thousands of teen-agers poured into the cities, the majority of whom were female. In Stockholm, over half the women above the age of fifteen were unmarried. Nearly two-thirds of the children born were illegitimate. In the newspapers, women advertised daily for employment without salary, so long as they would be fed, and "treated with kindness."[8]

Meanwhile, Finland was trying to shake off Russia's domination and Norway was trying to shake off Sweden's. In 1906, Finland partially succeeded, and one of the fruits of her victory was the first achievement of universal women's suffrage in the Western Hemisphere. Danish and Norwegian women were the next to succeed, and both won equal voting rights with men in 1913. Sweden was last, in 1919.

This was a period when Finland was decimated by war, and nearly one out of every five Swedes and Norwegians was to emigrate to the United States because of famine in the countryside.

The total collapse of the old order not only gave women the right to vote. It also presented them with a clean slate on which to draw a new image. All the old values, family patterns and laws, both written and unwritten, regarding what a woman could and could not do, were proved to be as inadequate as the haphazard farming methods of the times. Sweden, and to an extent Norway and Finland, became nations of strangers. New arrivals in the Industrial Revolution, they installed new ideas with new machinery and accepted totally new patterns of daily life with their new city apartment homes.

As trades and professions opened up to women, they joined the work force everywhere. They were elected to city councils and national legislatures. In Finland, it became an unwritten rule to have at least one or two women serving in the Cabinet.

Chronicling the vast changes were two Nobel Prize winners. Selma Lagerlöf, the first woman to be elected to the eighteen-member Swedish Academy, was the author of *The Wonderful Adventures of Nils, The Story of Gösta Berling* and *The Ring of the Löwens-kölds* trilogy. She won the Nobel Prize in 1909. Her books are marked by strong-willed, self-righteous and forceful women, who are the mainstay of the family and man's salvation. The Norwegian Sigrid Undset, who won the Nobel Prize in 1928, was concerned with religious morality, and the heroines of her best-known works, *Gunnar's Daughter* and *Kristin Lavransdatter,* are even more strong-willed and self-sufficient than Lagerlöf's.

During World War I, women in neutral Sweden became particularly prominent. Märta Måås Fjetterstrom was a leading textile chief executive. Pauline Brunius, the actress-producer, was appointed Director of the Royal Dramatic Theater. And Elise Ottesen-Jensen, the Norwegian-born sex pedagogue and peer of the American Margaret Sanger, formed the National Union of Sex Education in Sweden, and was able to win the introduction of compulsory sex education in the schools.

This was also the era of Alva Myrdal's report on Sweden's population crisis. She and her husband stated the problems of the average family simply. City landlords did not want couples with many children; mothers burdened by the classic "six stepping-stones" were both physically exhausted and unable to leave their infants to take gainful employment and thereby support them. In short, with child labor outlawed, it was too expensive to have children, and the pragmatic Swedes were thinking in terms of one child or no children at all.

The Myrdals concluded that society as a whole would have to shoulder the job of providing for the next generation. They proposed a four-part program: state-financed housing, giving the family with young children priority, a child-allowance benefit for all families, a commitment to feed a daily lunch to every schoolchild and the creation of mother-baby health clinics throughout the country. They also backed Elise Ottesen-Jensen's plea for sex education and family-planning advice, believing this to be a basic human right, and pointing out that, if every child is a wanted child, they will grow up to be better adults for society.

In 1938, when the Social Democrats first came to office, they immediately began to implement these programs. The concept that childbearing is a vital component of the GNP was clearly understood and emphasized. At this point, Sweden took the lead in social *trygghet* (security) from Denmark, which, since 1922, had been developing programs covering old age, disablement, health and unemployment.

Within a short period of time, Sweden had the lowest infant-mortality rate in the world. The replacement birthrate was reestablished and has held more or less steady through the ensuing thirty-five years.

Swedish rationalism always seems so simple after the fact.

Today Finland and Sweden lead the West in their efforts to make the working wife and mother a practical reality. Legal systems have been revamped in all the Scandinavian countries. Part-time flexible work hours are available, and taxes no longer penalize a two-career family. Men are encouraged to spend more time and creative energy as fathers, and the role of *hemmaman* (house husband) is now a viable choice for a man, even though examples are still rare.

Despite variations on which programs take priority and how they are to be implemented, the pan-Scandinavian commitment to sexual equality is clear-cut. The only valid area to question in a society as single-minded and forward-looking as this one is concerns the quality of life.

3

Cohabiting Companions and Sexuality

The first definition given in Inge and Sten Hegeler's *ABZ of Love* is: "Abnormal: Something that is unlike what we are used to, something that departs from the accepted rule, i.e., deviates from the norm."

Some 110 pages later, under "Genital organs, their appearance and size," the Hegelers return to the same pragmatic philosophy:

"Many people are worried about whether their genital organs look the same as other people's. Well, it so happens that we all look fairly different in the face, and the same applies to the other end.

"Some have large noses, others small.

"Some have large mouths, others small.

"Even so, most of us manage to find somebody who enjoys kissing us."[9]

When the *ABZ of Love* first appeared in English in 1963, people in both the United States and Britain were scandalized. Although the actual catechism of this Danish sexologist team was one of equality of the sexes and tolerance for the individual, the Anglo-Saxon community in general took the work to be one more piece of evidence that there was sin in Scandinavia.

"Look at the way premarital sex is openly permitted," it was said. "Look at the way the Scandinavian governments support the unwed mother. Look at the pornography. Look at the women in discotheques who don't hesitate to ask men to dance. Doesn't that all add up to an open and closed case of premeditated promiscuity?"

The sixties became a watershed decade for the codes of Western mores, spurred first by means of widespread and effective birth control, and second by warnings that the earth could not support the rising tide of humanity. Suddenly, sex for fun was no longer the craze of the frivolous, but a necessity for everyone.

Now, in the seventies, amid the shambles of what was once called "conventional morality," it is obviously time to reexamine the Scandinavian situation. A surprising fact emerges. Scandinavia today has the most clearly defined, coherent set of moral principles in the Western World. Their principles differ from those of other contemporary societies, and as such have often gone undetected. But the more people try to sort out the complicated wasteland of today's sexual politics, the more the Scandinavian solution makes sense.

There are several reasons why Scandinavian morality is so well adapted to today's world. Scandinavia moved into the Industrial Revolution late, and the biggest changes in life patterns have occurred during this century. Not only could Scandinavian society take advantage of other peoples' experiences, but its new codes of behavior reflect today's problems alone, without being weighed down by the dilemmas of the Victorian Age.

A more subtle, but perhaps even more important, factor is involved in the language. Conversational Swedish, particularly, is an intricate science with a devious form of direct address. The Swedes are forever commenting that they are more at ease speaking English than their native tongue, where there is always the possibility of making an error and/or insulting a colleague. As these perfectionist people moved into the industrial era, they became adept at communicating with each other via admirably constructed written reports. The most rewarding conversations were carried out on paper—point one, point two, point three.

Inevitably, the written analysis promulgated on a mass scale via newspapers, magazines and pamphlets became acceptable as a means of communication about private life as well. New nuclear families, half a country away from the grandparents, were hammering out new life-styles. It was relatively easy to discard the old way of doing things and make a commitment to experimentation with the flood of expert proposals invading every household. A quicker means to building an up-to-date and pragmatic code of behavior is hard to imagine.

Women have played an extraordinarily large part in formulating the new codes of intersexual behavior. Fredrika Bremer, Ellen Key, Sigrid Undset, Elise Ottesen-Jensen, Alva Myrdal, Birgitta Linnér, Dr. Kristen Auken, Inge Hegeler—all have had enormous influence. Being Scandinavian, they have presented carefully reasoned plans with realistic alternatives. Being women, they have highlighted the weaknesses and difficulties of the patriarchal system.

In the vanguard of these ranks are the "Dear Abby" columnists. The frankly outspoken and graphically explicit opinions of Dr. Auken have often been quoted abroad, as have excerpts from the *ABZ of Sex* and the columns written by the Hegelers.

Although not as internationally well-known as the sexologists, the columnists who write on emotional problems have been just as important in Scandinavia. One of the most articulate and widely read of these is the Dane, Tove Ditlevsen. A woman more different from Ann Landers is hard to imagine. Over twenty years ago, Ditlevsen began writing her column with descriptions of the problems she had experienced after she had had an illegal abortion. Not only did she suffer medical complications, but she also became addicted to morphine and other pain-killing drugs. She has been through several divorces and is the author of *Gift,* an autobiographical work built around the fact that, in Danish, *gift* means both "poison" and "marriage."

Her readers are looking for a wisdom that comes from a wrenching yet exhilarating life. They seek tolerance and resilience, qualities they believe are absolutely necessary for today's chaotic existence.

Ditlevsen says that her current beliefs differ greatly from those she held when she first started writing. "Now I don't think people should try to stick marriage out. A woman needs to be able to break off and start another life. She shouldn't feel guilty that it didn't work out."[10]

Purging guilt over infractions against yesterday's rules of behavior is a major part of the changeover to today's ethics. It is a task common to sexologists and social commentators in both the United States and Scandinavia. Where the Scandinavians differ is in the positive alternative that is also being taught.

This is being articulated most clearly in a logical place—the schools. Sex education is a Scandinavian institution, which is today a far more detailed and subtle craft than it was when it first became nationally available in Sweden at the beginning of the forties.

At first, everyone agreed on only one part of the program—the need for children to understand the physiology of an act which is to play a major part in their adult lives. Everyone also agreed that the best place to learn would be at home. A wealth of books had been written to help the parental instructor, and Scandinavian publishers of children's books had begun pioneering gaily illustrated "How I Got Here" reports for children. But this mode of teaching wasn't fast enough. Elise Ottesen-Jensen and her contemporaries contended that many parents were not only badly informed, they didn't want to bring up the subject at all. In their quest for new ways of life and in their acceptance of expert advice, the Scandinavians agreed to try having sex taught in school.

The program has always been controversial. It is still bitterly attacked from time to time in the press as contributing to juvenile delinquency. Other publications support the concept, and laugh off the conflicts. One recent cartoon features a twelve-year-old girl being asked by her father how the sex-education class went. "Oh," she replies disconsolately, "we only did theory today."

Among adults, theory is where the discord lies. There is still no consensus on whether or not "right" and "wrong" should be included in the classes. If ethics are to be integrated into biology lessons, the argument goes, then how can we decide *whose* ethics? The same debate has come up in every culture currently offering any measure of sex education in school. Most of the more recent converts to the system are opting for straight biological instruction, but the Scandinavians have tackled moral behavior as well. Norway, Finland and—to some extent—Denmark have all gone ahead explaining "good" and "bad" behavior. Sweden has sidestepped the issue by a semantical sleight of hand. They refer to actions as "practical" and "impractical." No matter what the labels, there is a coherent set of moral rules being taught to form a skeleton of ethics on behavior between the sexes.

Perhaps the best person to explain these principles is Birgitta Linnér, a Swedish lawyer who has also studied family sociology and psychology at Harvard and the University of Chicago. For the past twenty-five years, she has been with the Family Counseling Bureau of Stockholm and has written and/or edited many of the textbooks on sexual relations currently used in the Swedish school system.

Linnér is a small, dynamic woman, probably in her late forties, who is most often to be found in a crowded and cheerful office just off one of Stockholm's older shopping streets. Toys and games for the children of clients are tucked among the encyclopedias and law books. She is not an overly friendly or relaxed person, but she's easy to talk with because she's honest. She comes to the point immediately, and appears totally convinced that everyone can help himself or herself as soon as a situation is understood.

The Swedish moral code, she explains, is fundamentally honest and optimistic. It is based first and foremost on equality between the sexes. Its prime tenet is mutual responsibility.

"Sexual responsibility means three things," she says. "First, one must not force oneself on another—this means that a girl should not insist on attention any more than a boy should. Second, one must take the proper precautions against an unwanted pregnancy. Third, one must seek treatment for venereal disease upon discovery of the problem and refrain from sexual activity until all possibility of further contamination is cleared up."[11]

The dynamics of this pragmatic humanism are deceptively simple. Gone are the traditional, but once justifiable, fears of continual pregnancy and/or sexual exploitation of the woman when there was no work for her outside the home. The cults of self-denial, of the virgin, of the double standard, are all set aside as no longer necessary.

Just as important, there is also a rejection of many of the reactionary "With It" tenets propounded elsewhere. Sexual intimacy between friends is looked upon as *permissible,* but not as *mandatory* for the development of individual potential. Sex is recognized as the most intimate part of a relationship between dignified human beings. The need for mutual respect in order to avoid mutual destruction is clearly stated. Self-satisfaction has not been given the unqualified applause once won by self-denial.

I first saw the responsibility principles in action when I met a Scandinavian *au pair* girl in London. She was taking judo lessons, because, she said, there were those in England who hadn't realized that the freedom to say "yes" also meant the freedom to say "no." She was disgusted with the behavior of most men outside Sweden, and insisted that Swedish men were the only ones to have discarded the old belief that conquest equals status.

Crime statistics confirm her claim. Rape in Sweden is a rare occurrence. With a population and demographic profile roughly equivalent to that of Michigan, Sweden has only one-fifth the number of rape cases.[12] The number of child sexual abusers is also minute. On an egalitarian note, women can and are sometimes convicted of "seducing a minor under 15."

The low rate of intersexual violence points to only one conclusion: a system of mutual responsibility taught through the schools is the most viable philosophy being used in contemporary societies.

If accepting the mutual responsibility not to force one's advances upon another appears to be generally successful in Sweden, what about the second principle—the responsibility to avoid unwanted pregnancy?

Statistics on illegitimate births appear discouraging. In 1950, 10 percent of all Swedish babies were born out of wedlock. By 1970, the rate had risen to 18 percent—nearly three times as high as that of the United States.[13]

Linnér feels that this data is irrelevant. "One out of every three young couples are unmarried, today," she comments. "But these couples still give the child a stable home. They plan on having children—perhaps more carefully than married couples. The problems we have with these people if they decide to separate do not ordinarily concern the children at all. Conflicts arise over how to split up common property. The rights of the child are almost always observed by both parents."

Legally, the term "illegitimate" does not exist in Sweden. Children born out of wedlock have the same rights to their father's name and to equal family inheritance as any child born after marriage.

More important, tradition is not against them. Acceptance of illegitimate offspring dates back to the era of the Viking concubine. Donald Connery, who has done one of the most extensive recent social analyses of Scandinavia, explains that young couples were allowed considerable freedom right up until the first half of this century. "Trial marriages served to establish whether a girl was capable of providing the children needed for the family farm. Eldest sons, in particular, needed to be sure that they would have heirs. The pregnancy of an unmarried girl was not so much of a shock as a signal to set the date for the wedding."[14]

By the late 1950s, a new version of the old pragmatism was being propounded. Among others, two leading sociologists, Lis Asklund and Thorsten Wickbom, were already campaigning against "forced" marriages to legalize the child.

"To marry only for the sake of the child and without real affection for one another involves, as we see it, great risk," they wrote in a school textbook. "Many unhappy marriages began this way: 'We were forced to get married.' Afterwards, the couple may have more children and their resulting economic situation makes divorce impossible. But they never enjoy a really pleasant moment together. The question arises—how well has the emotional and material welfare of the child, for whose sake the marriage originally took place, been provided for?"[15]

If the rate of children born outside of wedlock does not constitute a setback en route to the goal of "Every baby a wanted baby," what other barometers are there? Checking the abortion rate is inconclusive because it has been regulated by artificial means, which will be investigated later. This leaves only one real gauge of the number of unwanted pregnancies—i.e., how many children are put up for adoption.

Swedish adoption procedures are a miracle of speed and efficiency. Unmarried mothers are given complete information on the process from the time they first contact medical authorities. The welfare of an adopted baby could be guaranteed by Lloyd's of London. And still the number of children placed with agencies has dropped until the waiting time for adopting a Swedish child is between three and six years. By this gauge, then, the "Responsible Pregnancy" principle seems to be working, after all.

It is the third and last rule of sexual responsibility which is in trouble. Prompt action to stamp out venereal disease has not been successful. Denmark and Sweden have been experiencing what the World Health Organization terms "an epidemic" in sexually transmitted diseases. In 1971, the UN registered 316 cases of gonorrhea per 100,000 people in Denmark. The rate in Sweden was 500. The United States, with a rate of 307.5 for the same year, came close to the Danish figure, but no country came anywhere near Sweden.

The high rate in all three countries can be partially accounted for by efficiency in tabulation. Both victims and medical authorities in these countries are cognizant of the necessity to report the situation. Sweden has strict laws compelling a person to reveal the possible source(s) of the infection, so again, the authorities are in a good position to keep count.

The fact remains, however, that these rising rates of infection reflect changing sexual behavior patterns. Statistics indicate that the group most consistently contributing to the increase is the teen-age girl. In the sixties, according to the Swedish National Association for Sex Education, the number of girls with gonorrhea exceeded the number of boys in all age groups. This was the first time more girls than boys had been infected, and doctors reported treating girls as young as thirteen and fourteen.[16]

These figures have scandalized the nation and caused innumerable debates on what can be done. Reactions are particularly salient because they are characterized by a subconscious reliance on two "traditional" moral values.

First, there is a great reluctance to characterize the girl as the aggressor and/or the culprit. Authorities depict her as more adventuresome than before, but still the partner most likely to "be satisfied with one relationship.'' The teen-age boy, on the other hand, is accused of greedily grabbing one sexual partner after another and getting them all into trouble.

In keeping with continued protectiveness toward the female, the male is the one who is required to shoulder responsibility for doing something about the problem. An Uppsala study indicated that 80 percent of the men reporting to the clinic did so of their own accord, while the remaining 20 percent were summoned by authorities. More than half the women, on the other hand, were summoned, and more than 33 percent were prompted by their partners. Only a tiny minority took it upon themselves to go to the authorities voluntarily.[17]

Swedish authorities are also surprisingly traditional and Puritanical in the ways in which they are attacking the problem. They are not mounting heavily publicized campaigns to develop a cheap inoculation or a simple means of testing. Routine blood tests are not a part of everyone's annual medical checkup. Any means of self-testing or self-curing is abhorred. Instead, authorities insist on a semireligious rite entailing confession of one's ''sins'' to the doctor, who then doles out a physical ''cleansing'' in as unsympathetic a manner as possible.

If it takes years before a cheap and efficient way of protecting society is developed, the reason will lurk somewhere behind a doctor's grimace of distaste at one Malmö clinic as he was explaining the sexual history of one of his patients. His attitude said louder than words: ''She *deserved* to catch syphilis.'' Like a medieval tradesman sanctimoniously conjuring up the wrath of God in his description of a competitor's demise from the plague, the doctor detailed his patient's musical-chairs sexuality, then wrung his hands as he bemoaned the difficulties of finding all her partners. Behind his desk hung a National Board of Health poster, admonishing, ''The only *sure* way to protect yourself against VD is not to enter into casual sexual relationships.''

It comes as a surprise to those who think of the North as a hotbed of casual sexual intimacy to find that VD is treated as a ''mark of shame,'' not because of the disease itself, but because of a fundamental censure against promiscuity, which is condemned everywhere. In 1964, the Swedish Medical Authority even petitioned the government for action against careless sex. Promiscuity, after all, carries the stigmas of irresponsibility, bad planning and lack of self-discipline. No more disgusting traits exist in the Swedish lexicon.

Taboos against promiscuity are even stronger once a person marries. A youngster can be forgiven moments of bad planning, but having taken on the responsibility of marriage, a person can no longer be considered a youngster. Scandinavian acceptance of premarital sex and the unmarried mother is based on the concept that the decision to marry should grow from a functioning relationship. Such a serious step should be taken outside the crosscurrents of either unfulfilled passion or premarital pregnancy. The rational individual who marries, then, is voluntarily assuming new obligations.

Fidelity is expected of both spouses. Conscious efforts to eradicate the double standard in Sweden means expecting men to be as responsible as women, not urging women to be as capricious as men. Both the Latin concept that a mistress makes a marriage tranquil and the American idea that the two marriage partners should join a swingers' club together are frowned upon in Sweden.

The ban on promiscuity is firmly rooted in the strongest motivating factor in the entire Scandinavian intersexual behavior pattern—fear of isolation. That fear is common everywhere, of course. It accounts for our being social-group animals in the first place. But the need to form groups—or "groupism"—does not by itself encourage monogamy. A more likely development would be polyandry and/or polygamy. Taboos against promiscuity develop only where the individual experiences *both* fear of isolation *and* fear of other members of the group. In that case, the individual tends to form a lasting and demanding pair bond with another trusted individual.

This is exactly what happens in Scandinavia, where people are standoffish with each other and extremely sensitive to criticism. As in the United States, family groups are small and mobile. Inside Scandinavia's highly fluid society, more and more pressure is put on the prime pair bond. There is a basic need for a marital relationship characterized by mutual trust and emotional harmony.

Serious analysts of Scandinavian society consider the widespread failure to meet this need a far more significant problem than the tangential but resolvable one of spiraling VD rates. Open any newspaper, any magazine, any study of Scandinavian suicide patterns, and invariably one point is immediately made—the Scandinavian suffers from *ensamhet* (loneliness). Alienation, isolation, inability to interact with others—translate it as you will—*ensamhet* dominates any conversation dealing with criticism of the Scandinavian scene.

In Sweden, *ensamhet* is considered a causal factor of everything from divorce to alcoholism to drug abuse to suicide. It is the pivotal dilemma in Swedish films, and the most common theme in Swedish literature. The Finns and the Norweigians are not quite as obsessed with the subject, but they still consider it a major issue.

Danish men like to believe that they are too gregarious to suffer from *ensamhet*. "When I asked a Swedish friend of mine if he talked to his wife during intercourse," one Copenhagen architect joked, "he looked surprised and said, 'Sure! I mean, if she's there, of *course* I talk to her!' Seriously, you know, the Swedes will never understand women the way we do." Danish women, however, are not so certain that sexual alienation lies only on the other side of the Öresund channel. The Danish suicide rate, which is higher than Sweden's, tends to support their complaints, for the majority of studies indicate that a broken love affair is the most frequent cause of suicide.

Ensamhet is blamed on many things, the two most common being the Nordic reluctance to talk about emotions and the long winters when people are locked into darkness for months on end. Ultimately, however, the majority of critics also point a damning finger at women—liberated women in particular.

"Our Scandinavian women don't like men," a recently divorced Norwegian told me. "They think most men are worthless, and they hate themselves for falling in love. They're taught to believe that the only way to atone for falling in love is to punish themselves and their lovers as much as possible."

While studying experiments in Scandinavian marriage, *Life* magazine reporter Mike Durham griped, "I seldom had to ask questions [of the Scandinavian woman] because most of them had some kind of compulsion to explain their actions in the starkest clinical terms. And when somebody talks to you clinically, you end up listening clinically."[18]

Paul Britten Austin, an English journalist who is married to Ingmar Bergman's sister and has spent much of his life in Sweden, is more lenient. He indicts Swedish men, who are "over-strained, over-worked, over-ambitious, they wear their social straight-jackets without grace of humour and their rigid behaviour is reflected in the highly specific dilemma of the women."

But Austin goes on to quote psychologists' feelings that it is the career mother, determined to force her infant son out into the world, who causes the egoistic, cold and demanding male. Finally, he speculates that Swedish women may be driven to hatred of Swedish men because of their four thousand years of inbreeding.[19]

Condemnation of the liberated woman goes back at least as far as the writings of Sweden's best-known author, August Strindberg, who was the Norman Mailer of the last century. Married and divorced three times, flamboyant, fascinated with women, he was a powerful but vitriolic writer who built his plays around his compulsive hatred of what he called the "man-woman" or the "Amazon-woman."

"I made up my mind to win you as woman by being the man," one of his heroes tells his wife.

"There is where you made your mistake," she replies. ". . . The woman was your enemy, and love between the sexes produces strife, dissension, conflict. And do not think I gave myself to you. I took—whatever I wanted."[20]

It is this chilly possibility of eternal animosity that makes Northern monogamy so delicate. Since the only alternative is total *ensamhet*, the Scandina..ans have worked hard at shoring up the system against its intrinsic hazards. This means that for the young, experimentation is overtly accepted but covertly treated with aversion—i.e., silence, distaste and references to disease. The result has been younger marriages and younger sexual intimacy, but little indiscriminate bed-hopping.

For adults, monogamy is so important that prostitution has nearly disappeared, and where it exists the majority of clients are reportedly foreigners. To ease the stress and claustrophobia, three outlets have been carefully cultivated—masturbation, pornography and serial marriage.

Masturbation is more or less accepted across today's Western society, but the rational Scandinavian approach to the other two practices needs to be more fully examined.

Denmark took the lead in liberalizing pornography laws when, in 1967, it abolished all restrictions on the sale of literature to adults. It now has the most liberal pornography laws in the world, although I was told by several editors of pornographic presses at the International Book Fair in Frankfurt that from time to time California has had as open a market as Denmark.

Being an open market, however, has not fostered a booming business in Scandinavia. The sale of material to Danes has dropped since the liberalization. Sex shops that once dotted the Strøget in central Copenhagen have now largely returned to a more lucrative trade in clothes and hairstyling. Those that are left report that the majority of customers are foreigners. Porno publishers indicate that more than 60 percent of their output is shipped abroad in plain, brown wrappers.

The change in the law was conceived by the Danish Minister of Justice in December 1964, when he asked the Permanent Criminal Law Committee to study Section 234 of the Criminal Code. The committee's report was published two years later. Unlike presidential reports in the United States, it had an immediate effect on lawmakers.

Its message was negative, but concise. It noted that existing pornography restrictions requiring "artistic merit" had become impossible to enforce because judges were asked to spend all their time being literary critics instead of arbiters of the law. No concrete proof had been discovered to the effect that reading about "descriptions of human sexual activity" caused psychological harm. Although there was very little practical research in the area, as far as could be rationally determined by the personal experience of psychiatrists and psychologists, written pornography had never been directly detrimental to society. As pictorial pornography was judged more likely to outrage public dignity, it continued to be forbidden.

That restriction was lifted in 1969, again on the strength of a negative development. It seemed that the number of pornographic books on the market had actually decreased after liberalization, while the number of picture publications had increased. One positive fact had come to light in the ensuing years, however. The prediction that pornography would not destroy the moral fiber of the country was proving correct.

The First Danish Sex Market Fair followed, with much fanfare. It flourished the first year and flubbed the next, and has not been heard from since.

It is intriguing that legalization appears to take the wind out of pornographic sales figures. But a far more important point that has been tested by the Danish experiment is the relationship of pornography to sex-related crimes.

Dr. Berl Kutschinsky, the Danish psychologist who has been carefully tabulating sex-related crimes since the changes in the law were first considered, published an initial report in 1970. In it, he noted that the number of sex crimes registered by the police from 1963 to 1969 *decreased by nearly 50 percent.*[21]

This overall figure is astonishing when compared to similar patterns in other countries during the same period. Kutschinsky, in a careful and understated way, takes pains to point out several mitigating factors. The fact that pornography offenses no longer existed, for example, would cut the overall figure directly. Homosexuality was also dropped from the books in 1967, eliminating another number of offenses. He is also suspicious about decreasing indecent-exposure figures, because authorities claim that nobody notices the exhibitionist anymore, much less takes the trouble to report him to the police. The same lack of public interest is also contributing to the decrease in the number of Peeping Toms reported to the authorities.

This leaves only one rate that Kutschinsky deems authentically relevant, that dealing with the crimes termed "physical indecency to women and girls." Again, there has been a significant decline, and the downward trend has continued, he told me in 1974.[22] It can now be recognized as one of the most significant facts we know about human response to unrestricted pornography.

"The availability of hard-core pornography is apparently particularly important in providing a valid substitute for the type of male afraid to approach women," the psychologist commented. "In the past, he sometimes became violent and/or took his frustrations out on children." Kutschinsky cautiously refuses to advocate the legalization of pornography in order to prevent sex crimes against children, but he admits that the Danish experiment has clearly destroyed the arguments of those who believed that legalization would cause an increase in intersexual violence.

Scandinavian acceptance of repeated marriage and divorce is starkly different from the rest of Europe. Divorce was easier and more acceptable among the Vikings a thousand years ago than it was among other cultures to the south. Even a hundred years ago, divorce could be initiated by either partner in most of Scandinavia, although the rate of incidence was low. Today, one out of every 2.44 marriages in Denmark is ending in divorce. In Sweden, the rate is one out of every 2.57. In the United States it's one out of every 2.72.[23]

The apparent paradox of a society that places a high value on monogamy and yet has a high divorce rate is not difficult to understand if viewed in the context of other cultural patterns. Divorce rates are the lowest in Latin countries, where perfection in marriage as an emotional partnership is not expected. The Latin Lady often marries for love, but rarely looks for camaraderie and emotional support as well. Nor does she want a potential competitor in her own sphere of influence.

The Scandinavian woman, like the American and other Anglo-Saxons, expects to find a friend as well as a lover. She has taken responsibility for choosing her own mate on an emotional basis rather than submitting to the wishes of her parents and/or practical considerations. In the past, she needed someone to spend a life with. Often she and her husband would be locked away for months in a homestead they both had to provide for and defend. Friendship, equal responsibility and equal dignity were all bound up in a way of life.

Today's Warrior Woman is not primarily interested in physical or financial protection for either herself or her children. She needs someone who will give emotional support to her career and back her efforts with practical help at home. She *also* needs constant reaffirmation of herself as an emotional being with a life outside her profession.

This double-barreled demand which she and her mate both place upon each other makes their life together exhilarating but vulnerable. Any problems are likely to be exacerbated by intersexual competition. I know Scandinavian couples where the husband feels miffed if you like his wife's scones better than his soufflé, and the wife is upset when he gets a promotion in the company where they both work.

To protect this tinderbox relationship, all Scandinavians except the Danes have tended to shy away from any social acceptance of the extramarital affair. In Norway and Finland, it's considered immoral. In Sweden, like any form of promiscuity, it is labeled impractical. Sometimes partners will agree to ignore temporary infractions, but society as a whole feels this practice is a mark against self-discipline.

Couples whose marriages are not living up to these high standards are expected to confront the situation, and either change their relationship or get a divorce. Those who elect to compromise with less than perfection are pitied for having lost self-dignity.

Widespread disappointment in the perfectibility of marriage has led a growing number of people to refuse to marry at all. The Swedes are particularly disillusioned. Not only do they have a high divorce rate, but their marriage rate is less than half that of the United States.[24]

The growing number of singles in Scandinavia, however, has not caused significant increases in the numbers practicing homosexuality. For adults of either sex, homosexuality is legal throughout Scandinavia, but it has not been hailed as a cure for *ensamhet*.

Instead, treading the path between marriage and aloneness, a burgeoning number of people have set up permanent but unofficial relationships. A partner in this kind of union is called a *samleben* (living companion), a convenient, bisexual designation that should be as welcome to popular English usage as *macho* has been.

Talking with women involved in these dyads, I was struck by the fact that they all deny the man-hating label that has been applied to liberated women.

"In the first place," one said indignantly, "it wasn't men's fault that everyone was so constricted by the old way of doing things. Swedish men have always tried to be fair—even Strindberg believed in women's rights. Both sexes benefit from shared status and shared responsibilities."

Strindberg, the notorious supposed misogynist, in fact did write a ringing women's rights manifesto. It not only included equal voting and equal-work clauses, but declared that a wife has a right to her own bedroom and should be paid a fair wage for her housework. In 1884, he insisted that women should pay for their own clothes and entertainment and "thus be spared from always being *treated*." He believed that true equality and a free relationship would eventually obliterate the war between the sexes.[25] Despite the length of the battle, today's *samleben* wholeheartedly agrees.

The women who choose to remain unmarried have several common characteristics. They are educated. They are occupied with a career. Often they have had a previous strong relationship with a man—sometimes a marriage—that went awry. Their *samleben* is also educated, career-oriented and previously divorced.

Authorities—as usual eager to classify people—have termed these relationships "loyalty marriages," and most Scandinavian governments are trying to bring these unions into the formal, socially sanctified lawbooks.

The reasons for forming the extralegal *samleben* setups, however, are anti-Establishment and strictly monogamous. Just as these individuals reject any parental guidance in selecting their mate, they also resent society's restrictions on their self-chosen and heavily emotional relationship. All their arguments about liberty and the nonviability of the traditional family come back to this. They have a partnership that they themselves must work at to keep going, and the sanctions they want are from each other. Society's approval only blurs the individual reward.

Of all the Scandinavians, the Danish woman seems best able to cope with living alone. "Living with someone is always a question of accommodation," a chic illustrator told me. "I'm attracted to men who are quite different from me. They make exciting friends. They make imaginative lovers. But they aren't necessary as a household appliance."

The Danish woman is the most individualistic in Scandinavia. Often redheaded, shorter, a bit plumper than her Northern sisters, she is more sure of her femininity and her right to do as she pleases. She is a spitfire. She rarely worries about disrupting social tranquility by a show of temper and has little trepidation about hurting someone's feelings.

"It's our women who are out of control," Søren Petersen, crime reporter for Copenhagen's largest daily, *BT,* told me. "We've had something of a murder wave the last two years, and who's been committing them? The women. They take up with some of these foreign workers, and they live together for a year or so. Maybe he pimps for her—she's often involved with the sexual underground. And then, one day she gets tired of him and sends him away. He comes back, of course, and they fight, and he beats her up. And the next time he walks in the door, he gets a bullet through his head."[26]

In ordinary social situations, the Danish woman often comes on as the shrew, belittling her spouse in tit-for-tat matches, sniping at others in the office hierarchy and generally resorting to malicious Corrine-type tricks for gain or entertainment. She writes books on "How I Trained My Husband," and has a militant Red Stocking feminist movement (the largest Danish Liberation Group) that is more antimale than any other organization in Scandinavia.

She is also, like the Frenchwoman, much more interested in creating a mystique all her own—a palpable aura constructed out of her own physical appearance and her tastefully decorated home that clearly expresses her unique personality. She is articulate, and her attitudes toward men alternate among motherly remonstrations, teasing and flirting. In short, she is the most Latin of the Northerners.

The Swede is at the other extreme. With a soft, musical voice and a retiring manner, it seems at first difficult to cast her in the light of the liberated Warrior Woman . . . until one sees her in an argument—still soft-spoken, but standing her ground as firmly as a wall. Neither she nor the Swedish man, of course, likes confrontation. The argument often winds up on paper, where it takes on a sexless hue.

An important advance of the seventies is that metropolitan Swedes have begun to drop the ancient formal-address system. It is now acceptable to address people in the familiar *du* form without going through the formal "dropping of the title" ritual. For the American, who rarely stops to think what title to use with a business acquaintance, much less with a friend, linguistic informality seems practical but hardly essential. For the Swedish woman, who was automatically the sex to use the first *du* at exactly the proper moment in a conversation, risking deep rancor if she was either too eager or too reticent, the change is equivalent to the discarding of whalebone corsets.[27]

Swedish women have less individualistic taste than the Danes. In their homes, they prefer beige drapes and clean lines. In their closets, they like pastel blouses and skirts or slacks. Few are fond of the maxi, and only the young wore the mini. Unlike the women of Helsinki or Copenhagen, they don't wear dramatic prints nor unconventional jewelry, they still often wear gloves even in the summer. The *du* restrictions may have disappeared, but Swedish women still prefer not to touch other people accidentally.

Norwegians are more bustling and cheerful. They, too, hold their own in a political argument with the opposite sex, and they're likely to look at their adversary directly while they do so, fully expecting total confrontation. Finnish women, in many ways the most confident of their equality, still do not join the verbal battle on the eye level. Neither do their men. Like the Swedes, they find direct confrontation embarrassing, and prefer pleasantries, smiles and a written report if any problem arises.

Scandinavian men also run a wide spectrum in their dealings with their women. The Dane, his hand on your shoulder and his conversation dancing with innuendo five minutes after you've met, tends to think of himself as far more sexually stimulating than his Northern neighbors. The odd truth is that the Dane is the only Scandinavian who is openly derisive toward women. The only Northerner who enjoys verbal fencing, he delights in attacking women in general and his wife in particular.

She is fully equipped to counterattack and even better at scolding. More often than not, the man comes out second best in these encounters. The more he loses, the more devious and vindictive he becomes. His banter creates a wall that leaves him difficult to know personally and difficult to deal with professionally.

The Swede, on the other hand, is slightly ill at ease talking with anyone of *either* sex. They only seem to feel relaxed when everyone present is engaged in nonverbal activity. This can be anything from the evening perusal of the newspaper (Swedes read more newspapers per capita than anyone else), to concentrating on a jigsaw puzzle (Swedes buy more jigsaw puzzles, too), to hiking and sailing. These activities, whether carried out in male groups or frequently shared by man and wife, are enjoyed without idle talk. As the Swedish sex manuals keep explaining, "Don't talk about it, *do* it."

Tall, often deceptively frail-looking, retiring and intellectual, the typical Swede in an office situation will open doors for his woman colleague, offer her a comfortable chair, then sit down on her side of the desk, to emphasize equality. He proceeds to thrash out details with her on a business level with no implication that she should play the part of sexual sparring partner.

The Norwegians and the Finns have a slightly rumpled appearance, as though they just grabbed a shirt from the same backpack they used for the weekend hiking trip. Their attitude toward women has the same sportsmanlike flavor. In the office, they open doors and offer chairs. In the home, they sit and expect to be served.

Scandinavian female-male relationships are dominated by a simple fact of life—Nordic men are much bigger than their women. They have a physical presence that a Latin can never approach. It emphasizes the difference between the sexes so starkly that one feels manufactured additions like hairstyles and high heels are silly and superfluous.

Perhaps this ever-obvious physical difference has made it easier for the Scandinavians to initiate emotional and intellectual equality between women and men. The challenge has been to make it possible for comrades to cohabit sexually. They have not solved all the problems of *ensamhet* or of intersexual competition, but they are molding a coherent system of mutual responsibility and dignity. Since the rest of us are now also faced with situations where emotional needs take priority over procreational ones, their example is vitally important.

4

Mother, the Secondary Parent

The newborn baby with the best chance of survival in the world is Swedish. Not only does Sweden have the world's lowest infant-mortality rate—12.6 per every 1000 births—but it also has the world's longest average life-span—74.2 years.[28]

Every pregnant Swedish woman is expected to visit the clinic regularly, take vitamins daily and exercise properly. Facilities to help her carry out her duties toward her unborn child are free and convenient to reach. Handbooks on how to care for one's body during and after pregnancy are everywhere—in the libraries, in clinics, in factory coffee bars, beside the pay desk in layette departments. They, too, are free. So are the parenthood classes for both mother and father.

Fathers are often present during delivery. Even in difficult Cesarean operations, some doctors encourage the father to be in attendance. "He gets in the way only if he hasn't been properly instructed on what to expect beforehand," one doctor told me. "The woman is always more tranquil if her husband is there, and, anyway, he has the right."

272

Motherhood holds little mystery for the Swedish woman. It is neither a rite of passage into adulthood nor an act of alliance with an ancient and magical sisterhood. It is a simple, physical function, without emotional appeal. "Why did I have two children?" one working mother mused. "Well, of course there was the pressure to conform . . . every woman does have a child, if she can. . . . And, of course, Edmund wanted children. And, well, I think it's one's duty to society, after all—our most direct contribution to the future. I think if I had been more aware, I might have chosen to adopt a foreign baby, but I don't know how Edmund would have reacted to that."

"None is fun" is not a slogan in Sweden as it has been in the United States, but the practice is there, all the same. Nearly 30 percent of the couples married between 1950 and 1961 were still childless by 1971. In fact, 64 percent of all Swedish households in 1972 were childless, but this includes new families and those with grown children who have already moved away from home. Seventeen percent of the households had one child, and 13 percent had two children. Only 7 percent had three or more.[29] In contrast, 51.7 percent of American households in the late sixties were childless, 14.3 percent had one child, and 17.1 percent had three or more.[30]

Swedish society in general gives the pregnant woman VIP treatment. Besides the medical support so freely lavished, she is shown extra courtesy by Swedish men who are already the most inclined of any European except the German to open doors and give women seats on the subway.

After the baby is born, the support is pervasive, thoughtful and well-organized. Maternity leaves, delivery payments and child grants arrive as a matter of course. Shopping centers are dotted with play facilities carefully walled off from the street. Opticians' and dentists' offices are stocked with a toy corner. Stairs in public places are always equipped with ramps to facilitate climbing with a buggy or a walker in tow. These, of course, accommodate wheelchairs as well, a fact that prompted one mother to snap, "Yes, you see, all these automatic doors and ramps and things are for those of us who are crippled. Of course the tram conductor helps you with the walker. It makes *him* feel so much bigger and freer."

Her comments reflect the other side of the picture. Pregnant women and women with young children are pitied by other women. "Oh, he's so small and you're expecting another?" a friend may comment. "How difficult! I hope your husband can help with the house."

Belittling of motherhood is particularly evident in school sex-education classes. Consciously, this is done to discourage teen-agers from having unplanned babies. Subconsciously, the desire appears to be to inculcate aversion.

"Is it a good idea to have children just because a person is sexually mature?" an instructress asks a sex-education class. One boy raises his hand and points out that having children means being tied down for the rest of your life. Someone else adds, "Besides, you're still in school," and the instructress observes that schools do not come equipped with nurseries for small children.

"At what age is it appropriate to have children?" she then asks.

"When you're twenty or thirty years old," says one girl.

"You should be old enough to support a child," the teacher adds.[31]

As already pointed out, premarital pregnancy is not labeled as sinful—the social taboos are only against an unpleasant or "unwanted" event. Aversion is built around the premise that "accidents" are impractical and irrational. Once a mistake has been made, however, society prefers to support the mother-to-be rather than insist on a forced marriage.

Paternity is established in 90 percent of the cases. Usually the man steps forward voluntarily; otherwise the mother can enlist the help of a welfare agent to settle the issue. Until 1974, this social service paraparent was automatically appointed to all children born out of wedlock, but this is now done only if the mother requests it, since so many of the children are born to *samleben* couples. Once fatherhood is established, the man assumes half of the monetary support. The mother is legally required to help with support, as well, and the state also contributes. All medical expenses and the first year in a maternity home are provided. Her child has priority on waiting lists in state-supported nurseries. The entire system is geared to helping her find a job—either through extensive employment networks or through free job-training courses, which are supplemented by living allowances from the state.

But what about the attitude of people in private? After all, in Sweden the government is the revolutionary and the people are the conservatives. The relevant question about society's acceptance of the unwed mother, as a British journalist once pointed out, is, "Does she entertain?"

Intellectual Swedes profess to be shocked at the question. Of course, single parents have no social problems, as such, they insist. "To us," the sociologist Dr. Kerstin Anér explains patiently, "their problems are economical. It is true, for example, that unmarried mothers do not often entertain. Not because they are social outcasts, but because they have neither the time nor the energy, and besides there is no one to look after the child.''[32]

In many circles of Scandinavian society, the unmarried mother *is* as accepted as the divorcée in New York City. Still, in the general community, a subtle social pall hangs over her.

Disapproval is devious. Children born out of wedlock find that the parents of friends are overly solicitous, and that they are cast in the role of class rebel. The mother finds her life-style no longer fits with that of her childless friend's, but she is reluctant to spend time with married mothers. Not that anything is ever said to her. Words play very little part in Swedish psychological interplay. "But," said one mother, who married when her child was three, "the pity they felt that I had to look after Thorolf alone was stifling."

In keeping with this subtle form of disapproval, the Swedes no longer employ the term "illegitimate"—a word conveying open confrontation and social discord. But somehow the expression "unwanted" still crops up. And "unplanned." "Unplanned" is hardly an invective in other countries, but in Sweden it's a word only slightly less negatively charged than the ultimate criticism, "stupid." Where rational behavior is worshiped, those unfortunate enough to have "unplanned" children must be looked after, of course, but society's support of them is physical, not psychological.

The Swedish father has a mystique all his own. His intense involvement with his offspring goes back to the Viking tradition of honoring the man with many children. It is akin to the authority and reverence enjoyed by *Herr Vater* in Germany. The Norwegian playwright, Henrik Ibsen, stated flatly that the father is the parent responsible for the rearing and moral character of the child. The name of the father is so important that sons of Sven were traditionally called Sven Svensson and daughters were called Svensdotter. Recently, redundancy has so encumbered telephone books and government records that the practice was declared illegal.

The fundamental quality of the tie between father and child is evident everywhere. It lies behind Sweden's initiation of a paid postnatal pregnancy leave for fathers, and behind the strong argument that fathers should take only part-time jobs, so that they can spend more time with their children as they grow up. It underpins the feeling that the father must be present at the birth of the child, not only to be with the mother but also to be with the child. It is reflected in society's total commitment to establishing the paternity of every child born out of wedlock (a practice also observed during the era of Viking concubinage). It plays a part in the widespread aversion to promiscuity, and even turns up in the fact that all pets in Sweden are pedigreed. Only one other country in Europe is so insistent on lineal certificates for their animals—the patriarchal Germans.

Patriarchal authority has developed in a particularly benign fashion in Sweden. The male preference for dealing with a situation physically instead of verbally has evolved into communication being achieved via exquisitely rational written reports. Society functions through systems that have been minutely examined and carefully tested beforehand.

Hysterical family confrontations are avoided in a similar manner. For an example, parents don't blurt out to their children news of an impending divorce. Instead they present them with the *Mia's Daddy Moves* book that details just such a situation in the life of a fictional little girl. The book explains how upset the mother and father feel, and how sad the little girl is, and how one of her mother's new friends finally explains that, "Everyone doesn't keep the same best friend for their whole life." The book is sensitive to emotions, but it is a far cry from the bitter, irrational denunciations a child might hear from her own parents, if they gave voice to their feelings.

Perfectionism, another common patriarchal trait, is instilled neither through corporal punishment nor through the current Germanic practice of patiently reiterated commands. Instead, parents, politicians and policemen trust the individual child and silently expect him or her to follow adult examples and do his or her best at all times. If a child makes a mistake, everyone looks embarrassed and tries to cover up the error. If a child excels, he or she is quickly praised.

Children grow up to respond not only with a high standard of social responsibility, but also with a reciprocal trust in authority. Social Welfare is accepted without guilt—in direct contrast to the shamefaced but defiant reactions of those on the American "relief" or the English "dole." Those entrusted with government and social discipline are expected to be accessible and rational.

Surprisingly, today's Swedish patriarch has lost control of an ancient right—he is no longer in control of family planning.

On the surface, evidence about this point is contradictory. Take the extensive and federally funded sex education and birth control programs, for example. Aren't both men and women solid backers of these projects?

The answer to this question lies in the fact that these programs were mounted not after legislators decided that they were a good idea of themselves, but after women had *already* reduced the birth rate to below ZPG.

At the time, the government simply professed the hope that the projects would help couples who were having trouble bearing children and would make "Every baby a wanted baby"—a concept that involves pedigree as well as healthy, happy, future citizens.

A second oft-quoted point in the argument that all Swedes must want small families is the supposedly liberal abortion law. Remembering the case of the American who flew to Sweden to have an abortion after discovering that her baby was threatened because of thalidomide (the fetus was subsequently found to be badly misformed), we are inclined to categorize Swedish abortion laws permanently as more liberal than ours.

Again, this is not the case. Until very recently, Swedish laws were not as liberal as those in the United States, England or Denmark. A woman was required to meet several "need" requirements (either physical or emotional), and fill out numerous forms before she could receive a legal abortion. A large percentage were turned down—the reason the number remained at a stable 5000 per year until the mid-sixties after a high of 6328 in 1951. Critics claimed that this meant there were 5000 to 20,000 illegal abortions every year.[33] When the law was somewhat liberalized in 1967, the number of abortions doubled and is still climbing. Abortion on demand was not available in Sweden until January 1975. It is now legal for residents until the nineteenth week of pregnancy.

A little-known fact relating to the image of the Swedish father is that until January 1976 male sterilization was illegal except in cases of chromosome defect, and female sterilization could be performed only when a pregnancy would seriously danger a woman's life or health due to illness, physical defect or weakness. The tardiness of this legislation is staggering to most family planners elsewhere. When I asked Birgitta Linnér about it in 1974, I was told quickly that the law was left over from old traditions. "Besides, we wouldn't need to change it, because everything else is freely available," she commented.

But by that time the family laws in Sweden had already been totally revamped. "Leftovers" must have been expressly protected from the change. As any woman with circulatory problems whose doctor has ordered her off the Pill would affirm, there is a strong continuing need for sterilization. There are no logical arguments against it, but there are some powerful emotional ones . . . all of them eventually leading back to the fundamental belief that man should never be robbed of his ability to procreate. A woman may be forced to choose sterility because of circumstances, but no contingencies of daily life—not even his wife's health—could affect the man.

I didn't realize the depth of the motivational force behind all the above material until I was asking the routine question about what a woman does if she wants another child and her husband doesn't. I was surprised to find that my Swedish interviewees didn't know of any such cases. But when I asked what happens when a husband wants another child and his wife doesn't, I was told that this was very common. "Almost every couple I know has run into that conflict at one time or another," one woman lawyer told me. "The wives don't want to go on being tied to babies, or they don't want children at all. Usually they compromise, but sometimes the conflict leads to divorce. I've known men who wanted five children, but I don't think any sensible woman would accept that."

Putting the many comments of this kind that I gathered together with the other factors that make up the pervasive Swedish social support of the joys of fatherhood, it seems incredible that the country's prosperity has not led to large Swedish families. The reason for their sustained low birthrate obviously must lie exclusively with the woman. How does she do it, and why?

Today, "how" is relatively simple. The Swedish woman takes the Pill. The next most popular birth-control devices are the diaphragm and/or vaginal creams. Condoms are predominantly used only by teen-agers—a result of doctors' fears that the Pill may be dangerous for the immature girl. The use of coitus interruptus, the rhythm method or total abstinence is not extensively tabulated, but sociologists feel these methods are rapidly disappearing because the woman puts so much emphasis on secure precautionary measures. Predictably, although family-planning advice is supposed to be directed at both women and men, illustrations on informational brochures always feature the woman, and opinions emphasize that the female is the partner "chiefly concerned in the case of an unwelcome pregnancy."[34]

Why Swedish women have continuously rejected motherhood for more than half a century is the much more imperative question. A comparative look at international birthrates immediately reveals the contrast with Italy. Examination of the role and status of the mother in the two countries also reveals a similar contraposition. The importance of the mother is almost ignored in Sweden. Her obituary is never front-page news in Stockholm as it is in Rome when her child is prominent in politics or films. Swedish women's magazines are likely to label mothers' tasks as humdrum and put them in the back pages, while lead articles explain the innovative and extensive research Scandinavia has done on the causes of juvenile delinquency. The finding most often emphasized? That increased delinquency, particularly among boys with divorced parents, stems not so much from increased money problems as from the lack of a father figure after which the child can mold his personality.[35]

The Swedish mother not only finds herself taking second place to the father figure, but she is also caught in a dilemma caused by the image of the Swedish child. Swedish faith in the integrity of the individual is deeply influential and reflected in the belief that the child is innately good. Responsible parenthood, therefore, is conceived as giving the child an honest and ethical role model combined with as much environmental freedom as practically possible. Children are expected to bloom on their own.

In direct contrast to the rest of Europe, Swedish children get the credit for developing into smoothly functioning adults, but they are rarely blamed for neuroses or antisocial acts. Criminality is considered the fault of the parents and/or society. Mistaken individuals, it is stressed, simply weren't *allowed* to reach their potential and should be helped and pitied rather than punished.

As a result of this philosophy, the Swedish mother finds herself criticized for making mistakes, but rarely lauded for a child who becomes a successful adult. Motherly pride in one's offspring, in fact, is often derided as "living one's life through someone else," a comment that sounds very familiar to the American. Meanwhile, the years of the woman's life which are dedicated to childbearing and childrearing are widely typified as a "sacrifice" to her husband and the future of society . . . but hardly as challenging or rewarding for the woman herself.

This same pattern appears to be manifesting itself in Finland, where birthrates have plunged from 17.6 to 12.7 per 1000 births in the past ten years. It is not so evident, however, in Denmark, while Norway currently has the highest birthrate of any country we are studying. Since all but Denmark share the emphasis on father-child ties, what has caused this difference?

Finland's declining birthrate is still too new to be conclusive. Authorities there insist that the major factor is urbanization with concomitant severe housing shortages that force young couples to live with in-laws for several years. Living with in-laws has never made much difference to Latins, but we will have to wait till the practical details of home construction are ironed out, as they have largely been in Sweden in the late sixties, before the strength of this argument can be fully assessed with regard to Finland.

The Danish situation is more intriguing. Abortion laws there have been more liberal than in Sweden. Sterilization has been possible, while the nursery system has long been more expensive, and *still* the Danish birthrate has been consistently higher. Despite Danish urbanization. Despite an articulate Women's Liberation Movement. Why?

The answer obviously lies in the Danish concept of the meaning of motherhood. Swedish women have been taught that bearing children is their duty, but patriotism is hardly sufficient motivation. A woman must feel proud and excited at the challenge and rewards of the role. Alva Myrdal believed that one could motivate motherhood with material well-being. She got a record percentage of healthy babies, but Swedish women are still opting out of motherhood because it lacks any mystique.

Danish and Norwegian women, on the other hand, don't talk about the "duty" of motherhood. Instead, well-organized Norwegian women's groups insist that career-oriented women are not enjoying life. And Danish writer Elsa Gress argues that a woman should relax and enjoy her work if she chooses to be a housewife and a mother. Economically, Gress points out, mothers contribute as much to the GNP as any secretary. Why feel guilty?

A Danish engineer explained the mystique on even more personal terms. She, like one out of every eight Danish mothers, has had a child born out of wedlock,[36] and she did it, she says, ". . . because single women also want the experience. It's something you can't learn out of books or buy in a department store. The Red Stockings haven't made us stop wanting to be with children. They've just made us realize that it's unnecessary to tie ourselves up with a man for all time in order to have a baby."

A 1974 study found that nearly three-fourths of all Danish married women between the ages of fifteen and thirty-four years either have or expect to have two or three children. This applies irrespective of the woman's age and social background. The study emphasized that more women wanted two children, that only a diminishing number wanted four or more children, and that the two- to three-child family has become more or less stable in Denmark since the fifties. A comment was made that the few who wanted four or more children were usually affluent and well-educated.[37]

The importance of the Danish mother is bolstered by a popular press that romanticizes her and her life. She maintains a health and exercise program that is just as rational as Sweden's, but it is administered by the Mother's Aid program, a name that emphasizes the mother's importance. The Danish mother does not think of herself as a progenitor of society. She sees her work as vitally important to the child. She is not afraid to chastise or encourage her offspring. Her discipline is bound up quite often in the concept of what the child owes her. "How can you just stay outside playing when you knew I'd fixed your dinner?'' she's likely to demand. "You know how much Mommy loves you. . . . You know how much your getting good grades means to me.''

Since the Danish mother feels directly responsible, her husband is inclined to leave the management of the children to her. "Do you know what happened when the children ran out in the snow in their pajamas?'' one mother said, laughing. "My husband started shouting. But not at them. At me to come and get them!''

It appears that the Norwegian father is more involved. "They have to teach their children skiing, so they spend much more time together,'' a Danish journalist observed. This may be true, timewise, but the mother still feels a heavy responsibility almost akin to the Italian. "Most of my friends work, but they intend to stop when they have small children,'' a Bergen woman told me. "We feel it is important that companies accept women back in the work force when their children are older, but a child needs his mother at home until he's ready to go off to school.'' And this fundamental belief in the importance of the mother is the reason why Norway has a birthrate of 16.6 while Sweden has a rate of 13.8.

5

Blessed Baby

          The philosophy that baby is born blessed is pervasive and powerfully influential. From the beginning, Scandinavian children are considered individuals. They have their own ombudsman to write to in the government as well as extensive legal rights. Most important, they possess the mystique of innocence, The child, running through the sun-soaked fields and the dappled woods of the North, is the most evocative image in Scandinavia. The Natural Being. Ingenuous, they are expected to select "good" naturally. When they don't, when they are greedy or destructive, excuses are made for them. Society hasn't given them the proper free environment, or they have made mistakes that they themselves will soon correct.

    This belief in the natural goodness of children is most clearly evident in Sweden and least in Denmark. It is amazing to observe the Swedish pattern of childrearing. A mother sits on a bench, her two toddlers playing in a sandpile a few feet away. They are carefully laying out the *gatan* (streets)

282

and *garden* (gardens) of a tiny play city—a favorite game of Swedish children of all ages. A bigger child invades and begins tracing out a new street in a different direction. The two little ones set up a howl. The mother looks up, but says nothing. If the conflict continues, she may suggest to them all that "We would have a nicer city if all the people liked their streets." If the outsider persists, she gathers up her two and leaves. If her own two set upon each other or attack her in one way or another, she says softly, "This isn't a very good way to behave, is it?" and then remains quietly watching until the children quit.

Walking down the gently curving streets of suburban developments, one occasionally sees children doing dangerous things, bothering other children or throwing stones. Passing adults glance at the activities, and hurry past, embarrassed. Other children often react the same way. The troublemaker is quietly, but firmly ostracized.

"The only time my little girl's class really gets rowdy," one mother told me, "is when more than half of them fight. Then it's okay; everybody feels they can start hollering."

"Usually arguing doesn't go very far, but we had a real brawl yesterday," said the teacher of a nursery school. "They got started, and suddenly every one of them was throwing things and pulling hair. When we got them quieted down, we had some cookies and milk, and talked about the problem. They decided we should have shorter turns with the puzzles, because they get bored waiting so long for their favorite."

When I asked if the two who had started the fight had been punished, the teacher said no; they had no way of punishing the children. They are not allowed to spank children or send them from the classroom. "We talked to them longer than the others, of course, because they obviously had the biggest problems. . . . No, we don't ordinarily call the parents to talk to them about a discipline problem. If the child feels that it would help to talk to his parents, then we try to get him to ask them to come. Of course, if he can't seem to get the message across—our students are all under seven— we'll see if we can talk to parents, but very unobtrusively. We don't want the parents to feel ashamed of their child in any way, as he can work his problems out more quickly if he doesn't feel they're pushing him."

The comment is often made that the Swedish Government makes progress through an exceedingly smooth process of nonconfrontation. Checking this theory against the experience of other nations, it at first appears untrue. The Italian Government, for example, also prefers to avoid confrontation and yet rarely makes radical changes in society. The ability to be effective by avoiding conflict has its origins in the way children are taught to channel resentment. While Italian children spend their energy in verbal arguments, Swedish children are encouraged to think out an alternative action, write it down and put it into operation as soon as possible.

As children grow, they find that the most important part of their lives takes place outside the home. First, it's the playground just a few steps from the door. Then it's the woods that are never more than fifteen minutes away. School is very important, but for the younger students, only lasts till one o'clock, when an organized-play group takes over. There are clubs for all ages, and extracurricular sports facilities and music classes in every community. Children attend these classes alone as much as possible, since city planners are supposed to provide walkways everywhere so there are no dangers to be encountered on the way. (This goal is not always achieved.) Sexual attacks on children, as we have already noted, are few.

The Scandinavian child is always encouraged to develop self-confidence. A recent cover of *vi Foraldrar (We Parents)*[38] emphasizes the ideal clearly. The lead article is "We Test Tricycles," and the cover picture shows a four-year-old girl, bundled from head to toe in a bright red and yellow plastic snowsuit, guiding her bright red tricycle. She has obviously had a tumble in the mud, but she looks happy and determined. She is wearing a crash helmet, has just crested a steep hill and is heading down, one long strand of blonde hair escaping from her crash helmet and blowing in the wind. There are no adults in the picture.

The concept that children will naturally try dangerous feats, and should simply take reasonable precautions is implicit; society provides the child with an open space to play; the magazine provides information on the reliability of equipment; parents provide the sturdy tricycle, a crash helmet and easy-care clothes in happy colors.

Financially, Scandinavian children have received more social benefits than any others in the world. State family allowances are 125 kr. (approx. $30) per month up until the children are sixteen, when they automatically qualify for student allowances if they continue schooling. If they are orphaned, they receive 425 kr. (approx. $97) per month, whether or not they have an independent source of income.[39]

More than that, Scandinavian children are legally protected against corporal punishment both at school and at home. As the Swedish Institute explains, "Swedish law, of course, forbids parents to assault their children, just as it forbids other citizens to assault each other . . . but the community does not otherwise interfere in the way parents bring up their children."[40] There are similar child's-rights laws in Denmark and Norway.

A child who has been slapped has the right to call BRIS (Föreningen

Barnens Ratt I Samhället), the pan-Scandinavian organization for the Promotion of Children's Rights in Society, and someone from the organization or the Family Ministry will come around. They talk about the problem with the parents, the child and perhaps the child's teacher, neighbors or others who know the family.

Once again, belief in the innate goodness and soundness of judgment of the child is breathtaking. BRIS reports that children *do* take the initiative in reporting maltreatment at the hands of adults, and that such accusations from children are rarely frivolous acts of rebellious anger. A teacher from a Lidingö school told me, however, that the majority of cases of child battering or maltreatment of any kind were not discovered through reports from the children, but rather through anonymous calls from neighbors or reports from the school nurse. Although the rate of maltreatment cases has not diminished through fear of discovery, the number of child deaths has, indicating that the program has produced at least one positive result.

An Englishwoman living in Stockholm told me indignantly that she believed the widespread BRIS campaign to inform every child of its rights is a major factor contributing to teen-age alienation. "Parents don't feel they have any right to discipline their children. You should see some of them, as young as six, riding their bicycles late at night, tearing around with no ideas at all about how to behave. Nobody ever pays any attention to them, or gives them any sense of direction."

Again, a journalist on the staff of *Femina,* the Swedish equivalent of *Glamour* magazine, said, "One of our biggest problems is that parents don't seem to be involved with their children. Look at the wars that go on in the sandbox right under the mother's nose! The sandbox is a real jungle! And she'll just keep reading her paper, without ever sticking up for anybody. It's no wonder that by the time they are teen-agers they feel deserted."

Sweden's teen-agers have been afflicted by all the blights of today's youth. Not only is the VD rate soaring, but alcoholism and drug abuse are also more widespread than ten years ago and start at an even earlier age. Some have turned to theft, vandalism of public property has appeared. The gleaming straight streets of city centers all have their gangs of blank-faced but surprisingly aggressive young beggars.

The overall rate of Swedish social disruption is still minute compared to other societies. The official interpretation of the problem is highly complex because of the intrinsic conflict between their belief that the individual is innately good, and their feeling that what children need is more time and attention from their parents, particularly their father.

The teen-agers, however, believe that the problem is caused by something else. In family-life classes, at discotheques, in student hostels, the conversations are not about feeling abandoned by the parents, but about feeling that they can't reach each other and that their lives have no meaning.

"I don't have anything I really have to work for," said a barefoot eighteen-year-old, who begs on Stockholm's Kungsgatan. "Everything has already been done for me. I feel like my life was planned by the Ministry of Life Planning five years before I was born. Even my protests have been programmed, and the posters are already printed. I've been living with a Dane—I thought he'd have more balls than a Swede. He had this big story about getting bashed by the French police in a student protest at Nanterre. But he won't fight with *me*. . . . I scream at him and spit in his face, and he just hides behind being *nice*. . . . We Swedes have a word for being nice, it's *snäll*. *Snäll* is never bothering anybody and never making a nuisance of yourself . . . and never letting your feelings come first . . . *snäll* can strangle you."[41]

In his analysis of Swedish temperament, Paul Britten Austin also comments on the importance and prevasiveness of *snäll*: "Every little Swede has it drummed into him that above all, he must be *snäll*: viz., not to make a noise, not cry, not place demands upon his elders, be polite to strangers, and be clean and tidy. First and last, he must not give vent to aggressions. To be *snäll* (good, kind, well-behaved) is to be as far as possible self-effacing. Which, it must be confessed, is a lot to ask of any little Viking."[42]

It *is* a lot to ask, and for the most part it has been asked for only a relatively short time. *Snäll* is a means to internalized self-discipline, a concept that had few adherents a century ago when the Swedes were sternly authoritarian. Corporal punishment was common, as were other harsh disciplinary measures, such as shutting children outside in the snow until they apologized. The transition to a society based on the child's internalizing *snäll* was hardly simple. Strindberg would have been aghast at the modern father who calmly states, "Mary does not need to be told to go to bed; she knows when she is tired."

The change in child-parent relations was one of the most profound consequences of the recent and rapid mass migration from the farm to the city. Forced to abandon the old way of life, the Swedes committed themselves to the new—new homeland, new homes, new life patterns. Doubts were cast on anything that was believed antiquated. Traditional parent concepts were exchanged for the bright hopes of the future that resided in the child.

Pragmatic values in personal lives became paramount. "Is it 'right'?"

gave way to "Is it 'practical'?" "Stupid" became a more serious indictment than "immoral."

In their newborn Nation of Strangers, everyone needed to be *nice* to everyone else, because that was the most practical way to avoid all antiquated social behavior. The *snäll* pattern is evident in all Nation of Stranger societies, with Australia and California being other notable examples. Of them all, Sweden alone couples the demand for *niceness* in public places with a low emphasis on the duties and rights of the individual, the factor that presumably accounts for their low rates of interpersonal violence.

A mark of a society's success is the way in which dissatisfaction is channeled. Dissatisfaction in a fast-changing culture often manifests itself violently because those who are attracted to change want it immediately at the cost of forcing a topsy-turvy existence on everyone else. An explosive confrontation easily builds up.

Sweden, with one of the most rapidly evolving societies in the industrialized world, has managed to maintain a land where there has been no string of Houston homosexual murders and no Baader-Meinhof gang has taken control of banks and department stores. There have been incidents of political terrorism—mild in comparison with those of the French students or the Provisional IRA in Northern Ireland—but they have been perpetrated mainly by foreign workers living in Sweden. Otherwise, Swedish home news is dominated by tax dodgers and the occasional gang of bank robbers, who are inclined to give themselves up voluntarily even after they manage to make their getaway.

Frustration is usually vented in only one direction—toward oneself. Suicide has an ancient history in Scandinavia, going back to the veneration of Valhalla—the Hall of Those Who Died by Violence. Today, even the most successful are not exempt from the desire for self-annihilation. The suicides of both Ivar Kreuger, the Swedish match king, and Marcus Wallenberg, head of Sweden's big banking family, are but the best-known examples of the modern businessman's abruptly ending his life in midcareer.

Alcoholism, another means of self-destruction, is also a classic scourge in Sweden, despite rigid laws restricting the sale of liquor and high taxes on every bottle.

It is important to note that neither the alcoholism rate nor the suicide rate has undergone much of a change since the advent of the Welfare State. Furthermore, these phenomena are not unique to Sweden. Austria, Denmark and Hungary all have higher rates of suicide, and Poland and the United States both consume as much or more alcohol per person.[43]

Both these problems register overwhelmingly on the male side of the ledger. Statistically, Swedish women commit one in three of the suicides and account for only one in fourteen of the alcoholics.[44]

It is often argued that when men hand over more responsibility to women, they will benefit from an equalization of these rates. The prediction is borne out to a large degree by the statistical trend in nearly every country participating in the current wave of Women's Liberation since the mid-fifties. Concurrently, the three places where women's suicide rate is most quickly overtaking men's are the United States, Sweden and Norway,[45] where a visible teeter-totter effect is evident, with men's rates going down as women's go up.

Although this is a positive sign that men are benefiting from sharing responsibility with women, studies in England indicate that this equalization is not a crucial factor in lowering the overall total of deaths. England's national suicide rate has decreased by one-third since the sixties, and many authorities there agree the drop is caused by a nationwide network of volunteer "befrienders," who are willing to talk things over with anyone day or night. This verification of the basic need to articulate one's problems gives pause to the hope of reducing suicidal stress in the land of *ensamhet*.

Whether or not forms of self-destruction constitute an indictment of Scandinavian parent-child relations, however, is debatable. Certainly, the Scandinavians are trying to ameliorate their problems with alcoholism, drugs and suicide. One of their approaches is encouraging families to spend more time and creative energy in each other's company.

Swedish policymakers further believe[46] that the answer to self-destruction and teen-age frustration lies in doing away with the admiration of the stoic. The stoic of either sex was valued by the Vikings for a good reason—he or she was well equipped to face the hardships of the person who lived out his or her life in the wilderness. In contrast, most adversity for today's urban individual stems not from nature but from the failure to communicate. Emotions, even intense emotions, are like a headache; no one knows you have it until you tell them by actions or words. The more precisely one can describe a problem verbally, the more others can help. Self-expression, however, comes easily only to the individual who has practiced it since birth. Today's Swedes believe that it is the task of each generation to work to make communication easier for the next.

Noncompetitiveness, another value currently believed to offer relief from Swedish emotional stress, is most evident and most surprising in the schools. Its widespread prevalence is surprising mainly because as recently as ten years ago it didn't exist. Social observer Austin, for example, commented at the time that it was "impossible to overrate, in Swedish eyes, the importance of an exam." Quoting other writers who describe Swedish exam-taking as more torturous than that of the French Lycée, Austin tied the need for exams to the perfectionist bond Swedes have to their work and their need for a job title to make them feel they are contributing significantly to society. The "race for high marks," Austin felt, was the "central ordeal of Swedishness. . . . Woe to him who fails! He hides his face and creeps out the back way."[47]

Today there are still remnants of this system. The teaching profession is highly respected, and, since the same teacher stays with a class through the first five years of schooling, she can assume an enormous importance in the child's life. Furthermore, at age eleven, children are still often graded and placed into secondary schooling that is designed expressly as either college-preparatory or manual-training.

Nevertheless, on the whole, the structure of the old system has been meticulously weeded out. For example, teachers are reluctant to show off children's work to visitors, and do not pressure parents with the problems of children at any age. The trend is away from competitive grading and toward evaluating students in the context of their own individual development. Although there is an extensive nursery-school network beginning at age three, academic schooling is delayed to a late age. With compulsory full-day attendance not starting until age seven and ending at age sixteen, Sweden has the shortest span of mandatory scholastic training of any industrial country.

Inculcating perfectionism by encouraging students to compete against their own past achievements is a technique that has been widely supported by the international educational community, but the Swedes, as usual, were the first ones to translate abstract theories from experimental situations into practice in the ordinary home. Parents will repeatedly say that they are not concerned if their daughter or son turns out to be academically weak. "There's no reason why my son has to be an intellectual giant," one wife of an architect explained. "If it doesn't work for him to enter a profession, there are many other jobs—probably ones that aren't as full of stress."

Her aplomb stems from two factors which illustrate how noncompetitiveness has been supported throughout Swedish society. First, she pointed out that she had faith in her economy's ability to provide jobs for people with a wide variety of skills. Under the Swedish system, factory workers have nearly as high a standard of living as lawyers, so job satisfaction takes top priority in career selection. Second, the mother said she was very proud of her son's ability to work with others and participate in sports. "You see, he doesn't have any problems with his future," she commented after a description of his organizing a boating trip with five others—both boys and girls.

If children get along with others and manage to organize their lives, they are never considered "stupid," regardless of test scores. Today's teachers quickly defend this attitude, and point to studies that have concluded that students who do brilliantly in school are not necessarily the ones who succeed in later life.

The girl's pattern of development is almost identical to the boy's. Sexual partnership is stressed everywhere. Most games are played by teams and rarely involve tests of strength. The most typical Swedish competition is "orienteering," a cross-country treasure hunt utilizing a map, compass and several check-in points. Run by either teams or individuals, the ability to navigate is far more important than physical coordination. Girls often excel, and mixed-sex teams are commonly preferred by all the children.

Children who hurt themselves rarely cry, regardless of sex. Both girls and boys chide their companions for any show of emotion, and cuts and bruises are given quick matter-of-fact medical checks—most schools teach first aid—and a minimum of Band-Aids and lotions.

An appreciable amount of time is spent indoors during the long winter months, when children are encouraged to work on intricate puzzles and all kinds of word, card and board games. Mothers and fathers often play these games with their children on snowbound evenings and weekends, but no one I interviewed said they had ever made it a habit to read to their children. The children do enjoy reading to themselves, and seem to have preference for books that avoid the traditional definition of sex roles. A study of 234 books for adolescent children published between the 1930s and the 1960s established the long-standing success of Nancy Drew. Kari Skjonsberg, the author of the study, stated that while girls were still more concerned with personal relations and boys with adventure, heroines over this period of thirty years had become much more aggressive and independent.[48]

Sexual equality, responsibility and mutual respect are taught by example in the home. If the mother has an outside job, both parents share the housework. Neither sister nor brother is expected to lend a hand until adolescence. At that point, they both pitch in equally.

The school's dedication to the ideals of sexual equality goes beyond the family-life classes and their emphasis on mutual responsibility. It is compulsory for boys to attend home-economics classes where they learn how to manage a family's budget, comparative shop, plan and cook meals, clean, sew and knit and care for babies and small children. End-of-the-year classes utilize real, squirming baby siblings to test the student's ability.

Lastly, sex integration means that girls must take metal, woodwork and car-mechanics classes. Advanced study in all of these fields, however, is not compulsory, and schools report that in those classes—particularly advanced mechanics—the student body tends to segregate itself along conventional lines. The other Scandinavian countries do not make home ec, woodworking and mechanics universally mandatory for both sexes. However, integrated sex-education and family-life classes are compulsory.

An important element in Danish upbringing is the sense of humor. The Danes, like the French and the Italians, encourage children to settle differences through verbal argument, and a disputatious weapon particularly cultivated is a child's ability to poke fun. For self-defense, children learn how to laugh at themselves as well as at others.

I spent an afternoon watching how this ability was being taught to a four-year-old girl zooming around the playground, turning somersaults, scaling fences and literally tearing the place apart. Her grandparents were watching, too, delighted. Whenever she fell—on the average of once every thirty seconds—both she and her grandparents would burst into uproarious laughter. Obviously this child will not grow up to be the sort of woman who can be stopped from entering any profession just because somebody else thinks it strange or ludicrous.

Mockery—both of oneself and of others—turns up in many places. Drinking companions invariably exchange derisive jokes. Tivoli and Deer Park shooting-gallery competitors jeer at each other and hoot at themselves. Even when a fifty-year-old woman stumbled and fell as she descended from a bus, two groups of watching girls giggled and the adults turned away, only partially concealing their smiles.

I was told later that the woman might not mind the smiles, but would have been embarrassed if someone had tried to help. That would have indicated that she was unable to manage by herself. After all, she was no doubt accustomed to using laughter for her own self-defense. This self-mockery and the training in verbal parries fosters the self-confident, spitfire nature of the Danish woman.

Both Sweden and Denmark are slightly more lenient toward girls than boys, and encourage the girlish "scamp" image. In Norway, however, an in-depth study of families interviewed repeatedly over a period of years found that boys were slightly favored.[49] For example, Norwegian girls

292   *The Female Factor*

were breast-fed on an average of only three months, while boys averaged six.

Describing the typical Norwegian family, sociologists Eva Eckhoff and Jakob Gauslaa note that the mothers treat boys with more emotional "warmth," give in to them more easily and punish them less severely than girls. Fathers, too, appear to treat the boys with more warmth, give greater consideration to their wishes and control them less than girls. Other in-depth interviews with children, teen-agers and parents in Oslo indicate that, as the children grow older, they feel that society accepts antisocial behavior on the part of boys, equating masculinity with aggression to the point that "bad" becomes almost a positive trait for the young male.

6

Efficiency Housekeeping

        Organization and perfectionism are as evident in the home as they are in other areas of society. Scandinavian design. Hasn't everybody heard about superconvenient Swedish kitchens and superdesigned Danish cutlery and superpractical Norwegian iron cookware and the superpsychologically satisfying Finnish home-furnishing materials?

        The modern government-owned apartments that house the majority of the Swedes and the Finns are designed with housework in mind. Floors are easy-care durable linoleum. "Woodwork" is made of quick-wipe plastic sheathing instead of wood. Kitchen and bathroom wall surfacing is waterproof. Electric-appliance plugs have safety barriers to protect children's fingers. Kitchen cupboards are built to a convenient height and placed to afford the most convenient work space.

        Scandinavian units everywhere are built with quality materials. Well-spaced buildings are restricted in height, and architecturally varied throughout a neighborhood, so there is not the same sense of monotony that characterizes the Paradise suburb outside Paris or the Centocelle area of Rome or the Levittown fields of the United States. Scandinavian green areas are abundant, well-tended and bright with children at play. There are supermarkets and shopping centers within walking distance of most apartment buildings. Spacious "nature areas" are also easily accessible.

And yet does the shining gadgetry show as much real consideration for the housewife as is supposed? The built-in freezers, for example, are irrelevant to the needs of the average small family, especially when neighborhood supermarkets don't stock many frozen foods. Then, too, although space and a drain are provided for a dishwasher, there are no facilities for ordinary washing machines. Sometimes there is an unoccupied corner in the bathroom where one can install a washing machine to hook up to the toilet, but the arrangement renders that vital fixture useless for two hours or more every washday. And there is absolutely no space allocated for setting up a dryer.

Planners told me defensively that apartments lack washing machines because every building has its own Laundromat. Untrue. Laundromats may have been on the drawing boards, but they do not exist in every building, even in the newest complexes of Stockholm. And until some planner does something about the Swedish winter, people will be forced to lug the weekly wash to the shopping center, and then cart it back through the sleet to do a final drying over the living-room heater.

Unfortunately, one must conclude that the famous Swedish efficiency home is not designed solely with the housewife's needs in mind. Not only are basic necessities missing, but there appears to be a calculated reason for their absence. It is not insignificant that Electrolux, Sweden's major appliance manufacturer, makes deep freezes and small refrigerators with small freezing compartments, but has not developed a medium-sized model because that market is dominated by Italian manufacturers. All government-housing equipment is made by Electrolux, which may provide more jobs for Swedes, but does not necessarily improve the lot of the Swedish housewife. Furthermore, the lack of washing machines may be due to the fact that that market, too, is dominated by the Italians.

These problems reflect a society where authorities play the role of benign father. But even the most benign will act out of self-interest. Society must keep the closest watch on the biggest benefactors.

Outside the home, there are similar problems. The biggest shortage lies in the area of public meeting places. There are plenty of pathside benches (Stockholm's suburbs have meandering paths instead of uninteresting sidewalks). But only large metropolitan shopping centers have places where people can meet easily. The central plaza of an ordinary neighborhood is limited to stores, libraries and occasional movie houses. There are no quick-service restaurants, no coffeehouses, no places to socialize after shopping.

Socializing with neighbors ordinarily occurs only at church, which holds regular *öppet hus* (open house) sessions. These get-togethers attract young married couples. They are secular, congenial and provide the opportunity for people to share coffee, watch a cartoon or enter a raffle, but there are few get-to-know-each-other rituals. No one is official hostess or host. There are no name tags; everyone smiles but appears unapproachable except to those who can already call them by name. For the young marrieds, this barrier is often overcome by their children, who develop friendships quickly. The ones who have the most problems are the single people who do not operate from a family base.

For the young married woman who accepts what is still the norm—i.e., the nuclear family living in the suburbs—the day is much less rigidly structured than that of her French or German counterpart. With stores open continuously, with the children taking themselves off to school, with a husband who may very well have the task of preparing breakfast, not even her rising hour is prescribed by necessity. And, despite snags in her housework facilities, she still has the most easily cared for home in the world.

If a woman has young children, they will be home most of the afternoon, even if they are already in the first or second grade. It is her job to take the youngest ones out to the play areas, to have cookies and milk ready for the older ones and to act occasionally as chaperone for sports activities, music lessons or children's club activities. But, again, even the smallest children want and can assume the responsibility for going places alone.

The young married woman may also have responsibilities to an elderly parent or in-law. Although the tradition of older relatives living with the young couple disappeared with the building of the efficiency apartment, Scandinavian women feel more at ease with older people than American women do. Increasingly, however, the ideal of individual self-sufficiency has coupled with the practicalities of old people's communities to make these projects less a natural form of family interplay and more a form of professional duty.

7

Freedom and the Career Woman

Pippi Longstocking as an adult is justly proud of her strength and status. The highest post held by a woman in the United Nations is that occupied by the Finn, Helvi Sipilä. Women totally control the city councils of Norway's largest cities—Oslo and Trondheim. Aase Lionaes is president of the Norwegian Lagting—a position roughly equivalent to that of United States Senate majority leader—and Cecilia Nettelbrant is Vice-President of the Swedish Parliament. Women are Supreme Court judges in both Norway and Denmark. All four Scandinavian countries always have women Cabinet ministers.

Finland and Denmark currently have the largest female proportion in their work force of any country outside the Eastern bloc. A larger percentage of women in their twenties are working in Sweden than anywhere else.[50] Scandinavian women have always been exceptionally important in the verbal arts. Their actresses have been better known internationally than their actors, and today the Norwegian Liv Ullmann holds a place alongside Ingrid Bergman and Greta Garbo in history's short list of cinema's top stars. Among Scandinavian film directors, Mai Zetterling is second only to Ingmar Bergman in international repute.

Women writers have made weighty contributions to Scandinavian literature ever since St. Bridget's renowned works in the 1300s. Today,
primary-school children recite Anna Maria Lengren's poems the way
Americans recite Gray's "Elegy Written in a Country Churchyard."
Women from both Sweden and Norway have won the Nobel Prize, and in
Denmark, Karen Blixen holds an outstanding place. Of her, social observer Connery says:

"When the Danes talk about their foremost writers of this century, they
mention [several names], but none of these achieved anything like the international following of a gifted, almost magical, Danish baroness named
Karen Christentze Blixen-Finecke, who wrote under the pseudonym 'Isak
Dinesen.' . . . Young Karen, who had published a few short stories when
she was twenty, also craved a life of adventure. She got it when she married her cousin, Baron Bror Blixen-Finecke. They became entranced by
Africa, and bought a coffee plantation near Nairobi shortly before World
War I. The marriage broke up after seven years. The Baroness stayed on
alone in Africa and managed the plantation until the bottom fell out of the
coffee market in 1934. She returned to Denmark, and within a few years
had established herself as one of the great poetic writers of her time. Her
Seven Gothic Tales became a classic, and *Out of Africa* was acclaimed as
one of the most moving books ever written about that continent. . . . It
was reported that 'she subsisted on fruit, oysters and champagne and the
resources of her own indomitable spirit' before dying in 1962."[51]

Scandinavian women have not been satisfied simply to fight for the equal
right to work. They have also challenged the old and rigidly entrenched ties
between status and decorum. They want both professional power and a
choice of individual life-styles—a dream that has never been realized in the
history of humankind by either sex.

Here, again, examples of their victories are easily found. Take Birgitta
Dahl, a respected member of Swedish Parliament. A divorcée with a *samleben*, she decided to go ahead with having a child out of wedlock because,
she insisted, traditional marriage has ceased to be meaningful. She suffered
little setback in her constituency.

Helle Virkner Krag, the Danish actress, might seem even more offensive
to the traditional voter, because she competed for the spotlight with her
husband, one of Denmark's most able prime ministers. The Danes, however, not only put her husband in their highest office, they also followed his
lead and voted the country into the Common Market. During that EEC
campaign, Helle Krag was playing a theatrical role as a notorious prostitute.

Obviously, Scandinavia has come a long way since Queen Christina decided to abdicate the Swedish throne because she wanted the freedom to observe a different religion and to enjoy a sex life without the decorum of marriage. Watching the self-confident Norse woman delivering a report in her Parliament or paying a group's restaurant bill, or—the height of role reversal—reading a book while her husband hangs out the wash, it is hard to believe how fast she's changed. A hundred years ago, it was not only socially unacceptable for her to follow almost any profession but weaving and teaching, it was actually against the law.

In the 1870s, the Norse woman did not have equal inheritance rights with her brother, there were more women than men and no one could be sure of marriage. Barred from working, she was often quite literally faced with starvation. If she did marry, she most often stepped into an agrarian life, where the roles of all members were respected but rigid. When she and her husband shared a traditional repast in the field before spring planting, their plow horse joined them. All contributors to the family efforts had to be equally honored.

Today's Scandinavian woman has built her life around the escape from the hardships of the last century. She has taken advantage of the mass migration from the country to the city and from an agriculture society to a highly sophisticated industrial one. Out of the resulting chaos and uncertainty, she has been free to mold a streamlined personality for a new era.

Her success makes her the international leader of the current Women's Movement, but she herself is not satisfied. In all four Scandinavian countries, women are frustrated by the fact that there are still ceilings beyond which they are not allowed to go. Women candidates for the post of prime minister in each of these countries are taken less seriously than they are in France and England. Scandinavia boasts of few widely known businesswomen on a par with the German Beate Uhse or the American Mary Wells. Female wages, at best, average out to only 90 percent of male salaries for the same work, and the majority of women workers are still clustered in low-paying service positions.

Scandinavian feminists are therefore still doing battle for equal work opportunities. A variety of experimental programs are under way. In Norway and Sweden, the government is financing programs where the husband and wife each work a half day, and the government makes up the difference in wages lost. Conceived by Evy Buverud Pedersen, Swedish Social Democrat and the mother of three children, the idea is not only to enable the woman to have a more varied life. "We're not trying to get the woman to work," Pedersen says. "We're giving the husband time to enjoy his children."

Fundamentally new approaches to the practical problems of equalizing work opportunities are facilitated by a surprising attitude toward work. The Scandinavians are some of the world's best-known adherents of the Work Ethic, but, examined up close, one can see that their dedication is very different from that of Germany or the United States.

"Work is *necessary*," a librarian told me, "but I don't know anyone who feels that organized work is *fun*. We enjoy getting our job done in the most efficient manner possible, but the real satisfaction lies in having it finished."

In other words, the key to the Scandinavian outlook is not joy in doing, as in the United States, nor is it joy in duty as in Germany. It's perfectionism. If a person has a job to do, she wants it done faultlessly, but she doesn't volunteer to do more for her own amusement.

Coupled with this unemotional outlook on work is an equally cool attitude toward materialism. "Industrial investment remains static here," Goran Ohlin, professor of political economy commented calmly in 1972. "This is not necessarily a bad thing. Do we really need more?"[52]

For an economist to make that kind of comment before Soviet grain purchases made huge inroads in world food surplus and oil prices made huge inroads on world budgets was sheer heresy.

It is this kind of heresy that has aided women's invasion of the labor market. Since the Swedish man equated his status not with how *much* work he did, but with how *well* he did it, and since he was not committed to forever building more, more, more, he has not been as threatened by the idea of women competing with him as men in other countries have been. Even in times of world recession, he is attracted to the idea of sharing the load, most probably through part-time work.

Anna-Greta Leijon, Minister Without Portfolio in the Swedish Department of Labor, explained how this system is working to the benefit not only of the workers, but also of society. "Just as we have found that group projects turn out better cars than do assembly lines, we find that part-time workers do a better job when they are at work. There is less absenteeism and fewer walk off the job. This is one more means of making both work and leisure time more enjoyable and individually rewarding. It also means that we have to pay higher wages for an hour's work, but if the worker responds with higher quality, this is not a major problem."[53]

With this kind of attitude in the government, with equal-rights laws both on the books and widely praised, with paid maternity and paternity leaves and nursery schools and husbands who help in the home, the Scandinavian woman will obviously be the first to enjoy full employment. Many anticipate that development with unconditional approval, but there are dissident views.

Roland Huntford, the Stockholm correspondent for the London *Observer* and one of Sweden's most-dedicated critics, violently attacks the Scandinavian trend toward women spending the major part of their lives in gainful employment. Insisting that the idea has been fostered by a governmental desire to mold a *Brave New World* collective mentality among the nursery-going children of working mothers, he details an amazingly swift metamorphosis of archetypes.

"[First] there was a rapid change in the language. The customary Swedish for housewife is *husmor,* which is honourable. It was replaced by the neologism *hemmafru,* literally 'the-wife-who-stays-at-home,' which is derogatory. Within a few months, the mass media were able to kill the old and substitute the new term. By the end of 1969, it was almost impossible in everyday conversation to mention the state of housewife without appearing to condemn or to sneer. . . . *Husmor* had been discredited; the only way out was to use *hemmafru* ironically.

"Connected with this semantic shift, there was a change in feeling. Women who, a year or so before, had been satisfied, and possibly proud, to stay at home, began to feel the pressure to go out and to work. The substitution of one word for the other had been accompanied by insistent propaganda in the mass media, so that it was as if a resolute conditioning campaign had been carried out. Very few were able to recognize the indoctrination in the linguistic manipulation; in the real sense of the word, the population had been brainwashed."

Huntford's belief that there is a concerted effort to weaken intrafamilial dependence in Sweden seems accurate. His fears that nursery schools will be used to inculcate the Swedish value put on nonconfrontation is certainly valid. But his conclusion and most important thesis that this development is bad because confrontation is essential to individualism is questionable and could be deemed deeply pessimistic.

For the moment Swedish women have the most freedom to develop their individuality of any woman on earth. There is, however, a serious question of how long this state of affairs will last if she totally accepts the concept that all women and men must divide responsibility equally in society and in the home. It is no real a step forward for either women or society to disenfranchise those who enjoy creative homemaking and motherhood.

Norwegian and Danish women are affirmatively attacking this question as well as the issue of *ensamhet.* Perhaps it is they who tomorrow will be able to offer the most freedom of choice in life roles—to citizens of both sexes.

Epilogue

The greatest forward strides in human history have always been made when large sectors of society were forced to carve out new ways of living because their old means of support and status had disappeared. Sometimes groups were driven from their previous existence by war or famine, sometimes by political or religious movements. Whatever the cause, the result was that a large group of people found itself in new surroundings, forced to make a living in new ways among peers who had little use for the traditional mode of doing things. These newly formed societies leapfrogged ahead. They had to, of course, and they had nothing to lose.

The group being forced into a new way of living today is one-half the world's population—women. The female life-span has nearly doubled in the past hundred years. Motherhood is no longer mandatory. The result has been a rising tide of women working to create a new life for themselves.

Ironically, we have arrived at this watershed at a moment when the world's economy cannot easily expand to accommodate women in the positions which men have occupied in the past. The likelihood is that women will spend the remainder of this century building new self-images and social patterns, and that the woman, as we know her, will be as foreign to us by the year 2000 as today's woman would be to the medieval peasant.

In the Western European societies that I have been examining, the greatest philosophical shift has been away from that of the Lady to that of the Warrior Woman. The Lady was never the only European feminine archetype, but she was dominant in most countries, and during the Victorian Era her value systems were codified into the vast social legislation being written across the Continent to cope with the Industrial Revolution. Even in Scandinavia, the traditional homeland of the Warrior Woman, her influence was reflected in the law.

The Lady, the innate Other so carefully diagramed by De Beauvoir, has carved out a contemporary empire in France as the Honorable Opposition. In Italy, as *La Mamma* and Maria, she rules the heart of the country, and has virtually demolished the direct physical confrontation and blind obedience that characterizes a male-oriented society. In Germany, and to an extent in England, she has become the sacrosanct Wife, but her power in these countries has never been clear-cut because there the values of the Warrior Woman have also been widely upheld.

The strength of the Lady is her verbal ability, and in the societies where she holds sway, verbal skill is highly esteemed. In the past, she spent her childhood as well as most of the rest of her life totally segregated from the male, but in today's rapidly integrating school systems she is unafraid to take on the other sex in verbal battle. This fearlessness extends into adulthood, but she still maintains the traditional Lady's reluctance to take on a challenge in the physical fields reserved for men.

For her marriage partner, she wants neither a friend nor an equal but someone totally different from herself. Ideally, the two develop a smoothly running symbiosis: she copes with the work inside the home, he copes with that outside, and both of them are strongly interdependent on a practical level. When they have children, she concentrates on the girls, he concentrates on the boys and the cycle of separation is perpetuated.

Besides being articulate, the Lady has another very important positive attribute—she knows and likes herself. These assets are related, for it is through her ability to define and compare that she has gained her self-appreciation.

The shift to the Warrior Woman has been caused by many factors, but the predominant one has been the male victory in expropriating feminine roles. Child-raising has been taken out of the home and assigned to the school and age peer groups; sewing and cooking have been assigned to the clothing and food industries; new homes have solved many of the problems of heat and water and they come stocked with appliances that "run themselves." Even childbirth has been taken away from the home and the supervision of the midwife and placed instead in the male-dominated world of the hospital. Women have been left with very few means of proving their worth, even fewer of competing for status.

The disenfranchisement took place over a long period of time, and until the sudden shift brought on by both the Pill and fears of overpopulation, there remained the possibility that the large-scale trend might still revert to the Lady. After all, the Lady offered the advantage of specialized marriage roles and this is an age of specialists. With the defrocking of the mother that we have witnessed in the past decade, however, a massive reversal now seems unlikely.

As Warrior Women in Europe and the United States have gone out to fight the same battles as men, their victories have been sporadic, but meaningful. Women are now able to do more than declare their equality; they can prove they *are* equal, and—more practically—that they are valuable participators. Until women can define their goals and their views of what is valuable along the way, however, they will still lack the power that the Lady has enjoyed. When they do reach that point, they will be able to begin making the kind of breakthrough contributions expected in a newly formed society.

The Warrior Woman has numerous strengths that are advantageous in today's world. Many have the ability to laugh at themselves, a trait denied every other serious archetype of both sexes. The ability to laugh at oneself is vital because it fosters the flexibility necessary to cope with sudden change. A successful navigator of modern living must be able to recast her self-image several times. Not only does she no longer have her mother's example to follow, but the profession she chooses at twenty may be extinct by the time she's thirty-five. Change is also the norm in personal relationships, and everywhere humor and flexibility are essential to easy adaptation.

The Warrior Woman readily accepts the idea that her primary role lies outside the home and motherhood. The concept has had a place in her culture for a long time, and the practice is supported in a million subtle ways throughout her society.

While it is true that the word-oriented Lady often moves easily into competition in today's business world, in Sweden both sexes have demonstrated the effectiveness of bypassing sheer oral skills to utilize the more concrete form of written analysis with its subsequent testing of proposed action.

On a personal level, the egalitarian Warrior Woman wants to team up with a companion in arms. She and her partner are well equipped to support each other because they value the same achievements and talk the same language. Conversely, however, this same couple demands much of their union, and are willing to destroy it before they will compromise their ideal of "perfect marriage." Further, wanting the same rewards and goals, they are susceptible to internecine jealousy when one wins and the other does not.

Women in every country I have observed are faced with more or less the same list of difficulties.

As children, many feel forced to choose between being a "second-class boy" in physical competitions or overwhelming the boys with verbal precocity. The Swedes and, to some extent, the Germans, are trying to circumvent this problem by a carefully considered program of team sports and by pitting children against their own past records instead of against each other. To date, the results of this kind of manipulation of individual initiative have been good as far as material rewards are concerned. Sweden also has an admirably low rate of explosive social violence, but the amount of implosive violence reflected in suicide and alcoholism rates indicates that noncompetitiveness is not a complete solution, even for those willing to applaud and trust social engineering.

This generation's girls and boys are being asked to adapt to more of a unisex approach to living than any group has ever known before. Margaret Mead has pointed out that no matter what duties a human tribe assigned each sex—no matter who did the heavy work, the hunting, the gathering and the storing, or the teaching of the children—every known society has always differentiated between the responsibilities assigned to women and men.

Today there is no logical reason why this should be, nor is there any practical reason why we cannot use unisex to build a true and lasting friendship between the sexes. Until now, however, even in Sweden, the society that has longest been attempting to bridge the gap, unisex has been associated not with more tolerance or friendship, but with intersexual independence and animosity. The fact that Scandinavia's intersexual violence rates are comparatively very low, however, is certainly a hopeful sign.

Throughout Europe and the United States, the pubescent girl is coping with yet another relatively untried pattern of behavior, that of open sexual experimentation. In contrast with unisex, trial marriage and promiscuity have been known throughout human history, so one would suppose that taboos against them would be easier to throw off. This has not been the case, however, because promiscuity in any form is at odds with the delicate but vitally important bonds necessarily forged between the true friends who mate and migrate through the complicated maze of today's postindustrial world. As a result, the Swinging Sixties are now somewhat passé, and even in New York's singles clubs, conversations hinge on "the need for a lasting relationship—not an ownership arrangement, of course, but something involving mutual trust and commitment."

Mutual trust and commitment, however, no longer mean a lifetime contract in any of the countries we have examined. The individual who does not have a divorce somewhere in the family is now exceedingly rare—a direct reversal of the situation fifty years ago. A pattern of repeated marriage and divorce has become acceptable among the perfectionist couples who seek sustained emotional support from each other. Many are refusing any official influence whatsoever over their individualistic unions, and formal marriage ceremonies and legal contracts are considered unnecessary encumbrances, particularly in Scandinavia, where the marriage rate is almost half that in the United States.

Societies all over the Western world are seriously attacking the problems of the workingwoman, and her contributions and conquests are clearly visible. Paid pregnancy leaves, child-care facilities, equal pay and equal opportunity, equal pensions—all are functioning with a notable degree of success in various countries. Since these societies have been rewarded for their liberalization with willing and responsible workers who have helped the economy, it is likely that this program will eventually be universal, despite current job shortages.

The biggest crisis looming ahead concerns the fact that soon there will be too few workers to operate the factories and the offices. Statisticians all over Europe are rerunning birthrate data through computers, then hurriedly sending the results to newspapers. The downward trend that had been expected to level off at just above zero population growth continues downward. Women are deserting the ranks of motherhood in droves. Past experience in such basically dissimilar cultures as Sweden, Tuscany and the Communist bloc indicates that women will not be herded back to motherhood by restrictions on birth-control devices or work rights. Even high family allowance incentives have not enticed Swedish women back to motherhood. An enormous amount of research needs to be done to find out what childbearing gives the mother, because, without emotional rewards, a woman simply won't take on the burden.

The countries where mother's continue to enjoy social importance and personal satisfaction are Italy and Norway, which are to be expected, and England, which is not. The Italian mamma has been more deeply disturbed by the contingencies of the industrial world than the Norwegian. Often her family is spread from Sicily to Turin and Milan and even on to Germany or Sweden. Like the Jewish mother, however, she has been relatively successful in maintaining familial fidelity, even when she herself spends most of her day at work outside the home.

The English working-class Mum has many of the same traditions and status rewards as *La Mamma*. Further, an interesting trend has developed among the middle and upper classes, where a hundred years ago everyone was firmly convinced that children should be raised by nonfamilial professionals. Owing to the work of Bowlby and a recently completed study of British people born during one week in 1946, the educated Englishwoman has become cognizant of her importance in the lives of her children during their first five years. This new sense of status and the repudiation of the Professional Mother are vitally significant to our understanding of the long-term needs and motivations of women everywhere.

Finally, there is the problem of the older woman. Throughout the industrialized world, women have a longer life-span than men, but women over sixty are still "protected" by law with an earlier retirement age. In the majority of cases, the older woman has nothing to look forward to but relative poverty and social ostracism. Scandinavian and German societies are making piecemeal efforts to reintegrate her with working society in child-care facilities, but only one culture, the Italian, provides a broadly based solution.

This is the traditional answer—a solution that was practiced universally in Europe and the United States until this century. The mother simply goes to live with her children after the death of her husband. She is expected. Her foibles are criticized but accepted, just as they are with any other member of the family. She is not treated as a guest (either welcome or unwelcome), but works with the family just like everyone else. Her experience with raising children is often resisted, but no matter how many struggles arise between her and the younger mother, her usefulness as surrogate—particularly if the other adults in the family work outside the home—is widely appreciated. In short, her status as *La Mamma* has vital manifestations.

Italy's solution is practical, but few people in other countries have the courage to adopt it in the face of social derision. Ultimately, what can be learned from the Italians is not that everybody should build an extra room for their mother-in-law, but simply that anyone who does take that option has no reason to feel guilty, oppressed or defiant for making the choice.

This will be, hopefully, the ultimate freedom we, as women, will enjoy in becoming knowledgeable about the choices now opening to us. It is the hardest one to realize, because it means overcoming prejudices not ordinarily attacked during periods of change. It is the freedom to go backward as well as forward.

The problems besetting us today are not easily solved. We will not solve them until we have reached a détente with the male half of the human race. We have to start solving them now, and we have already accepted the fact that we'll make many mistakes along the way. The exciting prospect is that we ourselves will be able to enjoy the fruits of our victories.

Appendix Tables

Table A Economically Active Males and Females Per 100 Population

Country	Year	Sex & F/M Ratio*All Ages		Ages 20–24
Denmark	1971	Female	37.8	61.9
		Male	59.6	87.5
		Ratio	1:1.58	1:1.32
Finland	1970	Female	37.5	62.6
		Male	55.1	77.7
		Ratio	1:1.47	1:1.24
England & Wales	1970	Female	32.2	—
		Male	60.4	—
		Ratio	1:1.88	—
W. Germany	1971	Female	30.2	91.4
		Male	58.7	71.7
		Ratio	1:1.94	1:0.75
France	1972	Female	29.7	82.6
		Male	55.0	62.3
		Ratio	1:1.85	1:0.75
Norway	1969	Female	23.6	81.9
		Male	56.4	47.7
		Ratio	1:2.39	1:0.58
Italy	1961	Female	19.5	88.8
		Male	61.1	40.6
		Ratio	1:3.13	1:0.45
Sweden	1965	Female	29.8	67.1
		Male	59.0	56.2
		Ratio	1:1.98	1:0.83
U.S.	1971	Female	30.4	44.8
		Male	53.9	86.4
		Ratio	1:1.77	1:1.93

SOURCE: UN Economics & Social Council, table 4, December 7, 1973.
*Ratios are computed without adjustment for sex balance in population.

Table A Supplement Economically Active Men, Women and Total Population 1975 to 1979 (in 000's)

Country	Year	Men	Women	Total	Women % of Total
France	1975	13,643	8,132	21,775	37.3
W. Germany	1978	16,793	10,159	26,952	37.7
Norway	1979	1,128	781	1,909	40.9
Sweden	1979	2,359	1,908	4,268	44.7
U.S.	1979	61,466	43,531	104,996	41.5

SOURCE: *Yearbook of Labour Statistics*, 1980, table 2,B, International Labour Office, Geneva.

Table B   Women's Position in Government

Note: T = Total number in body, W = Women in body, % = Female Percentage in body

Country	Ministers		Parliament			Other Legislatures	Supreme Court Judges	
	T	W	T	W	%		T	W
Denmark	16*	3*	179*	28*	15.6	Municipal 10.5% 1972	9*	1*
France	37*	4*	*Senate* 283	7*	2.5	671 mayors	No equivalent court	
			National Assembly 481	7*	1.4			
			Economic Council 200	6	3.0			
Finland	16	2	200	43	21.5	Municipal 14.9%	22	1
W. Germany	16*	1*	488*	30*	6.1		7	1
England & Wales	16*	2*	*House of Commons* 630*	26*	4.1			
			House of Lords 1079*	46*	4.2			
			(life peeresses in their own right)					
Italy		0	*Chamber of Deputies* 629*	27*	4.2			
			Senate 315*	5*	1.5			
Norway	16*	4*	155*	23*	14.8			
Sweden	18	2	350	50	14.3	State Govt 170T 35W Local Govt 22.9%	25	1
U.S.	UN Rep*	1	*Senate (1981)* 435*	18*	4.1	State Governors 50* 2* State Govt 9,463* 1,043* 11.0 Major City Mayors 47* 9* 19.1	9	1
			House (1981) 100	2*	2.0			
U.S.S.R.		0	*Supreme Soviet of U.S.S.R.*	35		Local Deputies 47.4% (1973)		
			Supreme Soviet of Autonomous Republics	38				

SOURCE: This chart was partially assembled by the UN Economics Social Council for the Committee on the Status of Women Report, December 7, 1973.

Blanks are unknown and do not necessarily denote 0.

*Denotes additional information for 1974 and 1975, which I have researched.

Table C   Political Milestones

1761 —1780—Women property owners have the right to vote in Virginia and under the Old Province Charter in Massachusetts.

1787 —1807—Women of New Jersey have the right to vote.

1790 —Publication of Mary Wollstonecraft's *Vindication of the Rights of Women*.

1848 —The First Women's Rights Convention in Seneca Falls, N.Y.

1862 —Women property taxpayers in Sweden win right to vote in all elections except national.

1865 —Widows and spinsters given local voting rights in Finland.

1869 —Women franchised to vote by the territorial legislature of Wyoming.

1870 —Women win right to vote in Utah.

1893 —Women win right to vote in Colorado.

1893 —Women win right to vote in New Zealand.

1896 —Women franchised in Idaho.

1901 —Women in Norway are enfranchised for municipal elections.

1906 —Finland is the first Western nation to enfranchise women for national elections.

1907 —First women win seats as Parliamentarians in Finland.

1907 —Women win right to vote in all elections in Norway with a small tax paying requirement that was lifted in 1913.

1907 —Danish women enfranchised for municipal elections.

1913 —Icelandic women gain universal suffrage.

1915 —Danish women granted universal suffrage.

1916 —Jeannette Rankin is first woman elected to Congress in the United States.

1917 —Englishwomen over thirty gain the vote.

1917 —Russian women win universal suffrage.

1919 —German women win universal suffrage.

1919 —Swedish women win universal suffrage.

1919 —Nancy Astor wins a seat in British Parliament.

1920 —American women win universal suffrage.

1920s —Women are elected to the legislature of all the countries where they are nationally franchised, and are particularly powerful in Germany. Finnish women win posts as ministers of education and of the arts.

1925 —Mrs. Nellie Taylor Ross elected governor of Wyoming.

1928 —Women in England win equal universal suffrage.

1932 —Mrs. Hattie Caraway is first women senator (Arkansas).

1933 —Frances Perkins appointed secretary of labor in the United States.

1938 —Birth-control and women's-right-to-work laws liberalized in Sweden after report by Alva Myrdal and her husband.

1930s onward—Women were elected to the national legislatures in all the countries where women were enfranchised. They continued to serve in the cabinets of governments in Scandinavia and England, but dropped out elsewhere until the sixties, when the movement began to swell again.

1945 —Italian women win universal suffrage.

1945 —French women win universal suffrage.

1966 —Indira Gandhi was elected prime minister of India.

1969 —Golda Meir was elected prime minister of Israel.

1971 —Women win the vote in Switzerland.

1971 —Divorce legalized in Italy.

1972 —Sirimavo Ratwatte Dias Bandaranaike was elected prime minister of Sri Lanka.

1974 —Francois Giroud appointed as minister of women's affairs in France.

1974 —Ella Tambussi Grasso elected governor (Connecticut) without previously having been a governor's wife.

1974 —Maria Estela (Isabelita) Peron takes over the presidency of Argentina after the death of her husband.

1977 —Elizabeth Blunschy-Steiner elected president of the Swiss National Council, the country's highest political office.

1979 —Indira Gandhi regains her seat as prime minister of India in a landslide victory after two years of being outside the government.

1979 —Margaret Thatcher elected prime minister of England, and as such becomes the first woman to head a European state through an election.

1979 —Maria de Lurdes Pintassilgo becomes prime minster of Portugal.

1979 —Nilde Jotte elected president of the Italian Chamber of Deputies.

1979 —Jane Byrne becomes the first woman to be elected as major of a major American city (Chicago).

1979 —Patricia Roberts Harris appointed secretary of health, education, and welfare, and becomes the first American woman to have held two portfolios (having been secretary of housing and urban development).

1979 —Simone Veil, ex-minister of health of France, is elected president of the Parliament of Europe Assembly of the nine European Common Market nations.

1981 —Gro Harlem Brundtland becomes Norway's first woman prime minister.

1981 —Sandra Day O'Connor appointed US Supreme Court justice.

Table D   Vital Statistics

Life expectancy at birth			
Country	Year	Women	Men
Denmark	75/76	76.8	71.1
Finland	1975	75.9	67.4
France	1976	77.2	69.2
W. Germany	75/77	75.2	68.6
Italy	70/72	74.9	69.0
Norway	76/77	78.4	72.1
Sweden	72/76	77.8	72.1
England & Wales	74/76	75.8	69.6
United States	1975	76.5	68.7
USSR	71/72	74	64

SOURCE: *U.N. Demographic Yearbook,* 1978, World Summary, Table 4

Crude birth rates and infant mortality rates											
Country	1950		1955		1960		1965		1970		1975	
	BR	IMR	BR	IMR	BR	IMR	BR	IMR	BR	IMR	BR	IMR
Denmark	18.6	30.7	17.3	25.2	16.6	21.5	18.0	18.7	14.3	14.2	14.2	10.4
Finland	24.5	43.5	21.2	29.7	18.5	21.0	17.1	17.6	14.0	13.2	13.9	9.6
France	20.7	52.0	18.6	38.6	17.9	27.4	17.8	21.9	16.8	18.2	14.1	13.8
W. Germany	15.8	57.2	15.3	42.7	17.5	42.7	17.7	23.9	13.4	23.6	9.7	19.8
Italy	19.4	63.8	17.9	50.9	18.1	43.9	19.1	36.0	16.8	29.6	14.8	21.2
Norway	19.1	28.2	18.5	20.6	17.3	18.9	17.8	16.8	16.6	12.7	14.1	11.1
Sweden	16.4	21.0	14.8	17.4	13.7	16.6	15.9	13.3	13.7	11.0	12.6	8.6
U.K.	15.8	30.0	15.0	24.9	17.1	21.8	18.1	19.0	16.1	18.1	12.3	15.7
U.S.	23.5	29.2	24.8	26.6	23.6	26.0	19.4	24.7	18.2	20.0	14.7	16.1

SOURCE: *UN Demographic Yearbook – Special Issue,* 1979, Historical Supplement.

NOTE: Unless otherwise indicated, population data are official estimates for July 1 of average year estimates. Crude Birth rates are computed per 1,000 population. Infant mortality rates are computed per 1,000 live births.

Maternal death rates per 100,000 live births						
Country	1968	1970	1972	1974	1976	1977
Denmark	10	6	3	4	1	
Finland	21	5	6	2		
France	202	185				
W. Germany	429	365	255	190	191	
Italy	542	446	366			
Norway	9	7	4	4	6	5
Sweden	10	11	8	8		
England & Wales	150	114	86	70	71	
U.S.	726	625	542	435	374	

SOURCE: *U.N. Demographic Yearbook,* 1978, Table 17.

Table E   **Which Contraceptive is Used by Married Women in Percentages**

	Italy	France	Great Britain	West Germany
Diaphragm	—	3	7	—
Chemicals	—	—	1	—
Rhythm Method	20	19	4	16
Pill	5	16	22	34
Withdrawal	32	30	10	9
Sheath	11	8	29	11
IUD	—	2	4	—
Douche	2	4	—	—
Total Abstinence	1	1	—	—
Nothing	35	25	23	27
No reply	5	—	—	6

SOURCE: Family Planning Study by the International Health Foundation of Geneva, done in 1969, interviewing 1000 women in each country from various backgrounds aged 16 to 45.

According to the Margaret Bone Family Planning study in England and Wales in 1973, a further 6 percent of couples there have one partner sterilized. Of these couples, 71 percent had the wife sterilized.

Male and female sterilization for family-planning purposes is legal in England, the United States, Denmark, West Germany (male sterilization is illegal in East Germany) and, now, Sweden. It is legal only in certain cases in France, Norway and Finland, and *illegal* in Italy except in cases of genetic deficiency.

Female sterilization may be obtained in Italy if the woman is so physically weakened that she cannot bear another child. This reason, however, is not justification for the husband's sterilization.

In Finland, one study showed that only 13 percent of the couples use contraceptives. The sheath is most popular, followed by the IUD and then abortion. Judging from the Finnish birthrate, withdrawal must also be practiced.

Table E Supplement   **Percentage of Women Age 15–44 Supplied With Oral Contraceptives 1970 – 1977**

Country	1970	1971	1972	1973	1974	1975	1976	1977
Denmark	27.5	27.5	29.9	32.1	24.9	20.3	23.2	32.2
Finland	11.9	13.7	13.6	11.9	11.4	11.2	12.0	12.5
France	6.1	8.8	11.3	15.6	19.6	22.2	23.9	24.6
W. Germany	18.9	24.4	27.6	26.7	28.6	29.3	30.0	26.9
Italy	1.2	1.5	2.4	2.9	3.6	4.3	5.1	5.6
United Kingdom	9.9	12.1	13.4	15.5	16.9	19.8	19.8	20.3
U.S.	12.7	14.4	15.4	16.7	17.1	16.8	14.5	12.2

SOURCE: IMS International/America, Ltd., Studies prepared for the Population Information Program, 1977 and 1978 (01 82)

NOTE: These percentages were computed by dividing the number of oral contraceptives bought by retail outlets and dividing them by 13 to arrive at the maximum number of women years of use. This was then compared to the number of women between the ages of 15 and 44, to arrive at the percentage in childbearing ages using the pill. No adjustments have been made for nonfertile women or other women not at risk of pregnancy for any reason, nor have possible inventory figures been used.

Table F   Percentage of Live Births That are Illegitimate

Country	1966	1968	1970	1972	1974
Denmark	10.2	11.1	11.0	14.4	*17.1
Finland	4.6	5.7	5.8	6.7	* 7.9
France	6.3	6.4	7.1	7.1	
W. Germany	4.6	4.8	5.5	6.0	* 6.3
Italy	2.0	2.0	2.2	2.5	
Norway	4.9	5.6	6.9	8.7	9.3
Sweden	14.6	15.8	18.4	25.1	31.4
England & Wales	7.9	8.5	8.3	8.6	* 8.6
U.S.	8.4	9.7	10.7	12.4	

SOURCE: *U.N. Demographic Yearbook, Special Topic – Natality Statistics*, 1975, Table 32.

*1973 statistics (latest available).

Table G   Number of Legally Induced Abortions

Country	1964	1968	1970	1973	1975	1977
U.S.	—	3,085	180,119	742,500	1,034,200	1,079,430
Denmark	—	6,450	9,027	—	27,884	—
Finland	—	6,288	14,757	23,362	21,547	—
France	—	—	—	—	—	150,931
W. Germany	—	—	—	—	—	54,309
Italy	(see notes)					
Norway	—	5,152	7,941	—	15,132	15,528
Sweden	4,671	10,940	16,100	25,990	32,526	—
England & Wales	—	23,641	86,565	110,568	106,224	—

Notes:

U.S. – Abortion was first legalized in Colorado in 1968. Other states followed. The Supreme Court upheld the legality as of January, 1973.

Denmark, Finland – Abortion legalized in 1966.

France, Germany – Abortion legalized in 1974.

Italy – Abortion legalized in 1978 after national referendum. Number of legal abortions not yet officially available. Previous illegal rate estimated to be approximately one million annually by the Planned Parenthood Organization.

Norway – Abortion legalized in 1968.

Sweden – Abortion legalized in 1964.

England & Wales – The Abortion Act went into effect in 1967 & 1968, respectively.

In all of these countries, abortion is now legal when:

1. There is risk to life of the mother.
2. There is risk to the physical health of the mother.
3. There is risk to the mental health of the mother.
4. There is risk that the child will be born physically or mentally defective.

Abortion on demand during the first three months of pregnancy is legal in all the above except Norway and W. Germany.

Source: *U.N. Demographic Yearbook*, Table 13, 1978.

Table H **Marriage and Divorce Rates per 1,000 Population and Marriage:Divorce Ratios**

Country	Year	Marriage	Divorce	Marriage:Divorce Ratio
Denmark	1978	5.6	2.5	2.24:1
Finland	1978	6.3	2.1	3.00:1
France	1977	6.9	1.2	5.75:1
W. Germany	1978	5.4	1.8	3.00:1
Italy	1977	6.1	0.2	30.50:1
Norway	1978	5.8	1.5	3.87:1
Sweden	1978	4.6	2.4	1.92:1
England & Wales	1978	7.3	2.6	2.81:1
U.S.	1977	10.7	5.1	2.10:1
U.S.S.R.	1977	10.7	3.5	3.06:1

SOURCE: *UN Demographic Yearbook*, 1978, World Summary Table 4. The ratios have been calculated from these percentages to give a comparative value.

Notes: Italy's divorce law went into effect in December, 1970, and was upheld by national referendum in May, 1974.

If both spouses agree, no-fault divorce is obtainable in all the above countries. A wait of nearly a year is necessary, however, in all but some parts of Scandinavia and the United States.

Child support by the husband is required by all countries, but is often difficult to claim except in Sweden, where the state automatically assumes the task of collection.

By far the largest alimony settlements are granted in the United States. Elsewhere, women are rarely awarded more than a minimum wage unless they had a large dowry or contributed financially to the family livelihood. In all of these countries, it is possible for the husband to claim alimony, although it is rarely granted — ordinarily only in cases where the husband is physically handicapped.

In Italy and France, it is common for both partners to settle on a lump-sum payment from the wealthier spouse before applying to the court with a joint petition.

Children in all these countries are usually awarded to the mother's care.

Table I **Suicide Rates by Sex**

Country	Sex	1961	1965	1969	Mid 1970's
Denmark	M	22.4	24.0	26.6	28.0
	F	11.5	14.7	15.2	18.7
Finland	M	33.2	32.2	37.4	
	F	9.0	8.1	10.1	
France	M	24.5	23.0	23.4	
	F	7.7	7.5	8.5	
W. Germany	M	25.1	26.8	27.7	30.1
	F	13.0	13.8	14.7	15.1
Italy	M	7.9	7.8	7.6	7.8
	F	3.4	3.1	3.3	3.4
Norway	M	10.6	11.8	13.0	17.4
	F	2.8	3.6	3.3	6.6
Sweden	M	25.6	27.7	31.2	26.3
	F	8.3	10.1	12.7	11.8
England & Wales	M	13.5	12.7	10.6	11.0
	F	9.1	9.0	7.2	6.1
U.S.	M	16.1	16.3	16.1	20.1
	F	4.9	6.1	6.3	13.3
(Hungary)	M	36.3	42.6	48.3	
	F	15.3	17.9	18.9	

SOURCE: *World Health Statistics Annual*, 1969 and 1979, vols. 1, *World Health Statistics Report*, 1969, 21,6, and the U.S. *National Center for Health Statisics*.

NOTE: Rate is crude death rate attributable to suicide per 100,000 population.

Table J   Percentage of Teen-agers in Secondary School During the Sixties

	Boys	Girls
France (1968) (age 11–17)	66	69
West Germany (1968) (age 11–18)	66	61
Sweden (1968) (age 13–18)	94	94
United Kingdom (1968) (age 11–17)	72	72
Italy (1969) (age 11–18)	54	49
U.S.S.R. (1966) (age 15–17)	65	71
U.S. (1968) (age 15–17)	universal education	

SOURCE: *Higher Education Reports on Population and Family Planning* (New York: The Population Council, September 1972).

Table K   Percentage of Population Aged 45–49 That Has Never Married

Country	1950/51		1960/61		1970/71		1975/77	
	M	F	M	F	M	F	M	F
Denmark	10.2	14.2	9.7	9.4	9.6	6.9	9.5	5.8
Finland	11.9	18.7	10.1	14.3	12.2	12.1	13.8	11.0
France	11.1	10.7	10.2	8.8	10.7	8.3	11.0	7.9
W. Germany	6.8	12.5	4.9	9.4	4.6	10.3	6.2	7.5
Italy	9.4	15.0	9.3	13.7	11.1	13.8		
Norway	15.5	20.5	13.4	13.0	12.8	8.3	11.6	5.9
Sweden	16.2	18.5	14.5	11.0	13.9	7.8	13.4	7.0
England & Wales	8.5	16.6	9.6	10.5	10.1	7.8	10.0	7.0
U.S.	8.7	7.9	7.2	6.5	6.6	5.4	5.6	4.4

SOURCE: *U.N. Demographic Yearbook,* 1979, Special Issue, Historical Supplement, Table 11.

NOTE: The percentage of single persons by sex for selected age groups is the ratio of persons classified as single (never married) at a given moment, to the number of persons of all marital status, including marital status unknown, for a given age group by sex.

Notes

Part One
The Englishwoman—The Eternal Teammate

1. Stuart Sutherland, *Guide to National Practices in Western Europe* (Brighton, England: European Business Communications, 1973).

2. Dr. Hans Bruck report to the 1972 Conference of Plastic Surgeons in Miami, *International Herald Tribune* (Paris), February 7, 1972.

3. *The Sunday Times*, (London), July 2, 1972.

4. Joan Goulianos, *By a Woman Writt* (Indianapolis: Bobbs-Merrill Company, Inc., 1973), p. 3.

5. Interview, Michael Griffiths, December 1971.

6. Anna Coote and Tess Gill, *Women's Rights: A Practical Guide* (Harmondsworth, Middlesex, England: Penguin Books Ltd., 1974), pp. 127–29.

7. Peter Lennon, "Encounter," *The Sunday Times* (London), October 24, 1974.

8. *The Sunday Times* (London), May 14, 1972.

9. *Time* (New York), October 28, 1974.

10. Coote and Gill, *op. cit.*, p. 21.

11. L. Chester and S. Boston, "Secret Memos Aim to Stop Equal Pay for Women," *The Sunday Times* (London), February 11, 1973.

12. *Daily Express* (London), May 14, 1973.

13. *Department of Employment Gazette* (London), October 1971, p. 906.

14. Peter Wilsher, "My New Charter," *The Sunday Times* (London), June 30, 1974.

15. Joan Rhoades. See "The Lady Who Practices Strongman Stuff," *The Sunday Times* (London), May 14, 1972.

16. *The Sunday Times* (London), July 22, 1973.

17. Arianna Stassinopoulos (talking to Peter Grosvenor), "The Women Who Feel Guilty," *Daily Express* (London), September 8, 1974.

18. Forty-two are listed as "Organizations to Promote the Interests of Women."

19. According to "a London spokeswoman" quoted in the *International Herald Tribune* (Paris), May 7, 1974.

20. Barbara Cartland, *Etiquette* (London: Hutchinson, 1972), p. 90.

21. *International Herald Tribune* (Paris), April 7, 1972.

22. Parliament Report, *The Times* (London), November 22, 1974.

23. The Statistical Office of the United Nations.

24. Jonathan Gathorne-Hardy, *The Rise and Fall of the British Nanny* (London: Hodder & Stoughton, 1972).

25. M. Kerr, "The Family in 'Traditional' Working Class England: 1," in *Sociology of the Family*, ed. Michael Anderson (Harmondsworth, Middlesex, England: Penguin Books Ltd., 1971), pp. 66–69.

26. *The Sunday Times* (London), March 29, 1972.

27. "Me and My Vas," *The Sunday Times* (London), March 25, 1974.

28. Interview, November 24, 1974, Linda Dicks, ex-Family Planning Worker.

29. Louise and Oliver Gillie, in "The Vital First Hours," *The Sunday Times* (London), October 20, 1974, quoted these statistics from the September 1974 *Midwife and Health Visitor.*

30. Jill Nicholson, *Mother and Baby Homes, National Institute for Social Work Training, Series* 13, 1968.

31. Under the Mental Deficiency Act of 1913, unwed mothers were frequently institutionalized as morally defective. In 1972, it was found that several never had been freed.

32. Dr. John Gibbens, *The Care of Children from One to Five* (London: J. & A. Churchill Ltd., 1961).

33. *Ibid.*, p. 151.

34. Elaine Morgan, *The Descent of Woman* (London: Souvenir, 1972; Corgi reprint 1973), p. 267.

35. *Ibid.*, pp. 272–73.

36. Barbara Cartland, *op. cit.*, p. 52.

37. "Where Have You Been To, My Pretty Maids?," *The Sunday Times* (London), May 27, 1973.

38. Auden, as quoted by Clive James, *The Observer* (London), April 28, 1974.

39. Judith Stone, "Back to Boarding School," *The Observer* (London), September 8, 1974.

40. Michael Pye, "The Anguished Child," *The Sunday Times* (London), November 17, 1974. Dr. Shaffer studied all child suicides from 1962 to 1968—of whom twenty-one were boys and nine were girls.

41. The National Union of Students Presentation to the Margate Conference, November 24–27, 1972, "Women in Society," pp. 2, 4.

42. Germaine Greer, *The Female Eunuch* (London: Paladin, 1971), p. 249.

43. Geoffrey Gorer, *Sex and Marriage in England Today* (London: Thomas Nelson & Sons, Ltd., 1971), p. 31.

44. *The Sunday Times* (London), February 26, 1973.

45. Drusilla Beyfus, *The English Marriage* (London: Weidenfeld and Nicolson, 1968).

46. M. Kerr, *op. cit.*, pp. 70–77.

47. Jack Trevor Story, "Cider with Kingy," *Manchester Guardian*, January 2, 1974.

48. Elaine Morgan, *op. cit.*, pp. 85–108.

49. Coote and Gill, *op. cit.*, pp. 169–97.

50. J. Klein, "The Family in 'Traditional' Working Class England: 2," *Sociology of the Family*, ed. Michael Anderson (Harmondsworth, Middlesex, England: Penguin Books Ltd., 1971), pp. 71–75.

51. *The Sunday Express* (London), April 29, 1973.

52. "Dear Marje," *Daily Mirror* (London), January 7, 1972.

53. Margaret Laing, *Edward Heath, Prime Minister* (London: Sidgwick and Jackson, 1972).

Part Two
The Italian Woman—Matriarchy in Motion

1. Ernst Bernhardt, *Mitobiologia* (Milan: Editore Rizzoli, 1970).

2. Eleanor Tufts, *Our Hidden Heritage* (New York: Two Continents, 1974).

3. *La Donna Oggi in Italia* (Rome: Inchiesta SHELL, n. 10, May 1973), tables 6.6 and 6.7. Based on extensive interviews with 4604 women and 1930 women above age fifteen. It was conducted by the best-known Italian pollsters, Doxa, under the direction of Professor Pierpaolo Luzzatto Fegiz. The interviews were carried out in all parts of the country and provide the most extensive statistical picture of the Italian woman compiled in recent times.

4. "Survey of 1958 Italian Women and Their Intimate Problems," *Novella 2000* (Milan), 1970.

5. Giuseppe Cattaneo, "Le Donne Italiane Accusano i Marití," *L'Europeo* (Milan), March 1971.

6. Paolo Pietroni, "L'Amore Coniugale," *Novela 2000* (London), 1970.

7. *La Donna Oggi in Italia*, table 4.2.

8. *Ibid.*, table 4.4.

9. *Ibid.*, table 5.5.

10. *Ibid.*, tables 5.6 and 5.7.

11. "Survey of 1958 Women and Their Intimate Problems," *loc. cit.*

12. Cattaneo, *loc. cit.*

13. Samuel Longfellow, ed., *Life of Henry Wadsworth Longfellow* (Cambridge, Mass.: 1886). Published by editor.

14. "The Geography of Inequality," *McCall's* (New York), 1971.

15. *Radioscope de l'Europe, Editions Européennes de Selection et du Reader's Digest* (Paris: Reader's Digest, 1970).

16. United Press International report, April 22, 1974.

17. *La Donna Oggi in Italia*, table 6.1.

18. Eugene Paykel, "Graduatoria deglia Eventi della Vita che Possono Provacare una Depressione Psichica," *'L'Europeo* (Milan), March 1971.

19. Luigi Vacchi, "Aborto al Buio," *Panorama* (Milan), February 11, 1971.

20. *Ibid.*

21. Giuseppe Barilla, "In Cerca di Un Nido," *Il Messaggero* (Rome), March 22, 1971.

22. *Radioscopie de l'Europe, Editions Européennes de Selections et du Reader's Digest.*

23. See Giancarlo Del Re, "Il Figlio di Scarpaleggera," *Il Messaggero* (Rome), February 13, 1971, for the life led by a school dropout.

24. "Ancora il Giratondo dell Scuola," *Paesa Sera* (Rome), November 1970.

25. "Parent Power Comes to European Schools," *The Times* (London), May 8, 1975.

26. Edward Magri, "Sex Course Meets Trouble," Associated Press Features, March 24, 1970.

27. Interview with Clelio Darida, Mayor of Rome, April 1971.

28. Luigi Barzini, *The Italians* (London: Hamish Hamilton, 1964), p. 191.

29. *UN Demographic Yearbook, 1972* (the latest compilation available).

30. Sergio de Risi, "Ogni Giorno Abbandonano la Famiglia Due Romane Sotto i 18 Anni," *Il Messagero* (Rome), November 18, 1970.

31. Interview, Jack Star, Bureau Chief, McGraw-Hill Business News Bureau, Milan, December 1970.

32. *La Donna Oggi in Italia*, tables 10.5 and 10.6.

33. Judith Harris, " 'Witchcraft' Conviction on Trial," Rome *Daily American*, July 24, 1970.

34. "So Many Helpless Children, but . . ." Rome *Daily American*, November 26, 1970.

35. *La Donna Oggi in Italia*, tables 2.10 and 2.11.

36. Statistics presented at the 1970 Milan Heart Specialist Conference.

37. A cross-culture survey of women simultaneously published in the magazines *Femmes d'Aujourd'hui* (France), *Brigitte* (Germany) and *Amica* (Italy) in February 1973.

38. "Vieni a Letto, se no, Ti Denuncio," *Panorama* (Milan), April 1, 1971.

39. *La Donna Oggi in Italia*, table 9.3.

40. *La Donna Oggi in Italia*, p. 286, gave the results of a pan-Common Market study, which indicated that Italy also had the fewest single workingwomen—only 24 percent of the Italian women polled were heads of their families, while 40 percent of the German and French women were family heads.

41. *La Donna Oggi in Italia*, tables 6.8 and 1.4.

Part Three
The Frenchwoman—"The Other" Nation

1. Molly Haskell, "Eric Rohmer in the Afternoon," *The Village Voice* (New York), October 12, 1972.

2. Simone de Beauvoir, *The Second Sex*, reissue trans. H. M. Parshley (London: New English Library, 1969), p. 433. Orig. *Le Deuxième Sexe* (Paris: Librairie Gallimard, 1949).

3. Dr. André Haim, *Les Suicides d'Adolescents* (Paris: Payot, 1969), p. 277.

4. André Malraux, *Man's Estate* (or *Man's Fate*, orig. *La Condition humaine*) (London: Methuen, 1933), pp. 56–57.

5. Brigitte Bardot in interview, *L'Express* (Paris), February 18, 1973.

6. Nelly Kaplan, film director, as quoted in interview by *The Sunday Times* (London), April 15, 1973.

7. See the Jean Bourgeois-Pichat report of the French National Institute of Demographic Studies in December 1971, and the 1938–70 comparative UN Statistics.

8. Sanche de Gramont, *The French: Portrait of a People* (New York: Putnam, 1969; Bantam, 1970), p. 390.

9. Jean-Paul Sartre, *The Age of Reason* (New York: Bantam Classic, 1959), p. 17. Orig. *L'Age de Raison* (Paris: Librairie Gallimard, 1945).

10. "Single Motherhood," *Time* (New York), August 25, 1971.

11. *Elle* (Paris), January 8, 1972.

12. "Une Nouvelle Manière d'Être Parents—Chacun Chez Soi," interview with Françoise Hardy and Jacques Dutronc, *Elle* (Paris), January 29, 1973.

13. *La Vie Catolique* (Paris), August 2–8, 1972.

14. According to a survey that I made of the 1972 editions of *Elle*, *Marie-Claire*, *Parents* and *Femme Pratique*, roughly the equivalent of the American *Family Circle*, *Cosmopolitan*, *Parents* and *Good Housekeeping*.

15. Franchon Pagès and Claude Lepage, "L'École des Mamans Parfaites," *Parents* (Paris), August 1972.

16. Benjamin Spock, *Baby and Child Care* (New York: Pocket Books, Inc., Giant Cardinal, 1962), p. 49.

17. According to a poll by *L'Express* (Paris) published in October 1972.

18. Pagès and Lepage, *loc. cit.*

19. Antoine de Saint-Exupéry, *Le Petit Prince* (Paris, Librairie Gallimard, 1943).

20. Elisabeth Schemla, "Les Derniers seron les premiers," *L'Express* (Paris), February 28–March 5, 1972.

21. "Le Grave Problème des femmes que travaillent: la garde du bébé," *Elle* (Paris), November 20, 1972.

22. Informations statistiques, Ministère de l'Education Nationale.

23. "At Home in Europe," *The Sunday Times Magazine* (London), January 1, 1973.

24. De Beauvoir, *The Second Sex*, p. 15.

25. A. Balint, *La Vie intime de l'enfant*, as quoted by Simone de Beauvoir, *Ibid.*, p. 13.

26. Martha Wolfenstein, "French Families Take Their Children to the Park," *Childhood in Contemporary Cultures*, ed. Margaret Mead and Martha Wolfenstein (Chicago: University of Chicago Press, 1970), p. 105.

27. An opinion reached in April 1971 in a Gallup poll of six nations, as reported by United Press International.

28. Christine Collange, "Des Mamans, Non," *Elle* (Paris), January 1, 1973.

29. Mary Blume, *International Herald Tribune* (Paris), May 5–6, 1973.

30. *France Soir* (Paris), October 14, 1972.

31. *Elle* (Paris), April 28–May 4, 1972.

32. R. Julliard and P. Charron, eds., *Rapport sur le comportement sexuel des français* (Paris, December 1972).

33. Conducted for the Presidental Commission on Population Growth.

34. Simone de Beauvoir, *The Prime of Life* (Paris: Librairie Gallimard, 1960).

35. Christian Kalt, interview, *Gente* (Milan), March 1973.

36. *L'Express* (Paris), October 23–29, 1972.

37. De Gramont, *op. cit.*, p. 398.

38. De Beauvoir, *The Second Sex*, pp. 129–30.

39. *Elle* (Paris), November 6, 1972.

40. De Beauvoir, *The Second Sex*, p. 206.

41. Georges Simenon, *Maigret Meets a Milord*, trans. Robert Baldick (Harmondsworth, Middlesex, England: Penguin Books Ltd., 1963), p. 40.

42. Georges Simenon, *When I Was Old* (New York: Harcourt Brace Jovanovich, 1972). Simenon is from French-speaking Belgium, but his views on wives' status are common to both Franco cultures.

43. De Gramont, *op. cit.*, p. 400.

44. Jean-Jacques Servan-Schreiber, as quoted in interview by *The Sunday Times* (London), February 18, 1973.

45. Margaret Smith and Meriel McCooey, "Other People's Homes," *The Sunday Times Magazine* (London), April 15, 1973.

46. SOFRES poll, November 1972, of 1000 men aged twenty to sixty-five.

47. *L'Express* (Paris), October 23–29, 1972.

48. As quoted in *The Sunday Times* (London), February 11, 1973.

49. Joseph T. Carroll, *The French, How They Live and Work* (London: David and Charles, Ltd., 1968).

50. Brigitte Gros, *Les Paradisiennes* (Paris: Laffont, 1973).

51. "7 Million de femme hors da loi," *Le Nouvel Observateur* (Paris), January 28, 1973.

52. Evelyne Sullerot, *Women, Society and Change*, trans. Margaret Scotford Archer, World University Library (New York: McGraw-Hill, 1971), p. 160.

53. Malraux, *op. cit.*, pp. 203–40.

Part Four
The German Woman—The New Brunhild

1. Esther Vilar, *The Manipulated Man*, trans. Eva Broneman (London, Abelard-Schuman, 1972), p. 15. Orig. *Der dressierte Mann* (Gütersloh: Bertelsmann, 1971).

2. According to the International Planned Parenthood Federation, the June 1974 law permitting first-trimester abortion on demand was immediately suspended by the Federal Constitutional Court, pending its judgment, which was negative in February 1975. The rest of the 1974 legislation, which replaced an 1871 law virtually outlawing any abortion, remains, and abortion for serious medical or psychological reasons is now possible in Germany.

3. S. K. Oberbeck, "The Unfindable Country," *Newsweek* (New York), November 27, 1972, p. 59.

4. Eugene Fodor, "West Germany," *Fodor's Guide to Europe* (The Hague: Mouton & Co., 1963), p. 285.

5. See Richard Barber, *The Knight and Chivalry* (London: Longman Group Ltd., 1970), pp. 88–89.

6. Robert-Hermann Tenbrock, *A History of Germany*, trans. Paul J. Dine (London: Longmans, Green and Co. Ltd., 1969). Orig. *Geschichte Deutschlands* (Munich: Max Heuber Verlag; Paderborn: Ferdinand Schöningh, 1968).

7. Anthony Sampson, *The New Europeans* (London: Panther Book, 1971), p. 249.

8. William Safire, "The Work Ethic, the Leisure Ethic," *International Herald Tribune* (Paris), September 4, 1973.

9. United Press International report, October 30, 1973.

10. Report by the Institute of Economic Analysis in Lausanne in September 1972.

11. Reginald Peck, *The West Germans, How They Live and Work* (London: David and Charles Publishers Ltd., 1969), p. 96.

12. *Cinema d'Oggi*, Rome, report on international box-office figures, September 11, 1972.

13. "Europe's Most Successful Society," *Time* (New York), May 26, 1975.

14. *Österreichischer Bundestheaterverband Bericht für 1971/72*, report on tickets sold to Austrian state theaters in Vienna.

15. Peck, *op. cit.*

16. Hilda Scott, *Does Socialism Liberate Women? Experiences from Eastern Europe* (Boston: Beacon Press, 1974), p. 84.

17. "Europe's Most Successful Society," *op. cit.*, and *Newsweek* (New York), February 26, 1973.

18. *Panorama* (Milan), November 23, 1972.

19. Although more German women work, on a proportionate basis, the Frenchwomen make up a larger percentage of their work force. Calculating from a February 1973 report by the Centre National de Sociologie du Droit Social in Brussels, approximately one out of every 2.4 adult German women work—in France, the ratio is 1:2. Also, according to the *Brigitte, Amica* and *Femmes d'Aujourd'hui* report documented in the Italian section, 52 percent of married women in *both* France and Germany are at work.

20. Massimo Conti, "Intervista con Beate Uhse, Vendere Sesso," *Panorama* (Milan), February 3, 1972, pp. 68–73.

21. The statistics on the East German economy were compiled in "The Rise of the 'Other Germany,'" *Time* (New York), October 1, 1973.

22. Evelyne Sullerot, *Woman, Society and Chage*, trans. Margaret Scotford Archer, World University Library (New York, McGraw-Hill, 1971).

23. The West German Grundgesetz (Basic Law or Constitution), Section I—Basic Rights, Article 3, paragraph 2 states, "Men and women shall have equal rights." Under the Weimar Constitution, only "basically the same" civic rights were guaranteed, and women's rights to equality before the law and within the family were not included.

24. Centre National de Sociologie report, 1973, found that, predictably, Italian grandmothers took care of the largest percentage of the children of working mothers—23 percent at the grandmother's home and 33 percent in the children's home where Grandmother is often a live-in baby-sitter. Surprisingly, Germany had the second highest percentage of baby-minding grandmothers—18 percent of the children stayed with their grandmothers while their mothers were at work, 24 percent were cared for by Grandmother in their own home.

25. "Hausfrau Liberation," *Newsweek* (New York), May 8, 1972, p. 53.

26. Scott, *op. cit.*, pp. 135–36.

27. *Panorama* (Milan), October 19, 1972.

28. *Quick* (Munich), August 30, 1972.

29. Associated Press wire story, November 15, 1973.

30. Reuters report, October 19, 1972.

31. Andrew Lang, ed. and collector, "Hansel and Gretel," trans. Ms. May Sellar, *Blue Fairy Book* (London: Longman Group Ltd., 1972), p. 249.

32. Rhoda Métraux, "A Portrait of the Family in German Juvenile Fiction," in *Childhood in Contemporary Cultures*, ed. Margaret Read and Martha Wolfenstein (Chicago: University of Chicago Press, 1970), pp. 253–76.

33. Christel Buscher, "Muss Eine Frau ein Kind haben?" *Eltern* (July 1973), pp. 13–19.

34. In February 1973, the U.S. National Institute of Neurological Diseases and Stroke published its findings of a fourteen-year study that involved 56,000 mothers and 40,000 of their children. They found tht the American ideal of gaining 16 pounds—i.e., the weight of a normal newborn plus the weight of the increased uterine size, the placenta and the amniotic fluid—was not as healthy as had been believed. Speaking on the report, Dr. Janet Hardy, of the institute, says that the minimal weight gain "in considerable part, accounts for the difference in neonatal and parinatal mortality between this country, which ranks 13th or 14th in neonatal death, and Europe, where the death rates are much lower."

35. "Was mit Mutter und Baby in den ersten zehn Minuten nach der Geburt Geschieht," *Eltern*, July 1973, p. 99.

36. Information taken from "Social Security in Germany," a report compiled by Dr. Rudolf J. Vollmer, Labor Attaché, Embassy of the Federal Republic of Germany, June 1975.

37. See Morton Schatzman, *Soul Murder: Persecution in the Family* (New York: Random House, 1973).

38. Wilhelm Reich, *The Mass Psychology of Fascism*, trans. Vincent R. Carfagno (New York: Farrar, Straus and Giroux, Inc., 1970), pp. 55, 153.

39. Rudolf Walter Leonhardt, *This Germany: The Story Since the Third Reich*, trans. and adapted by Catherine Hutter (London: Penguin Books, 1968), p. 122. Orig. *X-mal Deutschland* (Munich: R. Piper and Company, 1961).

40. Associated Press interview, June 22, 1973.

41. Erik H. Erikson, *Young Man Luther—A Study in Psychoanalysis and History* (New York: W. W. Norton & Co., 1958), p. 176.

42. As quoted in *Variety* (New York), January 23, 1973.

43. Rhoda Métraux, "Parents and Children, an Analysis of Contemporary German Child Care and Youth Guidance Literature," *op. cit.*, pp. 218, 224.

44. Elisabeth Plattner, *Die ersten Lebensjahre, ein Erziehungsbuch* (Heidelberg: Quelle and Meyer, 1951), quoted by Métraux, *ibid.*, p. 217.

45. Hermann Hesse, *The Glass Bead Game*, trans. Richard and Clara Winston (London: Penguin Books, 1972), p. 56. Orig. *Das Glasperlenspiel* (Zurich: Fretz & Wasmuth, 1943).

46. Walter Sullivan, The New York *Times*, March 28, 1972, quotes Einstein's sister Maja, on his inarticulateness.

47. Rhoda Métraux, "A Portrait of the Family in German Juvenile Fiction," pp. 253–76. *op. cit.*, pp. 253–76.

48. Ilse Aichinger, "The Bound Man," *Great German Short Stories*, ed. Stephen Spender (New York: Dell Publishing Co., 1960), pp. 224–39.

49. *World Health Demographic Yearbook*, 1973.

50. Alvaro Ranzoni, "Freno al Massacro," *Panorama* (Milan), August 2, 1973.

51. William Shirer, *The Rise and Fall of the Third Reich* (New York: Simon and Schuster, 1960; New York: Crest, 1962), pp. 64, 306.

52. Dr. Walter Langer, *The Mind of Adolf Hitler* (New York: Basic Books, 1972).

53. Vance Packard, *The Sexual Wilderness* (London: Pan Books Ltd., 1970), p. 482.

54. *Il Messaggero* (Rome), April 15, 1973, report, and the Pierre Simon *Report on the Sexual Behavior of the French* (Paris: Juillard Charron, 1972).

55. *Variety*, (New York), international box-office report, June 5, 1973.

56. Günter Grass, *Cat and Mouse*, trans. Ralph Manleim (London: Penguin Books, 1968), p. 32. Orig. *Katz und Maus* (West Berlin: Hermann Luchterhand Verlag, GmbH, 1961).

57. Barbara and Manfred Frunert, *Liebe ist deine Liebe nicht* (Munich: Kurt Desch Verlag, 1972).

58. Packard, *op. cit.*, p. 502.

59. As quoted by Hans Peter Bleuel, author of *Das Saubere Reich*, in *Panorama*, (Milan), October 12, 1972.

60. See the autobriography of Hannah Tillich, *From Time to Time* (New York: Stein & Day, 1973).

61. Harald Irnberger, "Frauen die im Schatten stehen," *Kürier Sonntags Story* (Vienna), November 25, 1973.

62. See also Alan Levy, *Rowboat to Prague* (New York: Grossman, 1972).

Part Five
The Scandinavian Woman—The Dynamics of Equality

1. Astrid Lindgren, *Pippi Longstocking*, trans. Edna Hurup (London: London University Press, 1971), p. 1. Orig. *Pippi Langstrump* (Stockholm: Raben & Sjögren, 1945). The first of a trilogy, the other two being *Pippi Goes on Board* and *Pippi in the South Seas*.

2. Vance Packard, *The Sexual Wilderness* (London: Pan Books Ltd., 1970). See his synopsis of this opinion given in Chapter 20, "How the Future Might Look," pp. 301–19.

3. Alva Myrdal, Foreword, *The Changing Roles of Men and Women*, ed. Edmund Dahlström, trans. Gunilla nad Steven Anderman (London: Gerald Duckworth & Co., Ltd., 1967), pp. 9–15. Orig. *Kvinnors Liv Och Arbete* (Stockholm (c) Studieforbundet Näringsliv och Samhälle, 1962).

4. Jacqueline Simpson, *Everyday Life in the Viking Age* (New York: G. P. Putnam's Sons, 1967), pp. 138–49. Much of the information on Viking life that follows is also from Simpson's work.

5. *Ibid.*, p. 140.

6. Much of the following information has been derived from the *History of Swedish Women*, compiled by the Swedish Federation of Business and Professional Women (Stockholm: Wicksells Tryckeri), p. 1.

7. Irene Scobbie, *Sweden, Nation of the Modern World* (London: Ernest Benn Ltd., 1972), p. 211.

8. Dr. Kerstin Anér quotes these ads in her paper for the Swedish Institute, Stockholm, "Swedish Women Today—a Personal Appraisal," p. 3.

9. Inge and Sten Hegeler, *AN ABZ of Love*, trans. David Hohnen (London: Neville Spearman Ltd., 1963), pp. 7, 100.

10. Tove Ditlevson, telephone interview, April 11, 1974, conducted with the assistance of *BT* journalist, Rimor Jessen.

11. Birgitta Linnér, office interview, April 2, 1974.

12. In 1967, according to *The American Almanac for 1970* (New York: Grosset & Dunlap, 1970), pp. 14, 139, Michigan reported approximately 500 cases of rape. Three years later, in 1970, Sweden reported only 116 convicted rapists. According to Swedish authorities, these figures accurately reflect the incidence of rape in their country, as 90 percent of criminals are brought to justice.

13. The Swedish statistics are from the *S.O.U.*, 1972:34, Familjestöd table 1:10. The American rates went from 4.1 in 1950 to 9.0 in 1967, according to *The American Almanac for 1970*, p. 50.

14. Donald Connery, *The Scandinavians* (London: Eyre & Spottiswoode, 1967), p. 38.

15. Lis Asklund and Thorsten Wickbom, *Brytningstid* (Stockholm: Raben & Sjögren, 1959), p. 140.

16. *Bad Luck, Or . . .* , booklet, trans. Richard Litell (Stockholm: National Association for Sex Education, 1966), 8 pp.

17. Quoted by Birgitta Linnér in *Sex and Society in Sweden* (New York: Harper Colophon Books, 1972), pp. 89–90.

18. Mikd Durham, "Editor's Note—A Solid Square in Scandinavia," *Life* (New York), September 15, 1969.

19. Paul Britten Austin, *On Being Swedish* (London: Secker & Warburg, 1968), pp. 55, 147, 149–50.

20. August Strindberg, *Seven Plays by August Strindberg*, trans. Arvid Paulson (New York: Bantam Classic, 1960), p. 40.

21. Dr. Berl Kutschinsky, *Studies on Pornography and Sex Crimes in Denmark* (Copenhagen: New Social Sciences Monographs, 1970).

22. Dr. Berl Kutschinsky, telephone interview, April 11, 1974.

23. See Appendix H.

24. See Appendix H.

25. August Strindberg, *Getting Married*, trans. Mary Sandbach (London: Victor Gollancz Ltd., 1972), pp. 44–48.

26. Telephone interview with Soren Petersen on April 10, 1974.

27. Austin, *op. cit.*, pp. 130–36.

28. See *UN Demographic Yearbook, 1971*.

29. *S.O.U.*, 1972:41, *Familj ock äktenskap 1* (Befolkningsförändringar 1970).

30. Department of Commerce, Bureau of the Census, Current Population Reports, 1968 series, p. 20.

31. Quoted by Birgitta Linnér, *op. cit.*, p. 94.

32. Anér, *op. cit.*, pp. 5–6.

33. Gunnar al Giejerstam, *Sexual Coexistence*, trans. Mac Lindahl (Stockholm: Delegation for Child Care of the Swedish Red Cross, 1966), 40 pp.

34. *Ibid.* For quite some time, the planned parenthood organization featured a woman, with the slogan *"Barn? Javisst—men när vi sjalva vill!"* ("Children? Of course—but only when you yourself want!").

35. Per Olav Tiller, "Parental Role Division and the Child's Personality Development," *The Changing Roles of Men and Women*, ed. Edmund Dahlström, trans. Gunilla and Steven Anderman (London: Gerald Duckworth & Co. Ltd., 1967), pp. 79–104. Orig. *Kvinnors Liv Och Arbete* (Stockholm: Studieförbundet Naringsliv Och Samhälle, 1962).

36. According to Mother's Aid statistics for 1971.

37. Jutte Ussing, *Family Life and Style of Life*, Report #60, I Kommission Hos Teknisk Forlag, Kobenhaven, 1974, pp. 85–86.

38. *vi Foraldrar* (Copenhagen), April 1974.

39. Information furnished during interview with Kate Wennerlund, Stockholm Social Welfare Inspector, April 3, 1974.

40. Swedish Institute, Current Sweden report #23, February 1974.

41. According to the statistics released from the "Suicide and Attempted Suicide" sym-

posium of September 1971, Stockholm, this is true—more than one-third of the Swedish and Danish male suicides are by hanging.

42. Austin, *op. cit.*, p. 159.

43. See the 1967 Central Sorbundet för Alkohol statistics.

44. Anne-Marie Bolander in *Nordic Suicide Statistics*, an offprint of "Suicide and Attempted Suicide" symposium, Stockholm, September 29–30, 1971.

45. See Appendix I.

46. The following assessment of Swedish thinking on teen-age problems derives mainly from interviews with Kate Wennerlund at the Stockholm Welfare Board; Anna-Greta Leijon, Minister Without Portfolio, Ministry of Labour; Ms. Britt Mogård, Chairman and Member of Swedish Parliament; and much of Per Olav Tiller's views (*op. cit.*) are also incorporated.

47. Austin, *op. cit.*, pp. 12–16.

48. Karl Skjonsberg, *Kjonnsroller og Miljo i Barnelitteraten*, report (Oslo: Universitetsforlaget, 1972).

49. Sverre Brun-Gulbrandsen, "Sex Roles and the Socialization Process," *The Changing Roles of Men and Women*, ed. Edmund Dahlström, pp. 59–78, trans. Gunilla and Steven Anderman (London: Gerald Duckworth & Co., Ltd., 1967), pp. 59–78. Orig. *Kvinnors Liv Och Arbete* (Stockholm: Studieförbundet Näringsliv Och Samhälle, 1962).

50. See Appendix A.

51. Donald Connery, *op. cit.*, pp. 169–70.

52. "Sweden: Troubles in Paradise," *International Herald Tribune* (Paris), July 11, 1972.

53. Anna-Greta Leijon, office interview, April 4, 1974.

54. Roland Huntford, *The New Totalitarians* (London: Allen Lane, 1971), pp. 222–25, 301.

Index